BECOMING A
CONSCIOUS
LEADER

BECOMING A CONSCIOUS LEADER

HOW TO LEAD SUCCESSFULLY IN A WORLD THAT'S WAKING UP

GINA HAYDEN

Published by Panacea Books
www.thewritefactor.co.uk

PANACEA
B O O K S
Reimagining the World

To Jessica, and all the generations
who come after her

TESTIMONIALS

"There is no higher calling than to be a truly conscious leader, one who is motivated by service to people and the organization's purpose, and not by ego, power or self-enrichment. In this highly engaging and very readable book, Gina Hayden has synthesized the wisdom of many conscious leaders. This book is an important contribution in helping us understand what conscious leadership is and how we can cultivate the qualities that are essential to it."
– Raj Sisodia, Professor of Global Business, Co-founder of Conscious Capitalism Inc., author of *Firms of Endearment* and co-author of *Conscious Capitalism – Liberating the Heroic Spirit of Business*

"Written from the heart, Gina has examined every aspect of being a conscious leader with reverence and deep understanding. Among the books on Conscious Capitalism, I hold this book as the most comprehensive guide for leaders on this sacred, heroic, fulfilling journey." – Sudhakar Ram, CEO, Mastek Limited

"The world needs more leaders and more effective leadership. This book makes a compelling case that we especially need more *conscious leaders* who can help organizations and communities become highly purpose-driven. Conscious leaders can help tilt the universe toward the greater good of humanity. If you want to improve yourself and improve the world, this is a must-read book."
– David Altman, Ph.D. COO, Center for Creative Leadership

"A well-researched and truly excellent book that describes what it means to be a conscious leader." – Richard Barrett, founder and chairman of Barrett Values Centre and author of *The Values Driven Organisation* and *The New Leadership Paradigm*

"Gina has written a practical, well-researched and integrated book on how conscious leaders think, act and lead. The challenges of being a leader in today's world require us to be responsible,

authentic and conscious of our own reactions and the impact we – and our organizations – have on others. This is a guidebook for any leader who wants to know how to lead with spiritual intelligence and make a positive and powerful impact in our world."
– Cindy Wigglesworth, Author of *SQ21: The Twenty-One Skills of Spiritual Intelligence* and President, Deep Change, Inc.

"In *Becoming a Conscious Leader*, Gina Hayden has robustly and beautifully described what conscious leadership looks like in action, as well as the winding journey of maturity toward it. Her work deftly weaves together insights and findings from adult psychology, neuro-science, Eastern wisdom traditions, embodiment theory and the latest in leadership studies. The result is an enlightening suite of principles and practices that will work in the unforgiving trenches of complex organizational leadership. Our responsibility and opportunity now is to embody these teachings, do the practice, and use them to help bring about an unprecedented flourishing of Humanity, Nature, and the Kosmos." – Barrett C. Brown, PhD, author of *The Future of Leadership for Conscious Capitalism*

"There is so much wisdom and practical knowledge in this book and it is a must read for those leaders who are ready to learn how to be a conscious leader. Gina has created a comprehensive guide-book that pulls together many aspects of what defines conscious leadership. No doubt this book will greatly influence organizational cultures around the world and I will be recommending it to my clients." – Diana Chapman, The Conscious Leadership Group and co-author of *The 15 Commitments of Conscious Leadership*

"Gina Hayden has expertly uncovered a way for leaders to go beyond filling skill, behaviour and knowledge gaps and move toward a deeper and more impactful development journey – one character-ized by greater consciousness, wholeness and humanity. By answer-ing this higher calling, leaders can generate greater energy,

commitment and creativity. An enthralling read."
— Michael Chavez, CEO, Duke Corporate Education

"Gina Hayden has gleaned so much practical wisdom from such a broad and deep set of different viewpoints and experiences, synthesizing it into tangible models and inspirational insights for personal growth and introspection that leads to the 'awake awareness' action so needed now. I am honored to be included and grateful this work is soon to be in the world. This is a handbook for leadership like no other I have ever seen."– Sally Ann Ranney, Environmental Leader, Conservationist and International Speaker

"As my realisation has emerged that so many things are simply not working in the world, I found myself with a sense of outrage... that outrage was quickly followed by a feeling of impotence. What was I going to do to help make a difference? This book helps to provide an answer. The world needs a new kind of leadership and Gina tackles this subject with grace and practical ideas. The book inspired me and made me realise that we can make a difference."
— Lorna Davis, Chief Manifesto Catalyst, Danone

"This book comes at a great time when businesses are under increasing pressure to justify themselves to the public, and leaders (and those they lead) are looking for more meaning in their work lives. It will help such leaders to see that a new type of thinking and leading is possible." – Paul Cleal, Partner, PwC

"I enjoyed reviewing the book and feel it is packed with observations from some wonderful people that will inspire and inform those who want to lead with a consciousness that we are all hungry for. Thanks for your outstanding effort." – Bob Fishman, former CEO, RHD

"Provocative and practical, *Becoming a Conscious Leader* is THE invitation to wake up to your highest self. Right on time with what's happening in the world, it will be your best friend as you transform into the leader you are meant to be so that you can take your organization where it has never been. Gina reminds us that we are in this together and she grounds us in what's important – connectedness. An inspiring read!" – Abigail Stason, author of *Beyond Ego: A Framework for Mindful Leadership and Conscious Human Evolution*

"What I love about this book is how grounded it is. And how rooted in her own real-life stories and those of highly successful leaders. And how clearly thought through, lucidly written and complete. And ultimately, how thoroughly Gina nails the reality that being a conscious leader is 180 very practical degrees away from airy-fairy." – Jon Freeman, author of *Reinventing Capitalism: How we broke money and how we fix it, from inside and out,* and *The Science of Possibility.*

"This timely book hits the spot! Brimming with insights at every turn, Gina Hayden provides us with a tractable guide through contemporary research, insightful case studies and her own hard won experience. This book is designed to aid our awakening as leaders and change agents. My hope is that a threshold of today's and tomorrow's leaders grasp the nettle of what these pages reveal." – Giles Hutchins author of *Future Fit* and Chair of The Future Fit Leadership Academy.

"This book demonstrates that leaders truly have the ability to change organisations and wider society for the better. Gina's exploration of conscious leadership is both an inspiration and a practical guide for those seeking a path to a new way of leading for positive impact on our world today and for the future." – Kathryn Kernick, Regional Director & Leadership Coach, Center for Creative Leadership

"*Becoming a Conscious Leader* is the most comprehensive assessment of what it is going to take for leaders in the business world to understand what is needed to expedite the evolution of the world of commerce." – Laura Roberts, CEO, Pantheon Enterprises

"At a time when seemingly everything is being democratized, transformed or disrupted, then it's essential that the way we 'do' leadership should also undergo a radical re-think based on deep reflection of our ways of 'being' and 'seeing.' Gina Hayden leads us gently on a journey of discovery into the rich, subtle but demanding terrain of conscious leadership by skillfully weaving the experiences and perspectives of 20 contemporary leaders into a robust, coherent framework that also integrates currently available research and practice. It's one of those rare, highly readable, jargon-free business books that will be read from cover to cover, becoming a well-thumbed source of inspiration and guidance for any individual intent on becoming a more effective, personally-fulfilled and inspiring leader." – Anna Pollock, Founder, Conscious Travel

"Gina Hayden's book is a must-read for people who want to lead and conduct business in a more inspiring and purpose-driven way. I have seen over and over that the success of executives stopped growing where they have stopped growing. This book will help you grow so that you can lead in a way that our changing world demands." – Peter Matthies, CEO, Conscious Business Institute

"It's about time somebody in the world had the immensely strong determination to share these stories and insights. This book is not only vitally practical, but a work of art. It threads together many layers of what the business psyche has not yet been made aware of. Gina's courageous questioning has gathered honest responses that are enormously useful to business leaders today." – Jennifer Wilson, The Global Centre for Conscious Leadership

"An amazing compilation of facts, economics, real case studies and thoughts from today's conscious leaders all in one place. Gina takes you on a personal quest to reveal what is a truly conscious business and a truly conscious leader and how you get there. A must read. You will be left inspired."– Prabhmeet Singh, management consultant

ACKNOWLEDGEMENTS

Writing a book can feel like the longest process and this one was no exception. Having finally, after several false starts, reached a version I feel is worthy of being sent out into the world is in no small part down to the collective efforts of an amazing group of people, all of whom gave generously of their time and their insights, who believe in the value of this work, who took risks to share their innermost worlds with me and who ultimately were instrumental in the creation of this book. Thank you so much for your generosity of spirit; I am immensely grateful to you:

To Lorna and the team at The Write Factor who guided me wisely and who patiently managed me while I thought of yet 'just another quick idea' that might improve the manuscript.

To the business leaders who gave so generously of their time and insights and who were willing to be asked some deep questions by me and be inspiring examples of conscious leadership. I am forever changed by our conversations: Tom Chi, Paul Cleal, Lorna Davis, Frederic Desbrosses, Bob Fishman, Neal Gandhi, GyanDev, Steve Hall, Ramesh Kacholia, Peter Matthies, Sally Ann Ranney, Sudhakar Ram, John Renesch, Laura Roberts, Dominic Sewela, Nithya Shanti and Jean-Francois Zobrist. And to the marvellous Millennials: Andrew Brady, Bethany Hilton, Prabhmeet Singh, and Jennifer Wilson.

I am indebted to Frederic Laloux, Mark Fraser-Grant, Rienzo Colpo, Julie van Amerongen and Malcom Stern for putting me in touch with several conscious leaders to interview, and to Barrett C. Brown for his wise words of guidance and suggestions for improvements of this book.

Thanks also to a number of people who have supported me by spending time reading the book and giving me their testimonials, recommendations and much appreciated encouragement: Richard

Barrett, Diana Chapman at the Conscious Leadership Group, Michael Chavez at Duke Corporate Education, Jon Freeman, Giles Hutchins, Peter Hyson, Kathryn Kernick and Dave Altman at the Centre for Creative Leadership, Louise Mowbray, Anna Pollock at Conscious Travel, Raj Sisodia at Conscious Capitalism, Abigail Stason and Cindy Wigglesworth.

Lastly, my deepest thanks go to Jessica, and to Sam, who waited patiently and hopefully while I worked on this manuscript, seemingly without end, during our evenings and at weekends, at airports and next to the pool on holidays when they would much rather that I was swimming with them. Your support in getting to the finish line has meant the world to me.

FOREWORD

John Renesch

The biggest crisis in the world today is not what fills our headlines – climate change, genocide, terrorism, environmental degradation – but a lack of wise leadership. While there seems to be no lack of people who want to be in positions of leadership and hold the title of 'leader', there is a lack of inspiring vision and know-how for today's major challenges, and the courage to do what's needed to address these.

Know-how involves the ability to inspire others, the skills to lead effectively in circumstances of great complexity and challenge, the courage to lead with conviction when others fail to do so and the self-awareness to know oneself well enough to have one's negative ego under control.

For years I have been calling this conscious leadership, which combines the personal awareness of what is needed (the self-awareness and vision) with the daring to stand for what has to occur in order to bring forth the vision.

In *Becoming a Conscious Leader*, Gina Hayden offers the reader some major tools in resolving this quandary and the alternatives, grounded in real-world experience of a new breed of leader, for inspiring, courageous and enlightened leadership.

Gina covers such important subjects as how to master the negative aspects of one's ego that play havoc with leadership; how to think from a systems perspective and be responsible for the whole; and how to take courageous stands and strive for personal mastery.

One of the commitments of the conscious leader is that of doing the right thing and acting for the whole rather than for personal gain. So many leaders capitulate when it comes to these tough decisions, subordinating what is the right thing for the whole to what is either more convenient or desirable for the benefit of themselves or some special interest group.

One example is the way politicians, elected to represent the will of the people, so often invert their priorities. They focus first on getting reelected, then on their political party and, only thirdly, on the people – reversing the priorities they were elected to value. Equally, in business, corporate executives so often make decisions based on fear of losing a promotion or their jobs, not on what is best for their companies.

Many people in positions of leadership are not skillful system thinkers and do not wholly appreciate the complex social systems we have created. In many cases, we have developed social systems that are more complex than our thinking can handle. Much like Frankenstein and his monster, our systems have become quite powerful and often beyond our ability to manage. While we intended the social systems to serve us when we created them we often find ourselves serving them – the exact opposite of the original intent! Changing complex systems requires a systems perspective. Gina addresses this question of systems knowhow in Chapter 17, with numerous examples of how successful conscious leaders go about impacting the systems they work within.

Becoming a Conscious Leader provides many answers for leaders – those who are now in positions of leadership and aspiring leaders – both of whom recognise the gap between what we have and what we need. It is a book for leaders who wish to step up and stand tall for a more conscious way of coping with and leading through today's challenges into a better world. These leaders might still be students, relatively new entrants into the workforce, entrepreneurs, or they might be executives already in the fray and aware of the challenges that present day leadership entails.

There are men and women who have risen to this challenge and who have demonstrated conscious leadership throughout their various sectors: private and public. This book's aim is to identify some of these leaders and to make public, through their inspiring stories, the insider's view into how they think and how they lead. Its purpose is to encourage many more such leaders to come to the fore.

Becoming a Conscious Leader is a rich and inspiring book that offers a leadership lens to address our current gaps and crises and to deepen the art and practice of effective, holistic and visionary leadership.

It is a must read for anyone aspiring to accept the role of leading consciously.

John Renesch
Futurist, Thought Leader and author of many books
including *The Great Growing Up*

CONTENTS

Introduction   1

1   Business is Waking Up   8
2   What is Conscious Leadership?   40

ZONE 1: SELF-MASTERY

3   Waking Up   70
4   Mastering Our Ego   108
5   Leading Authentically from Our Whole Selves   154
6   Radically Relative and the Value of We-Q   178
7   Taking Courageous Stands   196
8   Creating the Future   206
9   Practising Continuous Self-Mastery   226

ZONE 2: CONSCIOUS RELATING

10 Relationships and Connection   240
11 Redefining Competition, Reframing Innovation   252
12 Creating the Right Environment   264
13 Generous Listening, Generous Speaking   280
14 The Conscious Use of Power   292
15 Decision-Making as a Conscious Leader   316
16 Holding the Space   326

ZONE 3: SYSTEMS INSIGHT

17 Thinking in Whole Systems   346
18 Serendipity and Synchronicity   364
19 The Conscious Leader's View on Growth   378

ZONE 4: COLLECTIVE RESPONSIBILITY

20 Responsibility to the Whole   392
21 Leading Conscious Millennials   416
22 Advice for Conscious Leaders   446
Index   466

INTRODUCTION

When I was two years old, my mother packed me off to Sunday school. Each Sunday until I turned sixteen I went to church to be introduced to the ways of good living. Our home was that infamous hotbed of separatist thinking at the time: South Africa. Even the word 'apartheid' means separateness. I mention South Africa because it shows us that context is everything. We thought we were being upstanding citizens by going to church and learning good ways. In fact, seen in a broader context, from the perspective of the world, we were doing no such thing. We were acting in cruel and inhumane ways towards each other in a country that separated us by law. And although the world pointed out our faults to us, we did not have the consciousness at the time to see differently.

One evening, shortly after I turned sixteen, I sat on the comfortable church pew, listening to the minister, and a thought occurred to me: *How does he know this is the truth based on the book he is holding, when other religions have their own truth based on their own books and they believe they are equally right? Who is right?* In that moment, it was as if the scales fell from my eyes. The questions and the search began for me that, many years later, would culminate in this book. I was no longer convinced by other people's versions of the 'truth'. I was no longer interested in competing about these. I saw the craziness of attaching ourselves to one way of seeing the world which we are convinced is right, while making other ways wrong. Instead, I began looking for the common threads underlying all worldviews that join us together as human beings. Without knowing it at the time, I was looking for a greater context, one that includes all of us acting as one human race rather than separately. Consciousness is that context.

If you're reading this book, you might be experiencing similar thoughts; perhaps the foundations of your own worldview are being shaken. Many people are experiencing this – you are not alone. All around you people are feeling disconcerted about their current reality, as if it doesn't quite meet their aspirations and longings. Perhaps what used to satisfy you doesn't seem to hack it any more. What you took for granted as that which defines you – your goals, the pursuit of success, your achievements – might have lost its shine. You still want to be successful, but you are looking for a new definition of success, one that includes a better version of yourself. One that answers a call deep within you. You want to lead in a way that allows you to bring more of yourself to the game and doesn't ask you to cut off important parts, like your values or your sense of purpose. You want to do this for others, too, to make it more about everyone rather than just about yourself. You might be feeling an inner pull to be 'whole', to be connected to others, to find your 'tribe'. Perhaps you're wondering how to lead business for the greater good and perhaps you're experiencing the tensions of trying to be this kind of leader in a mainstream business environment that doesn't yet fully support all these ways of being.

This book is designed to answer this call to awakening, to deal with some of the very important questions that you and many other conscious leaders are grappling with. Tapping into examples from a wide range of conscious leaders, drawn from all over the world, we'll explore what it means to be a conscious leader operating both wisely and successfully in a conventional business world that is slowly waking up. My hope is that, through these stories, you'll get ideas, guidance and inspiration that will answer some of your questions and help meet your aspirations.

The world of business has been rather slow to catch up with the wave of humanity's 'waking up'. Business is the place where the battle lines that separate us are constantly drawn, and the traditional narrative of business is based on machinery and warfare (competitors, winners, losers, crushing the competition, stealing market share). Big business however has suffered severe consequences to its reputation through the infamous actions of some big-name corporates, their leaders and the most recent global financial crisis. Consequently, business, especially big business, is despised by many and seen as the enemy of all that is good, or at best, as a necessary evil.

But growing quietly alongside its flanks is an ever-strengthening quorum of large and small companies who are evolving to do business differently. These are accompanied by a clutch of movements that support this shift in our worldview about business. They go by many names: Conscious Capitalism, Inclusive Capitalism, Moral Capitalism, Blueprint for Better Business, and dozens of others across the world. In one study from 2014, conducted at Cranfield University in the UK, there were upwards of 130 initiatives identified worldwide, all dedicated to rethinking what we mean by 'doing good business'.

These movements share two important views: one, that business can have a higher purpose in the world than simply the act of making a profit; and two, that business needs to take responsibility for its impact on the world around it and factor this in to the way it conducts its profit-making activities. Companies that follow this trend are fast becoming the new normal. They are heroes that conduct themselves responsibly and for the greater good in a world that is waking up and becoming more exacting of business and the role it plays in society and in our lives.

Quite a lot has been written about this more conscious way of doing business and about these companies. John Mackey and Raj Sisodia's *Conscious Capitalism: Liberating the Heroic Spirit of Business* and Frederic Laloux's *Reinventing Organizations: A Guide to Creating Organizations Inspired by the Next Stage in Human Consciousness* are two excellent resources to further explore what's changing in the world of business.

Which brings us to the motivation for this book. While we know a fair amount about the companies themselves, we know less about their leaders and how they run their businesses in more conscious ways. How have they evolved and made the leap to leading consciously in mainstream business? How do they think, speak, behave and lead differently from other leaders? If we are to encourage more conscious leaders onto the playing field of business, then taking an up-close-and-personal look at those currently doing so can provide us with clues that make it easier for more of us to join in.

I am fascinated by how these leaders think, what makes them tick, how they got to where they are, and how this shapes the way they lead and do business. What can we learn from their example and how can this inspire those of us who also want to be on this journey? If we can map the territory of their characteristics and qualities, this can be a useful navigational tool for those of us feeling called to this within ourselves.

All this is in service of a possible future where many more conscious leaders around the world run their organisations differently, which in turn influences and positively impacts the lives of the thousands of people working in those organisations, and which ultimately has an uplifting effect on the world. Since so many of us are involved in business, it is a platform teeming with potential to elevate humanity.

I believe the key at this point in time lies with leaders and their power. Leaders set the tone of cultures; they influence many through their decisions; they set direction and make choices that impact, positively or negatively, on the lives of millions. Leaders therefore play a crucial role in the way business impacts the world. While there is evidence that we are moving towards a future where the traditional hierarchies of business will dissolve and companies become more self-organising, our current reality is that organisations are still operating in a pyramid-style structure. So, right now, the best way for business to play a role in uplifting the world is to impact the way we view leadership itself.

This is, nevertheless, not an evangelical crusade to convince business to be different: doing so merely creates resistance. To paraphrase Buckminster Fuller, to inspire change we need to create an alternative paradigm that is more appealing than the existing one. When this happens, those who are ready to make the leap, will leap. Those who aren't, won't. Ultimately, there's no one to transform and no transformation to be done to anyone. This book is simply a helpful guide to those who feel moved to play a different game of leadership and life.

All this talk of organisational leadership is not meant to replace the importance of self-leadership. This book is not only intended for leaders in the usual positions of authority; anyone can practise being more conscious as a leader, since this is as much about leading yourself from any point in an organisation as it is about leading others.

The number of conscious leaders in the world is increasing all the time. I've interviewed over 20 such leaders for this book, all of whom had fascinating stories to tell. I found them in all corners of the world: the United States, the United Kingdom, India and Africa, yet they shared similar worldviews, despite being spread geographically far and wide. Their perspectives on life and on business give us rich insights into how conscious leaders go about the job of leading.

One thing struck me, though. When I asked them at the end of our interviews, "Do you know anyone else like you that I can also speak to?" I was invariably met with a long, thoughtful silence before they responded, "I know of people like me, but I don't know them directly." This makes me think that being a conscious leader in the world at the moment can be quite a lonely place. Because you see the world so differently from your contemporaries, you might be inclined to think that you are alone in your views. It might seem like others don't quite 'get' you. You might feel a longing to be connected and to find your tribe. This book is also here to say: that tribe exists.

Something has made you pick up this book and read this far. You might be feeling the innate pull towards becoming a better version of yourself. You may not even have the words to describe that experience yet. I hope that you will find inspiration in these pages and get ideas for your own leadership and personal growth from the many examples on offer. I hope also that you will come to realise that you are part of an ever-growing group of new leaders who are at the frontier of leadership and business, and that business forms part of the very edge of our evolution as humanity. Most of all, I hope that many more of you will join.

Gina Hayden
November 2016

1

BUSINESS IS WAKING UP

f you've been around organisations recently – and it's likely that you have – you might have noticed that a sea change is afoot. At coffee stations and around the water coolers, in business magazines and on billboards, the word 'conscious' is popping up in places where it never dared show its face before. A new definition of success in business is emerging, and it centres on a company's ability to have a positive effect on society and the environment, in addition to the usual definition of being profitable.

Conscious business is becoming big business. It is shaping our new business narrative: we're seeing an increase in the importance of *purpose* as well as profit in companies that recognise the need to be values-led in order to get the best engagement out of their people. It also fulfils the expectation that the business is acting sustainably and responsibly.

CONSCIOUS LEADERS

These markers of change tell us that we are waking up to a new era in business – one that will also require us to 'up our game' in terms of leadership. The evolution we're party to in business must be accompanied by the evolution of the people who run businesses.

The kind of leader needed to embrace and shape this new business paradigm is the Conscious Leader.

Let's distinguish immediately between being a 'conscious leader' (the noun) and being more conscious as a leader (the adjective). Throughout this book I will refer to conscious leaders which can sound as if this is a state to be achieved, a kind of person who has passed through a gate and become 'a conscious leader'. This term is, however, simply used for shorthand. In reality, what it is about is becoming more conscious as a leader, across a variety of dimensions we will explore in this book. This is a process, one that continues for us and takes a different form in each of us as we all develop different facets of ourselves and become more conscious as leaders.

Conscious leaders have particular ways of thinking, acting and engaging that are best suited to the almost quantum leap that the new business reality is demanding of us. It is no longer enough for us to simply sprinkle more content on top of our existing leadership mindsets and expect to flourish in our leadership roles in this new world. Just as we can't run new software on an old operating system and expect a great performance, what's needed in our leadership is an upgrade of our operating system itself. This upgrade is what is meant by 'conscious leadership'.

Before we take a look at the qualities of conscious leaders, it's useful to set the scene. To begin with, we'll take a quick tour of the state business has got itself into and why this is so. We'll look at where business is headed and the factors contributing to this, and we'll explore how conscious leadership provides the key to unlocking what business can become in the best interests of all of us.

OUR CURRENT REALITY:
BIG BAD BUSINESS

The media loves a juicy story, and in the last decade or so big business has not disappointed. It's come up with some great examples of greed and a skewed playing field in which the little guy loses. There are disturbing statistics being revealed, such as that the richest 1% of the world's population now has as much wealth as the rest of the world combined, and that the richest 62 people in the world have as much wealth as the poorest half of the global population. In 2010, only six years ago, it would have needed 388 people (nearly six times as many) to have the same amount of wealth. This shows an alarming trend in the wrong direction.[1] The actions of those banks, traders and corporations, who have tripped and fallen due to the exposure of their own greed, has only made it easier to give capitalism a bad name.

It doesn't only have to be financial scandal that makes us look at business with a more-than-sceptical eye. Simply working in an organisation these days can be a painful affair. People are demanding that their workplace has meaning and purpose and fits with their values. Leaders have an enormous challenge on their hands, not only navigating the waters of more outspoken employees, but doing so while trying to solve the puzzles of complexity and globalisation that have never been attempted before.

Peter Matthies, who heads up the Conscious Business Institute in Santa Barbara, works with large corporates around the world and finds that 90% of the leaders he encounters are looking to work in a way that's more aligned with their authentic personality. As intelligent as these leaders are, they recognise that the world is changing, that they don't have the answers, and that the way they are currently operating is not sustainable. They have the headache of upcoming generations of talent leap-frogging traditional business models and joining Facebook or Google, while issues around climate change, shortage of resources and globalisation pile up on their already groaning desks. Peter told me that he hears a huge yearning in these leaders to make a shift towards a better world, even though they don't know what it is yet or how to do it.

It's not all gloom and doom, however. Many business- and thought-leaders find themselves getting excited by the prospects of a more evolved and responsible way of doing business. These leaders regard capitalism as the most powerful, flexible and robust system we have for creating global prosperity and enhancing the quality of life for billions of people all over the world. To adopt this attitude, however, requires us to look at our own mindsets towards capitalism. Instead of blaming capitalism – or money – or worse, being non-committal, if we can collectively shift the quality of our consciousness about it, we can imbue capitalism with a different set of values and intentions; ones which are about creating greater prosperity for all and acting for the greater good. We can have a different effect on the world at large.

Paul Monekosso Cleal, a partner at PwC, believes that business continues to be a force for good despite the actions of a misguided few: "I don't think there's a conflict between business and doing good in the world. Most of the wealth in the world has been created in a very positive way, through business. There have been markets for centuries, small businesses and individuals coming together for the purposes of trade. We all benefit and grow from this. The negative aspect, where people hijack it for personal gain, is what needs to be controlled, but this is more the exception than the rule."

Despite these first green shoots in the ways we are beginning to rethink our relationship to business, as a whole business continues to lag behind because it subscribes to the old-style model of creating value for shareholders rather than for a wider group of stakeholders. This unconscious and unquestioned belief drives leaders to prioritise profits and quarterly results over medium- to long-term sustainability. We've been guilty of living by two rules in business: as long as it's a) profitable and b) legal, it's good business.

How did we come to be this asleep?

WHERE WE'VE COME FROM:
OUR OUTDATED HISTORY

Our views about business are heavily influenced by economic theory. This is deeply rooted in the worldview of the founding father of economics, Adam Smith, the 18th century Scottish moral philosopher and pioneer of political economy. In the mid-1700s, Smith wrote two great works: *The Theory of Moral Sentiments* (1759) and *The Wealth of Nations* (1776). The second has greatly influenced how we've come to think about the way free markets operate.

Smith is most famous for his concept of the 'invisible hand': an organising principle that guides the markets and occurs as a result of the checks and balances brought about by the individual actions of many people. While many conscious business leaders recognise that Smith's ideas were actually about ethics and morality, the way many economists – and subsequently mainstream business leaders – have chosen to interpret Smith's 'invisible hand' is that it gives them free rein to act in their own self-interests because they are simply making individual choices while the checks and balances in the market look after everything else. This creates a whole ethos around the way we do business. The dominant narrative of 'it's nothing personal, it's just business' has come to mean that there is little need for us to take responsibility for the consequences of our actions in the world of business, if it is the invisible hand of our collective actions that is actually moving the markets. This view has not necessarily encouraged us to be conscious about the way our actions in business impact the greater system.

Our sense of personal accountability for our business choices has also not been helped by Milton Friedman (1912–2006), another prominent economist. Writing in 1970, he waded into the debate by launching a widely read and influential diatribe against the prospect of businesses having any social responsibilities whatsoever, other than to their shareholders. Friedman argued vehemently that the sole responsibility of a business is to use its resources to increase its profits. He insisted that businesses have no right to spend their investors' money doing social good and that corporate executives should spend their own money on these causes, if this is what they choose to do.

So all-embracing has been the influence of Smith and Friedman that business has been asleep for years, particularly over the last 50 years, acting under the unconscious and unquestioned belief that profit is the only bottom line that matters. 'Shareholder value' is a phrase that falls easily from many leaders' lips and, with it, leaders have carved out their role in concert, often regarding companies like machines in which components can be moved around and where humans are regarded as 'resources' to be allocated along with other resources like stationery and IT.

It doesn't take a great stretch of intellect to see that at the time of writing, in 2016, the world has moved on unrecognisably from when Adam Smith wrote about his 'invisible hand' 240 years ago. In fact, at around the same time, just 50 years before Smith wrote *The Wealth of Nations*, witches were still being burned at the stake. Janet Horne, the last witch to be killed in Scotland in 1727, died after being accused of using witchcraft to turn her daughter into a pony for the devil.

If anything, this is a sombre lesson to us to remember to take into account the context of any dogma we might unconsciously adopt. Adam Smith could not have dreamed of, nor comprehended, the challenges faced by the average person today as they navigate their lives – let alone the challenges faced by leaders as they steer their companies through the choppy, complex and unpredictable seas of a globally connected world. Even Milton Friedman, writing in 1970, would have had little idea of the unrecognisable context in which business operates today.

Of course, the way we view business is not the sole terrain of business leaders. We are all part of the system of capitalism and we all have inbuilt mindsets towards the ways we regard business and money. Jon Freeman writes widely on this topic and has spelled out some of what he believes needs to change to fix our broken system in his book *Reinventing Capitalism: How we broke Money and how we fix it, from inside and out*[2]. "The prevailing distortions in our attitudes to money are not only those in the minds of business people," he told me, "we all suffer from emotional issues and blind spots about what money is and whether we are its servants or its masters. At the same time, shifting our mindsets is only half the battle. We also have to upgrade some of the mechanics of the existing system so that it supports new mindsets, disable some of the recent changes to the system that have worsened its failures and add new features to it that bring sustainability inside the money system. At the moment, the inadequacies of the system are used as a convenient excuse for those who choose to abdicate responsibility for their own choices by claiming to be victims of the system."

While addressing changes in the system of capitalism itself is outside of the scope of this book (readers are referred to the work of Freeman and others on this topic), what we are concerned with here is the half of the equation that has to do with how we upgrade our existing mindsets about capitalism. It is high time that we update our beliefs about business – that we change our level of consciousness about it – and, fortunately, we are doing just that.

WHAT'S CHANGING: (R)EVOLUTION

In March 2014, Tim Cook, CEO of Apple, demonstrated his conviction that we address climate change at Apple's annual shareholder meeting when he told the group assembled there: "If you want me to do things only for return on investment reasons, you should get out of this stock." The climate change sceptics in the room, who were insistent that Cook committed Apple only to profitable investments, were on the receiving end of a further telling off when he retorted: "When we work on making our devices accessible by the blind, I don't consider the bloody ROI."

What on earth is happening when a company as colossal as Apple publicly flies in the face of the mainstream business narrative?

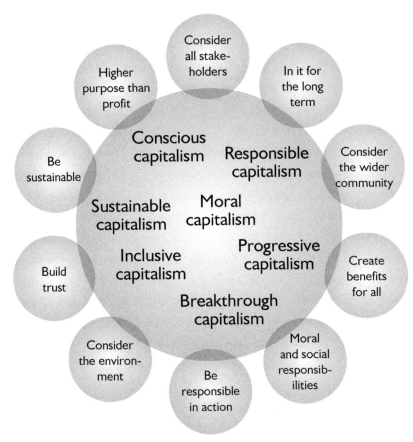

Figure 1: Qualities of the new business narrative

It is a sign of a tidal shift in business, which is the result of rising levels of consciousness in the world, and therefore in business leaders. This greater level of consciousness means that more and more business leaders believe it is no longer acceptable to regard business as anything other than an integral part of a greater whole.

The conscious leaders profiled in this book are part of the swelling ranks of business leaders who know that business is an interdependent part of a much bigger system. They are concerned not only with the consequences of their own and their organisation's actions on the world around them, but are actively looking to increase the benefits that are being created for other stakeholders. This is moving the needle of capitalism from a shareholder model to a stakeholder model.

As I mentioned in the Introduction, a cluster of new initiatives is emerging to reshape our business narrative: Conscious Capitalism, Responsible Capitalism, Sustainable Capitalism, Moral Capitalism, Inclusive, Progressive, Creative and Breakthrough Capitalism, to name but a few. Cranfield University's efforts to map these initiatives representing the movement reached 130, with many more besides.

There appear to be two common threads of aspiration across these initiatives: firstly, that business needs to consider not only its profits but also its purpose in the world; secondly, that business needs to contribute to the greater whole of which it forms part by considering how it impacts and benefits all its stakeholders. This is resulting in no less than a paradigm shift in business, a new system to replace the old, as our worldviews update themselves on a massive scale and the idea that business could be so much more than it is catches fire in the world's imagination.

In just some of the accompanying sparks, influential Harvard Professor Michael Porter and Mark Kramer, co-founder and MD of global not-for-profit advisory firm FSG, write in their article, *Creating Shared Value:* "The purpose of the corporation must be redefined as creating shared value, not just profit per se".[3]

This statement is important as it flies directly in the face of the dominant business narrative promoted by thinkers such as Milton Friedman.

"Even people within systems don't often recognize what whole-system goal they are serving. To make profits, most corporations would say, but that's just a rule, a necessary condition to stay in the game. What is the point of the game?"

Donella Meadows, systems expert,
Donella Meadows Institute

This change is also showing up in contemporary business thinking. *Fast Company* magazine writes: "... businesses built with purpose and run by inspired leaders can change the world and improve lives in the process, all the while creating outsized financial returns ... The idea that a corporation somehow exists outside [its system], subject only to the shareholder's profit motive, is not just short-sighted but irresponsible."[4]

Engaging with business in this way is exciting; it gives us hope. Bob Johansen, a futurist for the past forty years at The Institute for The Future and someone from whom we will hear often in this book, writes in his excellent volume, *Leaders Make the Future: Ten New Leadership Skills for an Uncertain World*, that corporations will play a major role in shaping the future for all of us. Although separate from governments, there need to be many ways in which business and governments work together. Profitability will shift over time from narrow economic criteria, like quarterly returns, to the larger question of sustainability. We are already seeing these shifts in business today. Leaders will need to think about the bigger system as part of their everyday decisions and they will also need to be looking generations ahead, at the long-term implications of their decisions and actions.

"Rebalancing," says Johansen, "will be an unprecedented leadership challenge."[5] Those leaders who remain conscious of the effects of their actions will have the opportunity not only to to be financially and operationally successful, but to make the world a more sustainable place for the future.

HOW BUSINESS IS CHANGING: THE NEW BUSINESS MEMES

There are six new memes emerging that show the shifts we are making in our thinking about business.

Meme 1: Greater transparency

"We live in an age where transparency and authenticity are the new kings," says Mike Radparvar, co-founder of lifestyle goods shopping site, Holstee. Mike and his brother, Dave, featured by *Fast Company* magazine under the heading 'Change Generation'[6], accurately represent the voice of a new generation in business.

It makes sense that we have a growing need for collective transparency in the wake of irresponsible and short-term behaviours that have led to so many mega-scandals and casualties, both in corporations and governments. Tolerance for executive mischief has run out and, because it's harder to hide what executives do, companies are being forced to act with greater transparency.

Andrew Brady, one of the Millennial conscious leaders featured in Chapter 21 of this book, relates how social media and technology create so much transparency that companies can't control their marketing messages any more. "You can't have the Nikes of the world putting out great commercials, but then behind the scenes they're having sweatshops," says Andrew. "Now it's much more transparent and you have to have more integrity and really look at all aspects of your business." Everything, it seems, is on show, and we are making our business decisions in the public eye.

In a growing number of conscious businesses, like Whole Foods Market®, for example, even pay structures are made transparent to all employees. In some companies, employees also define the parameters of their own salaries. Rather than keeping salaries a secret of the HR department, the idea is that transparency of financial information puts people in a better position to make more well-informed choices for themselves.

Meme 2: Conscious social media

Social media is an accelerator and an amplifier of our conscious choices

---

A growing number of people are asking questions about the clothes they buy or the brands they choose to support. Our increasing demands for transparency are a reaction not only to excessive business mischief, but also to our exponentially increasing technological connectivity and an ever-savvier consumer base. Consumers are choosing their brands more consciously and they're telling their friends about them. Posting on your social media wall that you are dissatisfied with the poor service of your bank is likely to be far more influential in the ever-growing social networks than those same friends reading the advertising billboard on their drive to work claiming what a great bank you have. Social media is an accelerator and an amplifier of our conscious choices.

Meme 3: Solving complex problems through collaboration

The more the internet drives our connectivity, the more it ramps up our communication and with it our potential for collaboration. We are becoming far more conscious of the value of 'we' rather than 'me' in solving some of our biggest challenges.

Collaboration features highest on the list of priorities in IBM's CEO studies, which survey thousands of global CEOs every two years. In 2008, these CEOs reported that their biggest headache was the unprecedented scale of change and the ever-increasing complexity they were consumed by and required to manage. More recently, in 2010 and 2012, they were interested in how they could capitalise on this complexity and leverage their organisation's connections and relationships. In the latest studies from 2015[7], what is becoming ever more clear to these CEOs is the importance of leading with bold creativity and connecting with customers and a wide range of other stakeholders in imaginative ways. In fact, the watchword for CEOs the world over is 'collaboration' and they expect to collaborate even more widely in the next three to five years.

Globally, these leaders are realising that the best way to deal with complexity and create a competitive advantage is through open and collaborative cultures that drive innovation. The best leaders favour 'purposeful partnership', which is collaboration with a specific goal in mind. There is widespread recognition that one person cannot possibly have all the answers to complex challenges and that the leader doesn't have the right or only path through this maze. The answer must involve many voices and many intelligences, a quality which is typified in Bob Fishman, former CEO of a highly successful service provider in mental health support, RHD (Resources for Human Development). We will meet Bob further in Chapter 6.

We are entering a 'collaborative economy' or an 'everyone-to-everyone' (E2E) economy[8], where everyone collaborates to create value and where retuned collaboration trumps small-minded competition. This is all about creating win-win outcomes, rather than playing zero-sum, win-or-lose games. It is about non-binary business. Companies who work in an innovative and collaborative way are able to think radically differently. These companies don't end at the walls and doors of their buildings – they spill out into the communities beyond and use these connections to create and innovate. Tony Hsieh, CEO of Zappos, is a great example of a conscious leader working in this way, and we'll visit his approach to leading his company in Chapter 17.

Meme 4: Innovating through We-Q

If greater collaboration is one way of capitalising on an interconnected and ever-changing world, then the purpose of collaborating is to innovate. Innovation keeps us on our toes and means that we can come up with multiple, fit-for-purpose designs and lasso our intellectual horsepower. It takes the collaboration of many brains working in unison, of extensive partnering in imaginative ways, to unlock the radical innovation needed to create fit-for-purpose solutions in the new world. It helps if employees are inspired by a higher purpose to what they are doing and if they can see the value and impact of their efforts, and it helps if they are able to bring their personal values to what they create.

How can leaders set up the right conditions for this to occur? Conscious leaders will be thinking about the value of 'we', the collective effort, and how to tap into this force by promoting the connections between the people in the room. Raj Sisodia, author of *Firms of Endearment: How World-Class Companies Profit from Passion and Purpose* and co-author of *Conscious Capitalism: Liberating the Heroic Spirit of Business*, sees human beings not as a 'resource' but as a 'source' where our infinite creative potential can, under the right leadership conditions, be released to fuel endless innovation and adaptation for a company.

In later chapters, we'll explore some of the specific ways conscious leaders use collaboration across previous 'no-go' boundaries as a tool to ignite innovation in their companies.

A Case of Innovation: Procter & Gamble

Procter & Gamble, the multinational consumer goods company, believes that one of the greatest challenges facing companies and their leadership today is the range and depth of innovation required to drive both top- and bottom-line growth. They are concerned with how to deliver one without trading off on the other. Their solution is an Open Innovation strategy called Connect+Develop.

P&G collaborates with inventors, suppliers, universities, competitors, joint ventures and start-ups. These external innovation partnerships drive more than 50% of their new initiatives, and their aim has been to make Connect+Develop deliver $3billion towards the company's annual sales growth. The company wants to be the partner of choice for innovation collaboration.

P&G sees their open-source model as a tremendous way of increasing their innovation because:

» It enables innovation beyond their specific areas of expertise.

» It offers access to many more innovative ideas that in turn improve the quality of the ones they choose to take forward to commercialisation.

» It reduces risks in innovation by transforming potential competitors into collaborators.

» It enables products to get to market faster.

P&G recognises that Open Innovation only works when some or all of these four advantages apply to all partners in the collaboration, not only to P&G. Deals only get struck if the proposition is strategically right for both parties and the terms are a win-win for each organisation. Get all this right, they say, and their experience suggests yet another benefit: a first deal significantly increases the chances of multiple deals and dramatically reduces the time it takes to get to them.

The positive knock-on effects of collaboration and trust in the service of innovating are highly apparent in the innovation practices of P&G.

Meme 5: Redefining the boundaries of competition

The Proctor & Gamble story illustrates how, in the new business paradigm, competition still exists, but it acquires a wrapper of collaboration. We are beginning to compete in our marketplaces at higher levels of inclusion than ever before, and we are evolving away from competition being an end in and of itself. It is no longer enough for us to compete with others for our market share in an unconscious and unexamined way. Conscious companies that innovate get to join forces with previously regarded 'competitors' and draw a bigger boundary line around the act of competition that, crucially, ensures that everybody wins, including communities, society and the environment. This takes a great deal of conscious self-management on the part of these leaders because we are primed as human beings to protect our own and to avoid losing out to the perceived 'other'.

In Chapter 11 we'll get to meet Laura Roberts, a conscious leader and CEO of Arizona-based conscious chemical company Pantheon Enterprises, who takes a radically different and inspirational approach to competition and embodies all of these new qualities. Conscious competition requires a more highly refined level of consciousness. It's about playing the game more intelligently, more inclusively and more consciously. Players unite around a common purpose and the context for winning is often huge, as big as the world itself. Conscious competition is about creating value for many others besides ourselves. In this new world, competition is reframed as 'How do I win without creating losers?' Winning at all costs is fast becoming a short-sighted disadvantage.

Winning at all costs is fast becoming a short-sighted disadvantage

---

The Japanese concept of *kyosei* means living and working together for the common good, enabling cooperation and mutual prosperity to coexist with healthy and fair competition. The new forms of competition are beautifully captured by two principles: kyosei and human dignity, which are incorporated in the Caux Round Table (CRT) Principles for Business, a code of ethics that sets the guidelines for how business can be conducted responsibly and ethically. Human dignity refers to the value of each person as an end, not simply a means, to the fulfilment of others' purposes. This captures the delicate balance of the new forms of conscious competition, a balance that leaders will need to hold in their hands.

Meme 6: A shift towards meaning and purpose

A sixth meme that deserves our attention is the simple but important shift that is occurring around how a company makes a positive difference in the lives of others. This is becoming more important for greater sections of the population. As consumers and as employees, we want to feel connected to something that matters, that has an impact, that we can feel good about. We want to feel whole and integrated, not act as if we are made up of separate boxes, some labelled 'work' and some labelled 'life'. For companies, the challenge is to be authentic about their brands, their purpose and their leadership in order to create this feel-good factor. It also leads to the knock-on effect of more stakeholder-centred forms of business as we consider the value we are bringing as companies to others in our wider system.

Across the age spectrum and especially at both ends of it, the volume of this desire is getting turned up. We are in the midst of experiencing a pull towards greater meaning and purpose. Values are becoming key to buying and working patterns. Armed with their smartphones, it is now possible for consumers to know much more about what is going on inside a company and choose to buy from somewhere else if it doesn't fit in with their values.

The older generation, living longer, has passed the point of relentless taking and is more concerned with giving back. They create a growing conscious consumer base who vote with their values and who have a different yardstick for measuring their choices.

At the opposite end of the age spectrum, the Millennials (those born between 1980 and 2000) are increasingly demanding that their work has personal meaning and value. They pioneer innovations that marry social needs with viable business models. Without the stability of life-long jobs that previous generations have enjoyed, it makes much more sense for this generation to create their own social enterprises where they have the freedom to earn a living doing the things they care about. Where they do work for companies, many expect these companies to fulfil their needs for connection, personal meaning and belonging while making a contribution and an impact on society – values that go far beyond simply having a job and making a profit. One of the most popular comments in the Millennial generation is that they are not prepared to occupy a desk for 20 years on the promise of a future big leadership job. They are far more immediate than that.

This trend shows no sign of subsiding in the generation that follows, the Digital Natives, who are defined as those who are sixteen years or younger in 2012[9]. We'll be meeting the Millennial conscious leaders later on in Chapter 21.

A Case for Meaning and Purpose: TOMS Shoes

Like many social entrepreneurs of his generation, Blake Mycoskie, founder of TOMS Shoes, saw a problem and wanted to do something about it. The problem he saw was children in Argentina who needed shoes to go to school, but couldn't afford them and so couldn't get an education to get out of the spiral of poverty they were caught up in.

Reacting spontaneously, as Mycoskie puts it, and without a business plan or any traditional company bells and whistles, he started selling shoes out of his apartment, and every time he sold a pair he gave a pair to a child in need.

As often happens in the new business models where social media, interconnection, collaboration, meaning and purpose are intertwined, the right people started wearing TOMS shoes and, as they got excited about it, they told their friends and followers via social media. It took off from there. Media attention created publicity and inches in consumer-facing magazines, newspapers and online blogs, and that led to a boost in online sales.

Seeing this many shoes being sold online not only drove up TOMS' revenue, but also captured the attention of the blue-chip retailers who wanted a piece of the action.

The TOMS story illustrates beautifully how feeling passionate about a cause and the agility of social media has the potential to create a successful business and revolutionise our view of business and leadership.

These six emerging business memes are causing us to think differently about business, humanising it more than ever. People, rather than just money, are becoming an important part of the business equation. "Business is not a maths problem, maximising here and minimising there. Business is about real lives and real people. It's one of the most human things we do," says Raj Sisodia, co-founder of Conscious Capitalism® and author of several books on conscious business. In our ever more technologically connected world, we are beginning to realise just how deeply connected we all are as humans. Old-style business, one of the last bastions of acting as if we are separate entities, is beginning to crumble.

We are being presented with the opportunity to shift the world through the way we conduct business and the prosperity we create for everyone beyond just ourselves. This has never before been possible to the extent that it is now – we simply didn't have the levels of awareness and connection prior to this point. Collectively, we have the chance to shape our future with our own conscious action through the medium of business. We have the opportunity to blend who we are with business and achieve a completely new outcome.

"Conscious business is one of the biggest frontiers we have to cross," says Peter Matthies. "We can go on a weekend trip to the mountains and be conscious, but what happens when we come back to business on a Monday morning?" The new frontier means combining new ways of being with new ways of doing in business. The scope is truly huge.

Futurist, conscious leader and author John Renesch, considered by many to be one of the forefathers of conscious leadership, says: "To me, the consciousness that is required in leadership is not just about your company, but about the world. Not just about your financial well-being, but the well-being of everybody that comes in touch with your organisation. It's about being conscious enough to ask ourselves, what kind of world is everyone who is connected to my business living in?"

Equally, John Replogle, former leader in Guinness and Unilever and now CEO of Seventh Generation consumer products, describes the new approach to leading and doing business in this way: "We need to be conscious, and we need to mobilise, and the only way that we're going to effectively do that is by harnessing the incredible power of business. If we do that well, if we lead responsibly, if we can ensure that the largest and greatest organisations on the planet think holistically and systemically, then I think we will make a huge, positive leap forward for humankind, and for all of the shared existence of this planet."[10]

What exciting times to be living in! As Michael Bernard Beckwith, spiritual teacher, wryly comments: "Kids in the future will look back and say – what, you were starting businesses just for the money?"

THE VALUE OF CONSCIOUS LEADERSHIP

We've spent this chapter so far looking at the changing context of business which is driving the need for a more conscious style of leadership. We explored the status quo of traditional business and the way it has been motivated solely by profit. We examined how it came to be this way; the unconscious narratives that have created our assumptions about how we should do business, and we've looked into the business revolution that's currently taking place and the accompanying memes that are beginning to reveal themselves globally.

Let's now dive into the topic at hand: what the new form of leadership looks like.

My fascination with conscious leadership, with how these leaders think and choose to act and lead, comes from a deeply felt sense I share with many others that business has the potential to be a huge force for good in the world. Its power lies in its universality: business is so much a part of our everyday lives across the globe. If we were to conduct business even marginally differently (not measuring success only by profit) and responsibly (keeping an eye out for how we are creating benefits for other stakeholders beyond ourselves), then we have the potential to make a remarkable difference for the greater good. The power rests in our hands, and in the hands of current business leaders.

Business has the potential to be a huge force for good in the world

---

We can tackle this topic from two ends of a spectrum: from an 'outside-in' approach or an 'inside-out' approach. Outside-in has to do with the shape of our organisations themselves: how we structure ourselves in our organisations so as to do business. At the other end of the spectrum, an inside-out approach has to do with the inner transformation of the leaders themselves, and not just the leaders, but anybody who is involved in business, at any level. Conscious leadership has a great deal to do with self-leadership; it is not only consigned to those in leadership positions.

This book follows the 'inside-out' approach. We are interested here in the end of the spectrum that is about the transformations of ourselves as leaders. What are those moments of realisation where we begin to see the world differently? How do we shape the way we lead and run our organisations? What can we learn from other conscious leaders if we feel the calling to follow the same path?

It's worth paying a fleeting visit to some of what's going on at the 'outside-in' end of the spectrum. There are many interesting shifts happening in the way our organisations themselves are being structured and compiled, with developments that are worth any leader knowing about.

THE OUTSIDE-IN APPROACH

As mentioned, this has to do with how the organisation itself is structured, and which systems, processes and practices support a different way of operating. Traditional organisations – the ones we know so well – are frequently pyramid shaped. The CEO sits at the top, with his or her board, and reports 'down' to many layers of senior leaders and then middle and junior managers who, eventually, filter the information and instructions down to the employees at the 'bottom' layer. Some organisational shapes are different: in the complex world we live in, lines of reporting are often blurred and people need to work across the matrix of relationships to get things done. The central question remains, however: how much freedom, self-determination and agency do people have within the organisation? What needs to come from the leaders in their positions, and how much can come from the employees themselves?

Frederic Laloux has done a deeply important piece of work in this regard, described in his book, *Reinventing Organizations: A Guide to Creating Organizations Inspired by the Next Stage in Human Consciousness.* In it, Laloux describes his research with various companies around the world that reflect some of the new business memes we explored earlier in this chapter. These organisations also radically break with tradition. There is not a pyramid in sight.

Using one particular scale that describes the levels of our own conscious evolution, these organisations are called 'Teal' organisations. Teal refers to those types of organisations which are fluid, ever-changing and which adapt as circumstances demand, all in service of achieving the organisation's purpose.[11] The organisation is not a vehicle for achieving management's objectives – an ego-based, mechanistic approach which requires leaders at the top of the hierarchy to control things. Instead, in Teal organisations, everyone across the organisation pays attention to the living purpose of the organisation and takes the actions that are needed to support and be in service to this. These organisations are naturally self-managing – a multitude of minds in concert is better at serving the organisation's purpose than one person at the top making all the decisions for everyone.

Laloux's work describes the ways in which these organisations operate at the outer evolutionary edge of our traditional approaches to business. Influenced by the edgy disciplines and practices of Holacracy, Spiral Dynamics and Integral Theory, Laloux found that there are three breakthroughs in these new-paradigm organisations, which are described more fully here:

» **Self-management**. These organisations use self-management practices to gather and dissipate, coalesce and morph, through the individual actions of many people around some well-defined 'big rules'. The key to operating effectively in this way, even at a large scale, is through a system of peer-to-peer relationships. There is no need for a traditional management hierarchy or the usual consensus that we think is required when we take away 'someone in charge'. Self-management has some pretty significant implications for how we regard leadership. It takes away the role of the traditional hierarchical leader and instead distributes leadership throughout the organisation. Leadership becomes a verb, rather than a noun focussing on positional 'leaders'. As we shall see in later chapters, operating in this way requires leaders to step above their egos and let go of their need for control. Letting go and allowing self-management to happen is a conscious act of trust and requires leaders to want to become more conscious.

» **Wholeness**. Instead of a traditional organisation which requires us to bring our 'business face' to work – that

rational, bulletproof part of ourselves that is cut out for
what we think of as 'proper business' – Laloux's Teal
organisations invite the whole person to come to work.
We get to include our values, our aspirations, our
purpose, our lives outside work, our emotions, our
hopes, doubts and our vulnerabilities in how we show
up in the workplace. This 'whole person approach'
honours the shift to meaning and purpose that was
mentioned earlier, in Meme 6. It suggests that we can
become more fulfilled, engaged and energised while we
are working.

» **Evolutionary purpose**. Teal organisations are living
systems, rather than empty shells, and have a life and
sense of direction of their own. Instead of leaders and
even shareholders controlling and forcing the
organisation into particular shapes to fit in with a
predetermined strategy, leaders of Teal organisations
'listen in', intuitively, and observe the patterns taking
shape in the organisation, so as to pick up a sense of
what wants to happen next to serve that organisation's
purpose. This is a much quieter form of leadership,
devoid of our ego's acts of will and force. Everyone in
the organisation acts as stewards of the organisation by
listening in and creating the future collectively, in a
highly self-managed way.[12]

To any traditional leader coming from a conventional business
paradigm, the above three paragraphs will no doubt read like
nonsense. But for some leaders, those who have woken up or who
are beginning to wake up to the possibility of a different way of
being, leading and doing business in the world, Laloux's paragraphs
tug at something important that sits just beneath the surface of our
awareness. Often, we feel an inward sense of 'Yes!' about the way

these organisations, and this form of leadership, is described, as it resonates with possibilities we hold deep inside us.

Bringing this inner recognition to the surface, and connecting it up with many others who are experiencing this same kind of recognition, is what this book aims to serve. There are many leaders such as you, who are experiencing this inner 'yes' but who are not yet hooked up to others. The purpose of this book is to facilitate that connection.

What Laloux's insights offer us is the wisdom of how to create a structure, a container for our own evolution, through the organisations we build. "The magic of these organizations," writes Laloux, "[is that] their processes can lift up employees to adopt behaviors from later stages of consciousness that they might not yet have integrated at an individual level."[13] Effectively, they encourage employees to act outside of the ego, to transcend their egos; a subject we will explore in more depth in Chapters 3 and 4.

In fact, the role of the leaders in Teal organisations shifts from providing direction and guidance (being the source of the answers) to creating and holding the space or the context for these kinds of organisations to manage themselves. Some even question whether the role of the leader will be required at all in the future, as the responsibility falls to self-leadership and our ability to self-organise in a collaborative, dynamic and creative balance with others.

THE INSIDE-OUT APPROACH

While these 'self-managing organisations' with Teal qualities might be the direction in which we're headed, right now many leaders still function primarily within traditional organisational pyramids, housing layers of management with the executives at the top. We are a way off yet from self-managing organisations being the norm.

While this movement gathers momentum – if indeed this is where we're headed as a critical mass – there is an opportunity for a transformation to occur in business through the existing struc-tures of business via the leaders themselves. This is the domain of the inside-out approach, where the mindsets, behaviours and actions of conscious leaders create more conscious organisations that operate differently and have a different, more positive ripple effect in the world. These kinds of conscious leaders have the poten-tial to transform their organisations, both outwardly and inwardly, as a result of their personal journeys.

For a business to evolve, the leader needs to evolve

This is also where the current leverage lies to harness the power of business for the greater good. In the current paradigm, leaders set the culture and role model it. They shape their organisations according to their consciousness. As John Mackey, co-CEO of Whole Foods Market and one of the founders of the Conscious Capitalism movement, points out, an organisation can only be as conscious as its leader, and for the business to evolve, the leader needs to evolve.

This principle applies even in Laloux's self-managing organisa-tions. He found that there are only two necessary conditions to create and maintain Teal organisations. One is that the founder or top leader must have developed a more highly evolved, integrated and conscious worldview to role model operating in this way to the rest of the organisation. It is helpful, but not necessary, to have a critical mass of leaders operating in the same way as well. The other condition is that the owners of the business must be willing to embrace the principles of self-management within their organisation.

What we see here is that even from an outside-in perspective, which looks directly at the structures of an organisation itself, it is necessary for a conscious leader to take a stand and hold the line on doing things differently. Without these kinds of conscious leaders in place, organisations easily revert back to being hierarchical structures. One of the conscious leaders we'll meet throughout this book is Bob Fishman. Fishman found, when he left RHD, that the organisation soon showed signs of returning to a more traditional, top-down entity under the new leadership.

It is not necessarily easy to be a conscious leader in any kind of organisation, traditional or otherwise. Even more difficult is the courageous and steady stance that conscious leaders may need to hold in the face of challenge from more traditional colleagues, board members and shareholders. It can be a tough call for a top leader to hold the space for a more conscious organisation to operate while shareholders or the board are calling for conventional measurements and results. Traditional businesses are short on patience when it comes to waiting. They may be willing to entertain a different approach as long as there are results to show for it, but where these don't arrive quickly enough, it's easy to want to get things under control with a top-down, command-and-control organisational style. Sudhakar Ram, Global CEO of Mastek, an IT multinational, is one of the leaders interviewed for this book. He wrestled with just this problem in relation to his Board and shareholders and worked through it. We'll meet him in later chapters and hear about his fascinating approach to conscious leadership.

Somewhere in the middle, between old-style traditional hierarchies and new and emergent self-managing organisations, is where we find ourselves right now. There is a wide gap in which to explore what conscious leaders can do to run their organisations both wisely and successfully in a world that is waking up all around them. Populating this gap with insights about the mindsets and practices of a range of conscious leaders creates a map which we can all follow, if we choose to, and builds a bridge from our existing, traditional ways of doing business to a fresh approach on the other side.

In the remainder of this book, we will explore all of these areas, beginning with a description of what we mean by conscious leadership and looking at how conscious leaders see the world, how they approach business and how they define success. We will look into how they lead by delving into such important questions as:

» How do you practise conscious self-mastery?

» How do you relate to others consciously when leading them?

» How do you ensure your employees are engaged and bringing their full selves to work?

» How do you ignite their passion and spark their energy to innovate?

» What does it mean to redefine the boundaries of competition?

» How does collaboration beyond competition work in reality?

» How do you increase your positive impact, and that of your organisation, on the world around you?

» What does having a purpose beyond profit look like and how do you find it?

» What is needed to become such a leader in the first place?

Knowing how these leaders do what they do can help us develop more of these qualities in ourselves and follow suit.

Endnotes

1   http://www.bbc.co.uk/news/business-35339475

2   Freeman, Jon. 2015. *Reinventing Capitalism: How we broke Money and how we fix it, from inside and out.* Salisbury, UK: Spiralworld.

3   Porter, Michael E and Kramer, Mark R. January/February 2011. 'Creating Shared Value: How to Reinvent Capitalism—and Unleash a Wave of Innovation and Growth'. https://businessethics.qwriting.qc.cuny.edu/files/2012/01/PorterKramer.pdf

4   Baird, Tripp. June 2014. '5 Myths Socially Conscious Entrepreneurs Need to Ignore'. *Fast Company* magazine. http://www.fastcompany.com/3031509/the-future-of-work/5-myths-about-the-freshest-iteration-of-capitalism

5   Johansen, Bob. 2012. *Leaders Make the Future: Ten New Leadership Skills for an Uncertain World.* San Francisco. Berrett-Koehler Publishers, Inc. 2nd edition, pxix.

6   Robischon, Noah. October 2011. 'Holstee's Mike and Dave Radparvar Are Doing What They Love, And You Can Too'. *Fast Company* magazine. http://www.fastcompany.com/1790496/holstees-mike-and-dave-radparvar-are-doing-what-they-love-and-you-can-too

7   http://ibm.co/1SlgTPt

8   http://adobe.ly/2eRbpi5

9   Johansen, Bob. 2012. *Leaders Make the Future: Ten New Leadership Skills for an Uncertain World.* San Francisco. Berrett-Koehler Publishers, Inc. 2nd edition, p10.

10 Repogle, John. Summer 2015. 'The Future of Seventh
    Generation'. *Conscious Company Magazine.*
    http://pinchot.edu/the-future-of-seventh-generation/

11 http://www.reinventingorganizationswiki.com/
    Teal_Organizations

12 Adapted from Laloux, Frederic. 2014. *Reinventing
    Organizations: A Guide to Creating Organizations Inspired by the
    Next Stage in Human Consciousness.* Belgium: Nelson
    Parker, p566.

13 Ibid. p243.

2

WHAT IS CONSCIOUS LEADERSHIP?

What do we mean by the term conscious leadership? And how is this different from any other kind of leadership? While it might seem redundant to define yet another style of leadership or introduce a new term to a box already crammed full of leadership theories, conscious leadership is of a different order from how we have typically viewed leadership in the past.

Becoming a conscious leader is less about adding knowledge, behaviours and skills on top of your existing leadership style and more about upgrading the operating system of your leadership itself. It's about taking a good look at how you've been functioning as a leader up to this point, at how you make sense of leadership and what it is for, and refining this. The lens of your leadership assumptions and biases that, as a leader, you might previously only have been able to look through, is now the lens that you are able to step back from and look *at*. Stepping back and seeing ourselves and our way of viewing the world in perspective, is part of the process of our own evolution.

Conscious leadership has the potential to take humanity to places that we haven't been before. It's definitely the kind of leadership needed to run a conscious business. In fact, conscious leaders go hand in hand with conscious businesses – one requires the other.

If business is to become the new frontier that can take us to the next evolutionary level as human beings; if capitalism is to come closer to fulfilling its potential to create benefit and uplift millions of people around the world – then conscious leaders are key. We have never before seen business in quite this way, with quite this degree of clarity and responsibility, and the potential is there within our grasp.

Conscious leadership has the potential to take humanity to places that we haven't been before

We have had glimpses of this new style of leadership over the years and seen hints of these qualities. For example, authentic leadership, which is closely linked to our sense of purpose, our 'true north', and to the quality of the connections we make with others, has been championed by Bill George, former CEO of Medtronic, in his book, *Discover Your True North*.[1] 'Servant leadership', popularised by Robert K Greenleaf, encourages us to be of service, to share our power as leaders and to put the needs of others in the foreground so that they may grow and develop as people, which in turn grows each of their communities.

More recently, Georg Vielmetter and Yvonne Sell of the Hay Group identified 'altrocentric leadership' as their version of the leadership required for the future. Described in their book, *Leadership 2030: The Six Megatrends You Need to Understand to Lead Your Company into the Future*[2], altrocentric leaders focus on others and on doing things for them, rather than focussing on themselves. They also see themselves as part of a bigger whole. This kind of leadership, these authors tell us, is crucial for coping with the complexity of what they call the 'megatrend storm' of global shifts and disruptions that we are experiencing today and which will continue to accelerate in the future.

In this chapter, we'll outline a model of conscious leadership that is helpful when reflecting on our own behaviour and qualities as leaders. It brings up questions of where within ourselves we may already be developed and where we might need to develop further. The aim of this model is not to uphold an ideal of perfection that we need to aspire towards and feel bad about not achieving: as with anything important, mastery and development of ourselves as conscious human beings is a process and not a destination. The questions are almost more important than the answers.

In many ways, the term 'conscious leadership' is a wrapper for many of the human qualities we are inspired to develop in ourselves. Let's take a look at what some of these qualities might be.

"The goal of becoming a more conscious person," says Kevin Rafferty, a conscious leadership coach, "is to be a continually evolving human being: more authentic, self-aware, caring, creative and effective. The goal of becoming a conscious leader is to be a conduit for others entrusted to you to become better humans and better people in the workplace: more engaged, secure, team-orientated, collaborative and innovative problem-solvers, who are focused on fulfilling a purpose. Conscious leaders are self-aware and motivated enough to drive their own personal evolution to become a higher definition of themselves and, through this, to impact the lives of others."[3]

Where do we find these leaders? John Renesch has been writing about conscious leadership since the early 1990s, long before this term even entered our collective awareness. He saw that these leaders already existed in government, business, education and other segments of society, but that their numbers were small, they were relatively low profile, and they were widely dispersed. Over the years, as he has been profiling and studying this increasing trend, John has noticed conscious leaders showing up in more and more situations and in greater numbers. Certainly, in the current shift towards conscious companies and social enterprises, more of these leaders are coming to the fore.

Conscious leaders exist at all levels in an organisation. They don't necessarily have to be in the traditional roles of power (although, as we'll see, this helps with the impact they can have) and, for many, it has a lot to do with how they manage themselves, no matter where they sit in the organisation. As John tells it, many have become disillusioned with corporate life and work as independent consultants or entrepreneurs. Some remain in their positions, though, running small, medium and large companies. It is these leaders in particular who are featured in this book. In John's words, these leaders remain, "part of the existing system but nevertheless see the wisdom in changing our collective worldview to one that offers greater hope, inspires a larger vision, honors the human spirit, and sets the stage for humanity to fulfil a higher destiny."[4]

A good starting point for thinking about the qualities of leading consciously is with high levels of self-awareness and skilful self-management. This enables us to move through life in a more conscious and choiceful manner. Beyond ourselves as individuals, the ways in which we relate to others and manage our relationships also defines us as conscious leaders. There are qualities in the ways conscious leaders connect to others that are worth taking note of and which we'll explore. Moving further out still, beyond their immediate relationships, conscious leaders are highly attuned to the greater system around them. They grasp the interconnections in this system and they have the ability to identify patterns and sense what is needed for the system to flourish. With this understanding, they feel called to take responsible, collective action that furthers the greater good, frequently in ways that have a positive impact on the widest possible reaches of the world.

A CALLING

What does it mean to feel called to something rather than simply having a career or a job? Nithya Shanti, a former forest meditation monk who has also studied business management and fulfilled a role in corporate Human Resources, distinguishes between these three[5]: "A job is something you do to pay your bills. A career is doing work to which you bring your heart, your knowledge and your identity. A calling, however, is when work doesn't even feel like work any more. A calling is an expression of our highest gifts and values. It's something you are delighted to do even if you aren't paid for it." Nithya regards conscious leadership as a calling. Conscious leaders bring their values to what they do. They fulfil their individual purpose through their work. "It's about awakening your inherent potential combined with service: how can I take my gifts and give them to the world in a way that makes a difference?" he says. "This has a certain magnetic quality to it because charisma comes from the heart. Doing this awakens the sense of possibility in others as well."

Being a conscious leader is not all easiness and flow, however. A steely determination and will is required to be a conscious leader, often because the vision you are upholding is different from the mainstream and sometimes others can find what you stand for to be tremendously challenging. In the previous chapter, we saw how conscious leaders in business need to hold the line when confronted by board members and shareholders who might want to force the business down a more unconscious or short-term route, especially under pressure.

John Renesch describes conscious leaders as mature 'stand-takers', willing to uphold a perspective even where this means they need to promote a new approach or buck a mainstream trend. "They stand for a new way for us all to exist in a sustainable world *together*, focussed on our commonalities, not exaggerating our differences," he says.[6]

No stranger to controversy and to being challenged himself, John Mackey, agrees. He believes conscious leaders are strong individuals who possess exceptional moral courage and are able to withstand the scrutiny and criticism of those who view business in more traditional, narrower ways.[7]

Mackey also regards conscious leaders as emotionally and spiritually mature. They are primarily motivated by serving something greater than themselves: the purpose of the business and its role in the wider stakeholder system. As a result, they are uncompromising in their commitment to taking a longer-term view of the business. It's about looking to grow and nurture their organisation in a sustainable way, rather than pursuing short-term gains.

Conscious Leadership in Action: John Mackey, co-CEO of Whole Foods Market

John Mackey is the co-CEO of Whole Foods Market, a global organic supermarket chain with a turnover in 2015 of more than USD 14bn. He is also the co-founder of the Conscious Capitalism movement. Whole Foods Market is held up as a good example of a conscious company following Conscious Capitalism principles. These four principles are:

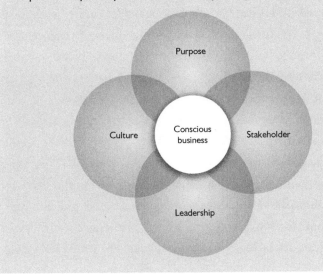

» Conscious businesses have a higher purpose in the world than only making profit.

» They act to create value for all of their stakeholders, from the shareholders to the employees, clients, suppliers, the community, society and the planet as a whole.

» They operate with a conscious culture.

» They are led by conscious leaders.

Mackey believes that conscious leadership is the most important component of a conscious business. "Without conscious leadership," he says, "little else matters. The quality of our leaders affects the quality of our lives. Every good leader contributes in ways, big and small, towards making the world a better place – one day, one life, and one company at a time."

More can be read about Conscious Capitalism's four principles in Mackey's book, *Conscious Capitalism: Liberating the Heroic Spirit of Business.*

Before we dive into our model of conscious leadership around which this book is arranged, it's worth looking at another fascinating study of conscious leaders which was conducted by Dr Mariana Bozesan as part of her doctorate. Bozesan was interested in finding out what shifts happen in the minds or 'interior worlds' of conscious leaders which makes them lead as they do. In this, she identified a number of qualities in these leaders. She found that they shared a strongly felt commitment to business being a service to humanity. As a result, they became involved in the creation of sustainable businesses in a number of ways: by promoting long-term over short-term thinking, by creating social enterprises, by taking an alternative stand to 'rampant consumerism' or through seeking political leadership. "Instead of running away from the business world," said one leader in her study, "I found myself running back to say that business has such an amazing framework and foundation to really help reframe, reimagine and redesign all the systems on this planet."[8]

This is probably the quality that is most prevalent in conscious leaders working in business: their ability to see how business itself can be the vehicle for transformation of humanity. They are inspired by the possibilities of this and they take action accordingly in their organisations.

Some of the other qualities that Bozesan found, and which are shared by the leaders interviewed for this book, are:

» A deeply held sense of the connectedness of life and of connection with others;

» A sense of service to others and the world;

» A feeling that there is no separation between our spirituality and our personal and professional lives;

» An ability to live life in the present moment and accept reality 'as it is';

» The ability to hold more than one perspective at the same time and to work with paradoxes and think outside of either/or boxes;

» The capacity to set intentions but to be detached from the outcomes; and

» Experiencing life with genuine joy, gratitude and a life-affirming attitude.

Let's begin building this collection of qualities into a user-friendly model of conscious leadership.

A MODEL OF CONSCIOUS LEADERSHIP

From the 20 or so interviews I've conducted for this book, and from the work of my colleagues around the world on conscious leadership, a map for a new model of leadership has begun to emerge. This map plots the qualities of conscious leaders who are ready to take on the challenges of leading in a new world and a new business paradigm that is significantly different from what has gone before.

As with any evolutionary step, we stand on the shoulders of giants – all the individuals who came before us – and this model does the same. You will recognise in it many of the aspects of leadership that you know, and some new ones as well; ones that traditionally belonged to a much more spiritual realm and had no place in business in the old paradigm.

What seems to be emerging differently, however, is how these qualities are constellated. There are particular facets of leadership that are coming to the fore in the present time and these qualities are showing up more frequently in leaders who are suited to wisely and successfully leading in the new world. It is these qualities that form the model of conscious leadership we're using here.

Conscious leadership, as a fairly new term, is often associated with just a single aspect of consciousness; for example, with the current trend of 'mindfulness'. Mindfulness, however, is only one facet of conscious leadership; it is not the full picture. There are many other attributes which we need to consider if we are to develop ourselves as conscious leaders and be fit for purpose leading in a world that's waking up.

In this model, the qualities of conscious leadership can be mapped into four broad sets:

1 Strong self-awareness and self-mastery;

2 Being conscious in the way we conduct our relationships;

3 A high level of awareness of the interconnectedness
   between ourselves and all of life which leads to strong
   systems intelligence and insight; and

4 An inner drive to contribute collectively and act
   responsibly towards the greater whole of which we're
   all part.

Within each of these four 'zones' of conscious leadership lies a
mosaic of personal and leadership qualities which we'll be exploring
throughout this book, using examples from real leaders.

For example, we'll be exploring such questions as:

» What does self-mastery look like in practice for
   conscious leaders?

» What are the attributes we need to engage consciously
   with our employees?

» How do we engage with the wider system to increase
   the level of innovation?

» How do we operate successfully in business while also
   contributing to and being of service to the
   greater whole?

» What does it mean to combine our personal purpose
   as leaders with the purpose of our business?

While the qualities listed here might seem daunting, read them
bearing in mind the 'Note of Caution', on page 61, and remember
that we are aiming for inspiration not perfection.

Figure 2 shows how the four-zone model creates a framework
for conscious leaders to better understand themselves and further
develop qualities of conscious leadership.

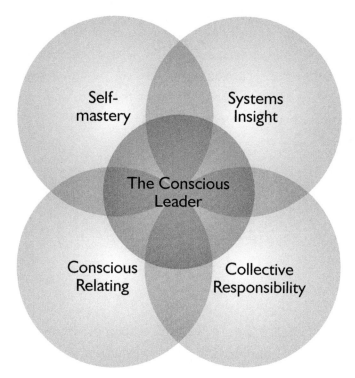

Figure 2: The four-zone model

ZONE 1: SELF-MASTERY

This is the zone of insight into and mastery of ourselves. An important first step on the journey towards becoming a conscious leader is to recognise the ways in which our **ego** plays itself out in our lives. We then need to create some distance from it and begin to build our muscles for transcending it. This moves us from a position of reacting to events, based on our automatic conditioning, habits, unconscious fear reactions and survival drivers, to being better able to consciously choose our responses. This is a key transition to unlocking all kinds of subsequent self-development and self-mastery.

Equally, what changes is the very nature of our **thinking** itself. We become less fixed on a particular point of view and the need to defend this, and more flexible in our views, being able to hold more than one position or perspective at the same time. We move from binary thinking to becoming more nuanced. This develops not just how we think but our very ways of seeing the world. We develop our ability to see how we are seeing and this is the essence of becoming more conscious.

> ## To 'see how we are seeing' is the essence of becoming more conscious

The self-mastery zone is also where we become deeply connected to our individual **purpose** (which in conscious leaders is often linked to their organisation's purpose). We become anchored in our **values**, which provides the framework for our decision-making. Through our clarity of purpose and being rooted in our values, we develop our capacity for enormous **authenticity**. In this, conscious leaders bring their whole selves to their role and encourage others to bring their whole selves to their roles too.

Gaining self-mastery within our lives and choice over our ego grants us the capacity to move from being reactive to being **creative.** Conscious leaders are highly creative beings – not necessarily in the sense that they create works of art, but that they create new realities in the world, new connections beyond the obvious. They are actively involved in articulating new futures. They take **stands** for creating or supporting something in the world that they believe is needed, and they uphold these stands with moral courage.

Essential to our self-mastery is our commitment to continuous learning and to our own **personal evolution**. We develop our spiritual intelligence, which Cindy Wigglesworth defines as, "the ability to act with wisdom and compassion, while maintaining inner and outer peace, regardless of the circumstances."[9] Our spiritual intelligence is, of course, carried through to all the other zones of our conscious leadership and of our lives.

Qualities in the Self-mastery Zone:

» An increasing ability to recognise and distance ourselves from our ego-based reactions;

» The ability to live more consciously through choice;

» An increasing sense of our purpose in the world, linked to our work and, ideally, to our organisation's purpose;

» Knowing what our key values are and using them to anchor ourselves in our decision-making and choices;

» Living and leading as a whole person, which involves bringing our physical, mental, emotional and spiritual sides into awareness and alignment, and being rooted in our values and connected to our sense of higher purpose or contribution;

» A desire to create and articulate new futures and to take stands that bring difference and benefit to the world;

» The ability to hold multiple perspectives at the same time without becoming too attached to any of them;

» Making an investment in our personal evolution and developing and refining our awareness to higher levels; and

» An increase in our spiritual intelligence.

ZONE 2: CONSCIOUS RELATING

If self-mastery deals with the individual, the 'I', then conscious relating deals with the 'We'. Conscious leaders might have huge amounts of self-awareness about their own patterns and drivers, a very strong sense of their purpose in the world and the ability to hold many perspectives at once and think at complex levels in nuanced ways, but the act of leadership takes place in the domain of other people. We are defined as leaders by whether or not other people are willing to follow us, and conscious leaders are defined by how they act in creating this followership.

Conscious leaders engage with others by staying **self-aware** during their interactions. They strive to be conscious, in the moment, which helps them to manage the reactions that invariably occur when engaging with others. As they embody their purpose and live through the stabilising influence of their values, they create an authentic and a congruent experience of leadership for others. They practise being **present**, listening fully and paying close attention to those they're with. This adds presence and weight to their executive authority and inspires others' respect and followership.

Conscious leaders have particular attitudes towards **power**, control and responsibility. These have to do with letting go of the need for **control** and a willingness to share power. Conscious leaders amplify **trust** in others. They are comfortable allowing others the freedom to make decisions and trust them to carry these through without having to control the outcomes themselves. This creates high levels of engagement. Conscious leaders recognise that they cannot be the source of all knowledge and decisions in their organisation and know that they don't hold the dominant or 'correct' point of view. Therefore they seek out **multiple points of view** and actively tune in to the richness of perspectives around them to help decision making and promote sharing of knowledge and information across all points of the organisation. This helps their organisation stay agile in responding to complex challenges and change. In many cases, they are concerned with **holding the space** and keeping everyone in touch with the organisation's purpose, listening for what is needed next and encouraging others to do the same.

Crucially, conscious leaders view **competition** differently – not as something that they or their organisation needs to win whereby others lose, but as an opportunity to create radical and fresh **partnerships** across previously perceived boundaries so that **innovations** can occur. These innovations are often motivated by and in line with their personal purpose linked to their organisation's purpose.

Innovation takes place where many minds can work in unison to combine ideas, and the conscious leader sets up the right environmental conditions for **collaboration** and diversity of perspectives to flourish. This encourages many joined up points of thinking and feedback so that refinements and improvements can be achieved.

Lastly, conscious leaders are also keen to create the right kind of environments for people to flourish and grow consciously themselves. This forms part of their intention to lead people not only towards better performance but also **personal growth**. They are skilful at creating a sense of place – of **community**, tribe or culture – connected to a purpose in which this growth can occur.

Qualities in the Conscious Relating Zone:

» Using our self-awareness in our relationships with others;

» Practising staying conscious and aware during our interactions;

» Being clearly aligned in our values, our purpose and our

behaviour, which creates an authentic and congruent experience for others;

»   Remaining present and attentive to others when interacting with them by listening deeply, which adds to our executive presence;

»   Being comfortable to devolve power, control and responsibility to others and trust them enough to let go;

»   Recognising that multiple viewpoints are better than one viewpoint and, wherever possible, encouraging people to share their views and create many connection points for better quality answers to emerge;

»   Conscious leadership is of a quieter nature, holding the space and purpose for our organisation and sensing what needs to happen next, rather than driving this through our own willpower;

»   Frequently looking for opportunities to join people up and creating radical partnerships across previous lines of competition in order to innovate; and

»   Making space for people to grow not only in their performance, but also in their own levels of consciousness, while connecting them to each other and to the purpose of the organisation.

ZONE 3: SYSTEMS INSIGHT

The third zone of conscious leadership is about being aware of and connected to the wider systems around us, of which we and our organisations are part. Conscious leaders are focussed inwardly as much as they are focussed **outwardly**, frequently on the **furthest** reaches of the system. Their focus often stretches as far as considering the planet and even our future as human beings.

Conscious leaders are highly **interdependent** thinkers. They think macro, not micro, **long-term**, not quarterly results. They are exquisitely attuned to the way the system is connected up and recognise how something that happens in one area, even across the globe, can have an effect on what is happening wherever they are. In the same way, they are conscious that their actions have similar effects on other parts of the system. This drives them to act in **responsible** ways and to encourage responsible action on the part of others. It also drives them to adopt a wider **stakeholder**-oriented mindset by seeing the consequences of their actions on the range of stakeholders in their business system and seeking to balance the value, benefit and health of this larger system. They realise that opting for a quick-fix solution in the short-term is a false economy as it will invariably have a ripple effect elsewhere in the system.

This extends to their attitudes towards **growth**. By taking a long-term view, they are more inclined to see things in terms of balance and **sustainability**. Because they think in whole systems, growth is seen as both a part of the system and as something that needs to happen in unison with everything around it. In comparison with most leaders driven by or pressurised into continual growth, conscious leaders regard growth as part of the bigger picture, something that sometimes happens and sometimes doesn't happen, not as an end in itself.

Conscious leaders see connections and patterns and use this ability to grasp trends and to help their organisations navigate through complex situations. It is not unusual for them to be highly attuned to episodes of **synchronicity** that occur in their world and the connected systems in which they operate. With high levels of connectedness and attunement to the system, conscious leaders can liberally use their **intuition** or inner wisdom to help them make decisions and sense what is needed next in leading their organisations.

In terms of their attitude towards the whole of life, conscious leaders have the capacity to see the reality of the world as it is while at the same time exercising a mindset of **abundance**. They **trust in life** and this leads them to allow life to happen and unfold as opposed to forcing and bending life to their will. Equally, they are leaders who **care passionately about life**, its systems, the planet and all of us on it and this inspires them to create outcomes and take action that shapes a better future for all of us. For conscious leaders operating in business, they believe that business can be a frontier to achieve this positive future.

> *"Leadership is not just what happens inside work, but outside work also."*
> Raj Sisodia

Qualities in the Systems Insight Zone:

» Noticing the systems around us and thinking in systems, which includes the interconnections and dependencies of all parts of the system;

» Taking an evolutionary perspective which considers the whole system, stretching out as far as the planet and beyond and our future as human beings on it;

» The tendency to think in stakeholder terms, including communities of employees, customers, suppliers, shareholders, local communities, society, the environment and the planet;

» Acting in ways, both individually and organisationally, that take responsibility for the long-term effects our actions may have on these systems;

» Seeing growth as something that occurs in balance

with the system around us and avoiding taking the unconscious view of continuous growth at all costs;

» Being attuned to trends, patterns and connections which inform our decisions and our leadership;

» Using our intuition and insight to read into the systems of which we're part;

» Allowing life to unfold rather than forcing it to our individual will; and

» At the same time, taking action and creating realities that shape a better future for us all.

ZONE 4: COLLECTIVE RESPONSIBILITY

As described above, because conscious leaders see life as one continuous interconnected whole, they are acutely conscious of the effects of their actions on others and the world at large. They don't see themselves or their organisations as separate agents, but rather perceive business, life and nature as **one connected entity**. This calls forth within them a deeply felt sense of responsibility to act in the interests of this greater whole of which they and everyone and everything else forms part. Not only do they think about the effects of their actions, and their organisation's actions, on the whole system, but they experience an inner drive to **contribute** towards it for the benefit of all.

Conscious leaders care,
a great deal, about all of life

Conscious leaders see areas that they believe need attention or reformation. Contributing or taking responsibility for these often informs their personal purpose, which in turn shapes their organisation's purpose – if they are in the position to set this up. This is where we see the potential value arising in the contributions that new forms of business can make in the world. Conscious businesses, run by conscious leaders, act in ways that benefit the greater whole and, in that, all of life and all of us.

Of course, conscious leadership is not limited to business. Leaders in government, education, non-profits and social enterprise all have the capacity to use these qualities to **contribute to the greater good** and to lead more consciously.

This last quality sets conscious leaders apart from being merely intellectually clever leaders capable of extremely complex thinking in systems. Conscious leaders literally care, a great deal, about all of life. They try to lead in such a way that benefits the world or at least creates the least amount of harm, and they take responsibility for their actions.

"Simply understand that you've been called to service.
Then love extends from you."
John Mackey

Qualities in the Collective Responsibility Zone:

» We no longer see business as separate from life but as part of it;

» We see business, life and nature as one continuous and connected whole;

» We experience an inner calling and sense of responsibility to contribute to this greater whole, for the benefit of all, through the areas we believe need attention and reformation;

» We look for ways to positively impact the greater whole, all of life and everyone collectively; and

» We see business as the new frontier to help make this happen.

A NOTE OF CAUTION

Although the attributes described in these four zones of the conscious leadership model may seem like a daunting list, the idea is not to get perfectionistic about it. None of us encompasses all of these attributes and the intention here is not to create a wish list which puts pressure on us to fulfil (and which we, invariably, feel we are falling short of), but rather to bring together into one place these qualities that conscious leaders demonstrate, so that we may ask similar questions of ourselves.

We are dynamic beings on an evolutionary journey

In my experience, it doesn't matter where we start (although beginning with creating some distance and choice from our ego-linked behaviours is a good starting point). For the rest of these qualities, we are all likely to be drawn to some more than others and we can listen inwardly to ourselves as to where we'd like to develop next and follow that trail.

It's also the case that each of these qualities is a continuum that has no end point. We are dynamic beings on an evolutionary journey and we can probably always go further than we think. The intention of outlining these qualities is therefore to provide a series of prompts for us to think about ourselves and the ways in which these qualities live within us, rather than to give ourselves a mark out of ten.

Throughout the rest of this book, we will delve into these four zones of conscious leadership and the qualities described above by means of real-life examples and stories from the conscious leaders featured. Amongst these pages you will find many inspiring and heartfelt stories of how these leaders live and lead that will give you insights into how these qualities come to life in real leaders running real organisations.

My hope is that you will be inspired, through the similar qualities in yourself, by the possibility of doing the same.

A CONSCIOUS LEADER'S DEFINITION OF SUCCESS

It would be useful to end this chapter with a look at how conscious leaders typically define success. Unsurprisingly, given the qualities described above, conscious leaders have a slightly different definition of personal success, one that is deeply anchored in their personal purpose and the contribution they want to make.

It may be tempting to think that because conscious leaders see the world as they do, they may not be interested in, nor even very good at, achieving success in the traditional way: those accolades and other bells and whistles that define to us and to others that we have 'made it'. In reality, however, these leaders are incredibly successful, running highly profitable companies and organisations, achieving what many of us measure as worldly success, such as financial success, while they enjoy rich spiritual lives, rewarding relationships and fulfilment of their own sense of their purpose. Somehow, they have incorporated all of the usual metrics of success and expanded the game to include more of life.

Below are excerpts from what some of the conscious leaders featured throughout this book told me when I asked them about what success meant to them.

Paul Monekosso Cleal, a partner in PwC, sees success as being about making a difference: "Making a difference means that other people recognise that you have created value for them. That probably makes me different from some other people who see success on a more personal or individualistic basis, as in, *what's in it for me*."

Dominic Sewela is Deputy CEO of Barloworld Limited in South Africa. Growing up in apartheid era South Africa has fed directly into Dominic's individual purpose and the way he lives this out in his leadership of the company. He told me: "There is a huge difference between success and significance. For me, success is a very simplified thing where people have set themselves targets, financial or otherwise, and when they achieve those milestones they celebrate it and say, 'I've been successful'. Significance is slightly more challenging – it's about making a difference, and more." We'll hear later in this book how Dominic brings to life this notion of significance in his company.

You might rightly wonder whether conscious leadership can be found in 'harder' industries like highly-mechanised production environments such as earthmoving equipment or engineering but, Dominic Sewela is a good example of a conscious leader flourishing in this kind of environment. This is mirrored in the leadership style of Jean-François Zobrist, the CEO of FAVI Enterprises, an engineering firm in northern France. Jean-François told me: "Success is where workers, clients and shareholders are happy. And it is in that order, because it is the happy worker who makes a client happy and it's a happy client that makes a happy shareholder." We can see in Jean-François' response also the tendency to make success about others, rather than only about oneself.

In a similarly industrial setting, Bob Chapman, Chairman and

CEO of Barry-Wehmiller (who was featured in a book on conscious leadership by Raj Sisodia[10], aims for what he calls 'Truly Human Leadership'. Success for Bob involves enabling people to have a life of meaning and purpose. He measures success by the way people's lives are touched within his business. "We must always measure success by the impact on human life," he says.

One of the other conscious leaders featured in this book is Lorna Davis, an executive committee member at Danone, the multinational food products corporation. Highly successful in business from an early age, Lorna ran a 250-million-dollar business as a General Manager at the age of 37. "By all external judgements I was 'there', but I wasn't happy," she says. After a transformational period, which is described more fully later on in this book, Lorna now defines success as, "using my talent and skills to make a difference in the world. I don't need money or power any more, except insofar as I can make a difference."

Difference. Significance. Human happiness. These are the qualities that shape a conscious leader's definition of success.

It's interesting to note that so many of these conscious leaders define success as the extent to which they're able to make a difference to the lives of others. They have built a foundation of traditional measures of success, but have taken this to the next level in the way they now regard being successful. It is a selfless sort of success, one that is defined less by personal glory and more by the way they seek to contribute to the world around them and make an impact. In the process, these leaders are changing the narrative of success, from a dominant paradigm where success is about 'me, not you,' to a paradigm in which success is about 'us'.

"We pursue a life well-lived, and the consequence might just be recognition, success, wealth, and love."
Frederic Laloux

Definitions of Success:
Luke Nosek, Co-founder of PayPal

When he was 27 years old, Luke Nosek, co-founder of PayPal, sold the company to eBay for $1.5 billion. Talking in 2014 at a conference about success, Luke's version of success has become whether he is making his own and others' experience of life better. "It's a subjective metric," he says, "measured by the quality of relationships around me and their experience while using our products."

As many people do, having had his experience of financial success, Luke started asking the, 'what's it all about?' question and found he couldn't come up with an answer. He had been defining success in the usual ways, by making more money and buying more products. One day, he realised he was caught up in the familiar cycle of, 'I've got this – now go get that' and he began to ask himself: 'Didn't I get that thing already?' This made him extremely uncomfortable. After taking a period of time out to explore, travel and reflect, success for Luke has also turned into, "a pure excitement for building new things."

Luke's account mirrors the arc of growth for many people as they look for happiness through the traditional routes of success – the move from 'stuff' to 'better stuff' to 'different stuff' – which ultimately leads to a search for purpose and ends in a desire to make a difference. It might be easy to think that it is all right for someone with the wealth of Luke Nosek to decide on a different and more humanitarian version of success. However, many leaders, in fact many people, follow this same arc through life. The difference with conscious leaders is that they are running their businesses and organisations successfully while making a difference at the same time, and this lends itself to a different form of leadership.

Often the most intriguing aspects of conscious leaders are those stories that describe their own transformation. The events that impacted their lives and caused a difference in the way they see the world are fascinating and prompt us to ask ourselves where similar events and influences may have happened in our own lives, and what we can learn from them.

Difference. Significance.
Human happiness.

Endnotes

1   George, Bill. 2015. *Discover Your True North*. New Jersey: John Wiley & Sons, Inc.

2   Vielmetter, Georg and Sell, Yvonne. 2014. *Leadership 2030: The Six Megatrends You Need to Understand to Lead Your Company into the Future. New York: AMA*

3   https://www.linkedin.com/pulse/you-conscious-leader-kevin-rafferty-the-conscious-leaders-coach

4   Renesch, John. 2012. *The Great Growing Up: Being Responsible for Humanity's Future*. Arizona: Hohm Press, p174.

5   Adapted from Wrzesniewski, Amy. Yale Professor of Organizational Behavior: http://som.yale.edu/amy-wrzesniewski

6   Renesch, John. 2012. *The Great Growing Up: Being Responsible for Humanity's Future*. Arizona: Hohm Press, p172.

7   Mackey, John and Sisodia, Raj. 2014. *Conscious Capitalism: Liberating the Heroic Spirit of Business*. USA: Harvard Business School Publishing Corporation.

8   Bozesan, Ph.D., Mariana. 2010. *The Making of a Consciousness Leader in Business: An Integral Approach*. San Francisco & Munich: SageEra, p239.

9   Wigglesworth, Cindy. 2014. *SQ21: The Twenty-One Skills of Spiritual Intelligence*. New York: SelectBooks, p8.

10 Chapman, Bob and Sisodia, Raj. 2015. *Everybody Matters: The Extraordinary Power of Caring for Your People Like Family*. New York: PORTFOLIO/PENGUIN.

ZONE 1: SELF-MASTERY

3

WAKING UP

A fundamental question for anyone looking to be a conscious leader is: *do I want to get better and better at the dream, or do I want to wake up from it?* This book has the phrase 'waking up' very intentionally in its title. In this section we'll explore the process of waking up – of becoming more conscious – and look deeply at how this plays out in the lives of conscious leaders.

When we wake up (in truth, life is usually a series of 'waking ups'), we begin to move away from being a smaller self, more contracted and focussed primarily on 'me', to a bigger and broader self, more connected to others and to the world at large, able to incorporate the viewpoints of others into our own. We shift, in effect, from 'me' to 'we'.

We can get captivating glimpses of the possibilities for our own awakening from the examples of others and their moments of realisation. These moments describe to us what happens, but they also touch on possibilities for our own transformation, for what we can become, that lie just outside the boundaries of our existing awareness. This can initiate moments of 'A-ha!' in us and inspire us to reach towards new and more conscious versions of ourselves.

WHAT IS WAKING UP?

Waking up is another way of describing the process by which we become more conscious. Just as the sun rises and becomes more illuminating, as we become conscious we are more aware of our mind-made conditioning that lies just beneath the surface of our awareness: those automatic thoughts, feelings, beliefs, values, habits and worldviews that operate often unconsciously, yet drive us and our behaviour every day. Until we become conscious of these parts of ourselves, they run the show for us and we remain on autopilot, but as we wake up, we start to see more and more of our own conditioning and become more aware of where we are simply functioning out of unconscious patterns. We begin to see the lenses through which we have been habitually viewing the world, almost like a pair of spectacles. What previously we were only able to look *through*, we are now able to step back from and look *at*. And, because we're no longer just acting unconsciously, we have a much greater degree of choice over our actions and our reactions, day by day, moment by moment.

We go about our lives walking the footpaths of our actions into freeways of habit, without ever questioning why

What is the value of becoming more conscious? We could just go about our lives responding to events that happen to us, or our own thoughts and feelings, and live an unexamined life. But, as Socrates said, the unexamined life is not worth living and it is unlikely that we would be lastingly happy as we get bobbed about like a cork in the sea of events.

Many of us, for much of the time, are inclined to live mostly from the neck up. In fact, many of us live only from the eyes up. Pete Hamill, an expert in embodied leadership, is fond of saying that for many of us, our bodies are simply a way of getting our brains around from meeting to meeting.[1] At our most unconscious, we go about our lives having the same sorts of reactions to the same kinds of circumstances, walking the footpaths of our actions into freeways of habit, without ever questioning why we are doing something or, indeed, whether we have any choice in the matter.

It is unlikely that many of us are unconscious to this degree, though we are all somewhere along this journey to becoming more conscious. The more we pay attention to and become aware of our own conditioning, the more choices we have over it, and the more we wake up.

As we become more conscious, we naturally begin to experience this benefit:

Awareness = Choice
No awareness = No choice

Waking up affords us tremendous power by giving us the opportunity to become creative agents in our own lives. We get to choose to respond rather than react, to shape ourselves, to be self-authoring. Conscious awareness gives us choice.

Another useful way of viewing our own consciousness is like a human operating system. Like any operating system, all of our functions, the way we think, feel, interpret things, our values, beliefs and habits, are built upon it, like apps. As Renesch describes in *The Great Growing Up: Being Responsible for Humanity's Future*[2], it makes a huge difference which operating system we use in the way we think about and see the world, because all other functions are based upon this underlying system.

The more complex the world becomes for leaders to navigate, the more they need to upgrade their operating system. Imagine you were still running on an operating system equivalent of DOS. Only certain functions or apps are going to be possible for you and you'd struggle to keep up with the changing demands and pace of your environment. Similarly, our leadership roles in a challenging and complex world require us all to evolve.

Old leadership styles simply won't boot up in the new leadership context

---

It takes a greater complexity of mind to lead in more complex environments and into uncertain futures. It also takes a greater complexity of mind to lead others in the collaborative and hyper-connected way that our new leadership paradigm is demanding. As with all evolution, our business context has expanded and is changing, and the old ways don't work as well any more. There are challenges, dilemmas and opportunities that are beyond what we have encountered. We need to expand our perspectives and increase our efficiency of processing. In effect, we need to adapt and evolve to become a more complex operating system if we are to be successful. The old leadership styles simply won't boot up in the new context – or they will run slowly and clumsily.

Figure 3: The leadership operating system

The questions to ask ourselves are: *have we upgraded ourselves as leaders? Are we still operating from our previous level of consciousness or are we working from the consciousness equivalent of the latest version of Windows or OS?*

ADULT DEVELOPMENT THEORY

One useful way of looking at how we might upgrade ourselves is through the lens of 'adult development theory'. Traditionally, we've thought that our development stops at some point around our twenties and that we're pretty much set as human beings from there on for the rest of our lives.

However, the body of work known as adult development theory shows how we in fact continue to develop across the span of our adult lifetimes. The difference, however, is that instead of developing physically or in the relative size of our brains, what we do develop – if we choose to, under the right circumstances – is the ability to grow our minds. This happens by integrating what we previously saw and knew to ever higher levels of complexity and nuance. We begin to make meaning of the world in more varied and more inclusive ways.

Through this mode of development, we leave behind the 'skins' of our old worldviews and evolve to seeing the world as more complex and integrated. It is this that shifts us from an either/or way of thinking to both/and. It is also what stops us from thinking and acting as if we are separate from others, somehow disconnected from them. Growing our perspective kick-starts the process by which we see that we are all connected and as one.

Adult development drives a different set of behaviours as a leader, that no longer looks to compete, win and achieve at all costs, but instead looks to compete, win and achieve together with others, for the benefit of all. The creative tension and diversity implicit in collaboration around many viewpoints is what gives advantage. We move away from more ego-driven (me-first) to less ego-driven (we-first) ways of seeing, being and acting in the world.

This trend has been called 'vertical development' which, incidentally, is identified as one of the most critical factors in developing leaders of the future.[3] Vertical development is distinct from 'horizontal development'. Horizontal development involves the development of our behaviours, our skills and our competencies as leaders. Vertical development is about how we develop our ways of making meaning in the world. How we do this can be seen in the diagram below. As we become more conscious of ourselves, we move from a perspective which is a single point of view to collecting around us similar points of view to form a group; to being able to see that group in context amongst other groups; to joining groups together;

and to finally being able to see in systems – essentially, a collection of many, many groups, all interconnected.

All the while, we begin to look for factors that differentiate us and make us similar, and in the process we become able to see the great many interconnections that exist between us all.

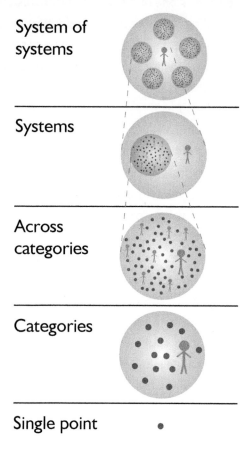

Figure 4: Adapted from Robert Kegan, In Over our Heads: the Mental Demands of Modern Life (Cambridge: Harvard University Press, 1994), pp 314-315, by Peter W. Pruyn. http://developmentalobserver.blog.com

We can see how this evolutionary process by which we 'see how we are seeing' enables us to think at ever greater levels of complexity, subtlety and refinement. Where previously, certain things were excluded from our viewpoint because they didn't fit in with our worldview, now many points of view become available to us and we are able to hold these multiple positions in our minds at the same time and see each in relation to the others and to ourselves. This breadth of perspective is one of the many advantages that conscious leaders have in dealing with a complex and interconnected world.

The way we grow in consciousness is often described as being like a fish that sees the water it is swimming in for the first time: prior to this moment the fish only saw water – or, in fact, it didn't even know there was water, it just swam. Its context was defined by water and that is where the boundaries of its perception lay. Transferring this metaphor to the human context, as we begin to 'see our own water' – those beliefs, values and perspectives that we take for granted as the way the world works – we, too, become capable of seeing the water we're swimming in. From here on, we have some choices: to continue as is or to grow.

As leaders, this growth has been mapped in a very useful way by Bill Torbert[4], Principal of Action Inquiry Associates, and his colleagues at Harthill Consulting, who have defined several stages or 'centres of gravity' which we go through as adults, particularly relating to our ways of operating in organisations. These stages refer to our levels of vertical development. (See Figure 5.)

According to this framework, the development of our conscious-ness as leaders follows an arc, from being highly self-orientated in the Opportunist stage (driven by our own egos) and wanting to win and survive at all costs, to wanting to belong and fit in with a group (Diplomat stage). We move on from there to prizing ourselves and others for our expertise and skills and primarily valuing logic (Expert stage). From here, we develop the thinking associated with the typical leadership stage, the Achiever. Approximately 52% of the management population sampled in 2015[5] are profiled as operating from the Achiever stage. They are driven by personal and team achievement and well-suited to achieving goals and juggling managerial demands – but, crucially, they don't actually yet question why they are chasing these goals. The meaning of life at this stage of adult development is mostly made up of pursuing goals and achieving them, which are typical leadership and managerial actions in most organisations.

At some point in our lives, it may occur to us to ask why pursuing these goals is so important; why we need to get more 'stuff'. There are some engaging stories at the end of this chapter about the journeys of conscious leaders who have come up against this question. In fact, questioning our worldview creates a significant breakthrough in our level of awareness. What we previously took for granted – even that which was unquestioned – is thrown open to the light of day. We have begun to wake up. (In adult development terms, this important shift is called the breakthrough from 'conventional' to 'post-conventional' thinking.)

What it means, effectively, is that the game we were playing is up. When we wake up, we undergo a fundamental change in our way of thinking and making meaning in the world, and this change is irreversible. Just like the fish that sees the water it is swimming in for the first time and can never go back again to not knowing water, we cannot go back to our previous levels of knowing in which we were less awake than we are now. Each step beyond this point is a more expansive act of waking up, bringing with it more structural changes in our consciousness.

By the time we experience these kinds of awakenings, most of us recognise that these changes in us are irreversible, because we realise that our previous worldviews were just an illusion, merely made up[6]. It is this kind of realisation I had at sixteen, while sitting in church, as described in the Introduction, when I realised that all models of religious truth were constructs and there was no way of distinguishing better and worse between them on the basis of their respective 'books of truth'.

The breakthroughs described above are part of what, in adult development theory, is called the Individualist stage. At this stage we become fascinated by the fact that everything is relative; all viewpoints have merit to us. Individualists account for about 27–33% of leaders[7].

Moving on beyond this point, we might develop even further towards the Strategist stage. These are the leaders who are most interested in generating personal and organisational transformation and they are effective transformational leaders. They imagine and articulate a vision for their organisation's future whilst at the same time ensuring it is running effectively in the present.[8]

Strategist-stage leaders, using this model, represent only about 8% of the profiled leaders today. There is a real need in organisational terms to grow more leaders operating from the Strategist stage because of the increased demand for working with complexity and transformation in organisations.[9]

Beyond the Strategist stage of adult development we find the Alchemist leaders. These are the kinds of leaders who are interested in integrating material, spiritual and societal transformation. They take the widest and most inclusive view possible and are closely connected to the system, looking to create transformations that affect the furthest reaches of it. Some of the leaders in this book demonstrate several aspects of this level of adult development thinking both in the ways they look to create change that has implications for the entire planet and humanity and in the ways they go about this. This kind of meaning making is very rare – around 2% of us operate at this level, according to adult development theory.

Seven Transformations of Leadership

Alchemist	- Integrates material, spiritual and societal transformations	2%
Strategist	- Generates organizational and personal transformations	8%
Individualist	- Reframes complex problems in unique ways	27%
Achiever	- Driven by personal and team achievement	51%
Expert	- Focuses on logic and expertise	12%
Diplomat	- Wants to belong and fit in	0%
Opportunist	- Wins for self in any way possible	0%

(c) Harthill Consulting Limited, 2016, percentages (rounded figures) based on 6,000 consultants, managers and executives profiled worldwide.

Figure 5: Sourced from Torbert's Action Logics

Since latest figures suggest that around 37–43% of us have 'broken through' the proverbial ceiling into post-conventional ways of thinking, this tells us that a large proportion of leaders are operating from the earlier stage of Achiever, driven by their personal, team and organisational ambitions of *doing*. They see attaining these goals and targets as their *raison d'être* and may not necessarily question why they are doing this but instead take it as read that their roles as leaders requires them to do so.

For those leaders becoming more conscious, however – and probably if you have picked up this book and have read this far you are one of these leaders – you are likely to have undergone some kind of process that got you to ask *why*. You are also more likely to be interested in transformational change, and the transformation of all within your organisation – and possibly even your organisation's role in the transformation of society – as you move through the stages of Individualist, Strategist and even Alchemist.

What's important to bear in mind about this model is that you cannot force the pace of your own development along this continuum. Later stages are not necessarily 'better than' earlier stages, since we need to take care of our own development and build stable structures upon which our personal evolution can rest. Like buildings without strong foundations, the floors of our own personal development will not be held up if we have not taken the time to develop at each stage, to allow our own cement to set, as it were. Therefore, the horizontal development of our personality attributes, skills, qualities and competencies is equally important to make us whole as leaders.

It would be wrong to approach adult development theory, and the development of our own levels of consciousness, as some kind of competition by which we need to race ahead and get there first – wherever 'there' and 'first' may be. In fact, doing so would be reminiscent of an earlier stage of meaning-making – probably Expert or Achiever. Integration of our previous worldviews and ways of making meaning in the world is what builds strong foundations for our own personal evolution. Many practitioners of adult development theory suggest that it can take at least three years to move from one stage to the next. What might cause these shifts is explored later on in this chapter.

IS THERE ANYBODY OUT THERE?

Leaders who are more conscious, and who might be thought of as operating from the worldviews of the later stages (Individualist, Strategic, Alchemist), have a peculiar challenge on their hands; one that you may be intimately acquainted with as you read this book. The challenge is that you may find yourself seeing the world in fundamentally different ways from many of your colleagues – sometimes even feeling as if you are speaking a different language from them.

While you might see the importance of having relative viewpoints and holding many perspectives at once, and while you may be very interested in the transformation of your own organisation and the way it becomes a catalyst for growth of everyone in it, as well as being a positive influence on society whilst making a profit, those around you may still be thinking in terms of traditional objectives, measurements, competencies and yardsticks.

How you go about making yourself understood is fairly critical at this stage, while conscious leadership is still in its green shoots phase. As others have described, people at earlier stages of adult development have difficulty fully comprehending or appreciating the thinking of those whose viewpoints are more developed and complex than theirs currently are. In addition to this, at the earlier stages of our development as adults, our egos are invested in holding on to the rightness of our own views. The suggestion that we might need to let go of these and move on to something more vague, and seemingly less stable, can be very threatening to the ego.

As conscious leaders, therefore, how we speak in ways that will reach everyone in our organisation, no matter what their stage of development, becomes important. What we know is that forcing the process doesn't work – it simply breeds resistance. As Laloux describes: "From all we know, climbing the developmental ladder is a complex, mysterious, spiritual process. It happens from within and cannot be imposed on somebody from the outside, not even with the best of arguments."[10] It is not a logical process; it is one that needs to be experienced, and even that experience cannot be rushed.

The really influential question, according to Peter Matthies, is: how far can we move the needle of our consciousness along the continuum from where we are towards an ever more conscious

paradigm? He says: "That's why I think consciousness and awareness is at the core of it. We need to become aware of our thoughts
that drive our behaviours and the ripple effect we create out in the
world, if we want to change the way we do things."

Going really big-scale for a moment, other authors and thinkers,
like integral philosopher Ken Wilber, point out that the changes
humanity needs to make in the external world, need to be matched
by changes in our internal world as well. The outer reflects the inner.
Conscious leaders can hold in place a more developed and sustainable world, especially if this leads to the development of consciousness in others as well.

Evolving on purpose is the adult
choice made by humans who are
engaged in their own development

The development of our inner worlds – that is to say, the development of our consciousness – is critical at this point in time as we
face the challenges on the global stage. This is the first time that
we have, at the level of critical mass, been purposefully engaged
with our own conscious evolution. In *The Great Growing Up*, Renesch
points out that being conscious of this choice differentiates us as
human beings from the animal kingdom and confronts us with the
question: *How do we want to evolve?* Do we want to have a hand in
creating a future we all want, or will we evolve by accident? Evolving
on purpose is the adult choice made by humans who are engaged
in their own development and who take responsibility for their own
collective future.

THE ADVANTAGES OF WAKING UP IN BUSINESS

Let us now bring the vastness of this worldview right down to the reality of business, by looking at some of the advantages that conscious leaders can create. As business is a powerful influencing force in the world at large, it makes sense to develop as many conscious leaders as possible because of the benefits they can bring by transforming organisations, their employees, their stakeholders and their systems.

This book is filled with examples of how conscious leaders use their expanded awareness to run their organisations, and their lives, differently. This extends to the cultures they create in their organisations, how they source insights and continuously innovate, how they encourage collaboration and co-create in order to do this, and how they use their own levels of presence and awareness to lead and have a different kind of impact on others. Their influence as conscious leaders also extends to the effect they have on the world at large: how they look to transform society, for instance, or innovate with the purpose of having a positive influence on the future of the world.

A couple of examples serve as an introduction.

Peter Matthies tells a familiar tale of how companies try their hardest to change their culture, but whatever they do it doesn't seem to take effect. He was once working with one of the world's largest IT companies which wanted to change its culture. They were employing the biggest strategy and consulting houses in the world to help achieve this, but nothing was working. In the process, they had let 25% of their top managers go, and still they couldn't get their people to collaborate properly. "This is because 'changing culture' is not a behavioural thing," said Peter, "it's a mindset thing. A consciousness thing. And the million-dollar question is: *how do we change people's mindsets; the way they think?*" He used one of the many programmes his company offers to do just this, to develop levels of consciousness in the leaders and employees of this organisation. The lesson learned? Changing levels of consciousness throughout an organisation by encouraging people to think differently, fundamentally changes the game of culture, and this has positive effects on engagement, energy, motivation, collaboration and purpose.

When it comes to accelerating innovation and insight across an organisation, Barrett Brown, MD at Apheno Advisory, conducted his PhD on conscious leaders who were engaged in complex change. He has a fascinating story to tell about the way conscious leaders source information. With greater levels of consciousness, Brown points out[11], comes our increased mental capacity to join the dots and make links across different disciplines, different sectors and different projects. There is, literally, a 'cognitive ramping up of intellectual horsepower' in conscious leaders since, with their greater capacity to think at more complex levels, they are able to see patterns and glean information from these patterns that less aware leaders might miss precisely because they are attached to their own viewpoint.

What is needed is to turn up our intuitive insight

As well as seeing patterns and links in information around them, conscious leaders are also more present and open in how they access their intuitive faculties alongside their rational faculties. Intuitive insights go deeper than the rational mind. These leaders recognise that many of the more difficult problems their organisation face are too complex to deal with using logical thinking. As Brown describes it, you can't map out all the variables and the rational mind simply runs out of tracks. What is needed is to turn up our intuitive insight.

He describes the arrival of intuitive insight as 'lightning bolts' and 'sunrises'. Lightning bolts are those moments of insight that take you by surprise (such as the proverbial 'eureka!' moment, while sitting in the bath). Sunrises are those occasions when the landscape that you've been working on gradually becomes clearer and you begin seeing what you've not seen before. It's not about throwing away the rational mind, advises Brown, but about turbocharging it with additional power of our intuitive capacities.

While conscious leaders experience their own intuitive insights, they also demonstrate another key skill, namely sourcing insights from the collective intelligence of others. All conscious leaders have travelled a sufficient distance away from their own egos which means they are able to get out of the way and allow the answers to come from many voices rather than just their own. In fact, as we shall see, they actively seek to put in place structures, processes and activities that enable many voices to be heard and for collective intelligence to be harvested.

Tomorrow's leadership will be largely defined by distributed and collective leadership. It is essentially about moving from leadership that is heroic to post-heroic.[12] This means tapping into the collective intelligence of those who are directly involved in the challenge. Conscious leaders are adept at bringing these people and communities together to co-create the best solutions. They engage others in ways that release our capacities to contribute and move the situation forward a step at a time.

The era where we needed to be the smartest person in the room in order to shine is rapidly being replaced by conscious leaders who prefer to share power and convene the widest range of stakeholders in a collaborative dialogue around purpose. They know how to get the most from combining the insights of all of those present. Distributed, collective leadership is certainly one of the key qualities shared by all the leaders featured in this book as they talk about some of the ways they put this into action.

It's worth highlighting one other advantage of conscious leadership, which is the value of having awareness and presence in business. Part of the path we walk to wake up and become more conscious is to become more present and aware of ourselves *in the moment*: of what is driving us, of our unexamined assumptions, biases and beliefs, of our own conditioning. As we saw earlier in this chapter, the more aware we are of the landscape of ourselves, the more choices we have over it, whether to re-enact this or to choose something different for ourselves.

Self-awareness not only gives conscious leaders more choice in regard to how they manage themselves, but also gives them a heightened sense of presence. Because they are present, in the moment, attending closely to what is going on and being tuned in to the people around them, this lends them a particular quality of presence and sometimes even charisma that the busier, more distracted leaders don't have. Presence is great for getting people engaged, for building trust and for noticing patterns that produce insights.

We are at our most potent, our most influential and our most powerful in the present moment

---

What takes presence away from us? The current mindfulness revolution has many answers to this. We know that we lose presence because our minds are always busy, our thoughts forever chattering, commenting, drawing us away from and out of the present moment, either into the past (and, frequently, our regrets and guilt) or into the future (and frequently our anxieties and fears about what will happen). We can become lost in our stories of the past and future and lose the potency to deal with the situation we find ourselves in in the present. It renders us only partially available to all the data and possibilities with which to make our decisions. It interferes with our ability to access intuitive insights and see the connections and the patterns all around us.

We are at our most potent, our most influential and our most powerful dealing in the present moment, withdrawing our energy from distractions and placing it in the here-and-now. We enjoy greater creativity and insight and being present also enables us to stay centred and open, and look at events rather than react to them. What all this adds up to is that leaders need not be asleep in their circumstances. The array of mindfulness techniques available to us are all geared towards strengthening our ability to stay in the present moment.

An example of the benefits of being present comes from conscious leader Frederic Desbrosses, General Manager at Mars® Turkey. He describes the advantages in this way: "A good level of self-awareness is basic for good leadership. I have never seen a great leader without a great central awareness. And you don't need to filter out your environment any more. Decision-making becomes clear. People are always telling me, 'Frederic, you are not stressed,' but I don't think it's stress because I have the same pressure as everyone. It's just that things come clearly to you when you're self-aware. You are connected, you feel your environment, you feel the people around you and it helps you to get it very clearly."

Advantages of being conscious in business:

» Creating a culture of energy and engagement.

» Accelerating insight and innovation across the organisation.

> » Being present, aware and focussed on dealing effectively
>   with the situation at hand.

HOW DO WE WAKE UP?

In the final section of this chapter, we'll be looking at some of the experiences that leaders might go through in waking up and becoming more conscious. In many respects, it has to do with shedding our old 'skin' and becoming a new version of ourselves.

Waking up has to do with shedding our old 'skin' and becoming a new version of ourselves

---

How we become more conscious is well documented in various spiritual texts the world over. Often we undergo a life experience that rattles the foundations of our worldview, leading to a loss of the certainty we once felt and upon which we were contentedly resting. Sometimes we are simply shaped by the experiences of life in a less dramatic way, leading to a more gradual experience of waking up. Occasionally, we have a deeper knowing about life from an early age that shapes our interpretation of the world and how we relate to it. And, sometimes, we simply experience 'the end of achievement', where the things that used to satisfy us, the ways in which we gained our sense of value and validation, simply aren't enough any more.

Let's take a closer look at these four types of experiences of waking up, as told by the leaders interviewed for this book.

A CRISIS OF CERTAINTY

Having one's worldview cracked open is often a painful experience. "You can transform through agony or ecstasy. But most people choose agony," says John Renesch. John can pretty much be regarded as the 'forefather' of conscious leadership, having been a frontrunner in the field for many years before it even had a name. His agony or ecstasy theory certainly holds true for another leader, Sudhakar Ram, Global CEO of Mastek, an IT multinational, who told me: "In my early thirties, I had a level of certainty about everything, about myself. I was confident that I could always make things happen. I thought I knew a lot. The financial crisis of 2009 was probably the first time that these ideas about myself were shocked into a rude awakening and I started to question, *do I really know anything?* I tried every strategy at that time and it just didn't work. In a business that was always growing, it is sad when you start declining, and then declining in a rapid way. And we are a public company, so investors came around and they put me under pressure and asked me questions that I didn't really have the answers to. With the benefit of hindsight, it was a beautiful moment, but at the time it was not."

This kind of awakening, of breaking out of one's previous self, is often excruciatingly uncomfortable, and it is only with the benefit of time passing and looking back that you begin to see that this was the path towards greater personal growth. At the time, we feel under attack, confused and bewildered as our previous certainties begin to disintegrate and we have nothing, other than trust, to hold on to.

Undergoing personal coaching at the time, Sudhakar's key decision was to stop trying to make things happen and to let go. He realised that there was no need to hang on to something which he wasn't doing his best at. "That was a very important moment for me, personally," he says. Surrendering his usual control and certainty led to a period of intense personal and professional growth. He took his entire executive team to Otto Scharmer's Presencing Institute in Boston, where they underwent training on Scharmer's Theory U programme (see Chapter 13).

"What came to me in a flash while I was there," Sudhakar says, "is that I cannot play at this as if I'm a traditional business while at the same time trying to do something and be something different. I had to declare my game, my intentions to be different, and by doing so, I realised that everything else would fall in line."

Sudhakar is talking here about the conscious leader's essential trust in life greater than his or her individual will. The clarity of his insight meant that Sudhakar was able to be completely clear and open in the way he articulated Mastek's future to his shareholders, customers and employees. His intention was to establish Mastek as a self-organising company system of hub teams with decision-making powers, very much along the lines of what Laloux has since described in *Reinventing Organizations*. As time passed, Mastek as an organisational system self-corrected and settled. Virtually the entire executive team realised they no longer wanted to have a role in the company in its new guise and they left on positive terms, having simply decided that they and the company did not fit together any longer.

John Renesch experienced similar challenges to his worldview. "The transition for me," he recounts, "was when I started New Leaders Press. It was a good business idea, connecting up credible business people in the world who were having conversations about spirituality at work. In the process, I started changing from an entre-preneur into a writer and thinker and, when I woke up to it, I realised the company could have been doing a lot better than it was, because writing about ideas had become far more interesting to me than making the business work. I hired a CEO to run it for me, but it was a case of too little, too late."

This experience, combined with a significant relationship that broke up at the same time, was the archetypal 'crisis of certainty' for John, who says: "I realised that the way I was moping around was disproportionate to the reality of events. I saw that I was in the midst of a midlife crisis and that the relationship I was in was essentially a distraction. After a couple of years of seemingly being in pain, I got involved in the human-potential movement and got my first realisation that my life does not need to be the same tomorrow as it was yesterday."

THE END OF ACHIEVEMENT

Sometimes it is not a specific life event that cracks open the shell of our existing self, but simply a gnawing and ever-growing dissatisfaction with the way our life is, no matter how successful we are. These kinds of leaders have been naturally successful and are achievers, but there comes a time when this achievement and success becomes empty and they begin to ask themselves, *is there something more?*

Neal Gandhi is a British serial entrepreneur who has enjoyed significant material success and is now an angel investor. Throughout his life, he has built a number of businesses but, by his own admission, "the purpose of those businesses was pretty much to make me money. That's what they were about; that's what I went off to do."

Even though his businesses were financially highly successful, at another level this drive was causing massive destruction in his life: "I'm twice divorced, and there was destruction of the people around me, a mess. I'd done four consecutive start-ups over 20 years and I'd taken no time out in between. I was on a treadmill where no matter what we achieved, there was never enough money for home improvements or to take time out to be a family, because it was all about making the next lot of money."

Even before his second wife told him she was leaving their marriage, he had begun to question why he was chasing achievement in this way. Was he really meant to be doing an average of one start-up every five years? He wasn't entirely sure he had the energy for it! The breakdown of his second marriage stopped him in his tracks and made him think about who he was, what he was here to do, what his values were and what the principles were that he was living by.

Life dealt him an additional stark dose of reality in the form of a new business idea: "About a year later, a distant relative contacted me to ask for help in setting up a cleaning company. I knew nothing about cleaning but I thought it couldn't be that hard. This business got me exposed to what it means to be earning a living wage and how people cope. My consciousness began to emerge around how people live and the impact that business has on the lives of its different stakeholders. I got to a place in my head where I was thinking about conscious capitalism without even knowing anything about the term."

Neal continues to invest in companies that are purpose-driven for the greater good, and some of his stories are featured throughout this book. What is notable about Neal is his way of being. He is now blessed with an abundance of time and choice, free of the scarcity mindset that was driving him before. On the day I spoke to him, in addition to managing significant interests in a number of companies, he had just returned from Arizona, where he had been training himself in eliciting alpha brainwave states at will and was on his way that evening to Switzerland, to a lecture on the Hadron collider at CERN, "because this whole journey for me has awoken a real interest in quantum physics."

Another conscious leader for whom achievement began to lose its appeal is Steve Hall, who is now CEO of driversselect, a US-based second-hand car company. driversselect specialises in the 'nearly new' car market and is aiming to revolutionise the way business is done in this industry. It does this through radically upgrading the customers' experience and by adhering to certain core values. This approach makes the company a great place to work and turns it into a conduit for each employee's expression of what makes him or her unique.

Steve, who comes from a family of entrepreneurs, learned about how business works in various companies and then started his own businesses, discovering he had a knack for growing a business based on financial results. "At the age of 40," he says, "I had pretty much hit all my financial targets and I had achieved everything I thought about how successful business should look – yet I was surprised by how unhappy and unhealthy I was. My marriage was not healthy, I didn't have a good connection with my family and I was constantly exhausted. That's when I realised that I was living a life that was not true to myself and my own values; that I was living a life that was about the expectations of other people, and what they valued."

He set up driversselect and, in the process, Steve has created a growing business that fulfils both his own values and the values of each of the employees who work for the company. "It occurred to me," he says, "that people often come to work thinking they have to be someone they're not. Then they want more work-life balance because they want to be who they are, and be around people who have similar values. So I thought, wait a second, why can't we create that balance in our work environment? If we need to be here 50 hours a week in this industry, why not make work life mirror personal life?" driversselect achieves this through its four key values and the company defines success as people being fulfilled and able to be themselves at work.

Another leader who experienced the end of achievement is Peter Matthies, whom we met earlier in this chapter. He recalls how his high-flying consulting career lost its shine: "When I look back at my life, sitting in my VC office in Munich for Andersen Consulting (now Accenture), I was scratching my head and saying, 'This sucks. I need to do something different.' One of the moments when I woke up, I was at a client assignment in Holland. I looked at myself in the mirror and said: 'What the hell am I doing here? This isn't how it's supposed to be; this is not inspiring. I can't do this for the rest of my life.' I went back to my office and asked a lot of my colleagues the same question and they all said the same thing: it's work and we have to do it; this is the way it is. But for me, those answers weren't satisfying. I thought: there must be something different out there. This was a big source of pain for me for a very long time, because I felt very alone with that."

He quit his job at Andersons and started his own software company and built that up for a while – and came to exactly the same point of realisation. One day, looking out at the Alps, he had another epiphany. "I saw the beauty of the Alps and it completely stopped me in my tracks. I asked myself, what are we doing here? And what do I want to do with my life? Because this is not it." This time, Peter sold his share of the company and took a completely different path to California, where he became involved with a mentor who changed his life.

This story has a happy ending: Peter realised that there was no pathway, no curriculum to get from 'here' (where leaders are dissatisfied and beginning to wake up) to 'there' (being a conscious leader in business). There was only a scattering of personal development courses and practices available. So, he has created an online curriculum to develop conscious leaders through the Conscious Business Institute.

Sometimes conscious leaders think that they need to leave the corporate world in order to be true to the person they are becoming. Often this is the case. They look to set up their own enterprises or turn to consultancy. However, the story of Lorna Davis shows how it is possible to blend your growing awareness with your role in a very corporate structure, if you can find the right environment to do so.

We met Lorna in the previous chapter, talking about her perspectives on success. In her life, she had always been achievement-focussed and driven by action. She says: "My life has genuinely been a meandering wander through the world, saying yes to whatever challenge anybody offered me. It's very unfashionable to speak like this when people talk about their burning passion and their vision of success. Quite frankly, all I wanted to do was have a great time, make lots of money and get stuff done. I was always very active and I wanted real achievements."

Lorna went from business success to business success, culminating in running a 250-million-dollar business as a General Manager in the Far East at the age of 37. "I was very interested in what I could control, and I liked business because I could get things done. I also liked being a leader because I could get things done. The underlying motivation was very masculine." After a while, it became clear to Lorna that she was ticking off achievement myth after achievement myth, but this was not making her happy. At the same time, she was doing a lot of personal transformation work and developing her own levels of consciousness. This brought her an important insight: by going about things as she was, she wasn't meeting her value of freedom and she wasn't happy.

The starkness of this realisation was enough to make her leave the corporate life that had been such a key part of her identity up to that point. Although she was convinced she would never return, she did in fact re-join the corporate world, but this time as Chief Manifesto Catalyst for Danone, a role which sees her leading the company's innovative and ambitious social purpose transformation programme. Lorna is responsible for strengthening the economic and social impact agenda for Danone by 2020, and for amplifying the bottom-up innovations she finds that meet the company's social purpose. She finds examples of social impact innovation in Danone's teams on the ground and promotes these across the company and within the local communities.

Lorna now defines success very differently from the way she did before, when it was all about reaching achievement milestones: "I'm realising that it's about being in every moment, getting the best blend of the inside and the outside yourself, and doing the best you can to make a difference."

BEING SHAPED BY LIFE'S EXPERIENCES

Dominic Sewela was born in apartheid-era South Africa and his company, Barloworld Limited, is based in South Africa. It's hard to overstate the enormity of this transition, from growing up on the wrong side of the tracks in a country split by racism, to Deputy CEO of a large multinational today.

Dominic's experiences growing up have instilled in him a deeply held set of values about the importance of contribution, not only to business but to the society around you. When I first met him, on a consciousness transformation programme in 2009, Dominic recalls how he had stumbled upon, "this thing called consciousness coaching because all the other coaching programmes that I saw were not appealing to me." He learned an important lesson about humility in the process: "When I first walked in there, I expected to see other CEOs and, to be honest with you, I was probably the only one. The first day I was questioning why I was there, but I had to just let that go because I was so preoccupied with myself I was not thinking about the objective, and the objective was to listen. People were sharing their personal stories and asking me about my challenges, and at that point I challenged myself to get off my ego trip and allow myself to think about what I had come there to do. When I did that, I got a lot more out of it."

The work Dominic put in, and continues to put in, to his personal transformation plays out in the way he leads his company and the ideals he holds for his employees. He has spearheaded a learning initiative where the external coaches who work in his company coach not only for performance but also for what he calls 'significance'.

Dominic describes significance in the following way: "I'm a child born in South Africa during the era of apartheid, coming from a very poor family. In that context, when I've achieved an element of significance is when I've been able to see the eradication of poverty in various communities, particularly the communities I've come from. The way I'd like to do that is by creating self-sufficiency in people, where people can literally lift themselves and their kids out of poverty. In doing so, we will be able to bring a much safer, much more egalitarian environment to the country because, in South Africa, due to the disparity of means that currently exists, there is a lot of crime largely driven by poverty."

Dominic's approach to increasing significance in communities is partly through his own employees, who are coached to achieve their own significance. This is a prime example of the value a business can have in how it uplifts its employees, and through this, directly impacts and uplifts society.

Another conscious leader featured in this book is Paul Monekosso Cleal, a partner at PwC, who is currently based in Lagos, Nigeria. Paul manages to combine a well-developed instinct for 'right action' with a very matter-of-fact, commercial pragmatism. Talking to him, you get a sense of calm, principled goodwill in the way he goes about his life and his business.

What goes around really does come around

While he can't recall any particular moments of 'waking up', he does see that his life experiences shaped the conscious leader he is today. He says: "At its heart, my approach was formed early in life. I've always been quite conscious of the balance of giving and taking. I've noticed that over time there is a benefit to helping others – they'll help you. This 'business karma' is something I've seen happen often. What goes around really does come around."

Perhaps the most significant life experience Paul has had is his mixed-race heritage, something that he is now taking a stand for through his role in Nigeria. "Growing up in a mixed-race background in London and living in only one of those places (his father is from Cameroon in Africa) leaves a bit of a gap. So, over the course of the second half of my life, I've spent more time in Africa and I feel like I've now got a much better balance between the two halves of my background. A lot of it is about my search for identity and complete-ness. To be authentic, you have to be true to yourself and know who you are."

Paul is currently contributing as a leader in ways that help Africa make sense of its future and its progress. "I'm trying to bring what I've learned in the past and deploy it here," he says. "I've benefited from people investing time in developing me and I try to give the same back. It's another part of the whole business karma cycle."

BORN WITH AN INNER KNOWING

For some conscious leaders, they seem to have been born with an inner, evolved knowing, which revealed itself at an early age and required very little 'breaking open' to appear in their lives and in the world.

> *What are the conditions in business*
> *that are needed to sustain life?*
> Sally Ann Ranney

Sally Ann Ranney is an environmental visionary and strategist who has worked with three US presidents and serves as an environmental consultant and advisor to business leaders from some of the world's largest companies. What is noticeable about Sally is her natural and honed ability to think about whole systems. This means that, in a world where business is so often unconsciously thought of as separate from the system in which it exists, Sally's voice as a conscious leader calls on us to take a broader perspective and to consider business in the context of the larger whole of which it is part.

She asks how sustainable business can be if it doesn't consider its host, the planet. Specifically: "We have to change our narrative," she says. "Language is how we think. Currently, our narrative around business results in our hearts becoming closed. We need to change our narrative so that our hearts can become open."

A good question we can ask ourselves is: *what are the conditions in business that are needed to sustain life?* This kind of question invites us to come at business from a different angle, from one that considers the greater system within which business sits and to make decisions as leaders that preserves the system of life.

Sally's style fuses business and nature. She described how what she calls her 'internal compass' has always been with her, something she experiences as a deep, principled centre that can't be rocked. In a way, it serves as ballast for her life. She tells a charming story of how, at seven years old, she had an epiphany at Sunday school. "On this particular Sunday, I shut the book, stood up, said to the teacher, 'You're not telling the truth and I'm not staying here any more', and walked out." Fortunately, her mother was an understanding woman. When asked by her mother, "Where would you rather be?" Sally said, "With God." When her mother asked where that was, Sally pointed to the field opposite and said, "Over there."

She spent many Sundays in that field thereafter, watching nature. "The greatest gift my mother gave me is that she never made me go back to church. She didn't try to reprogramme me. That was my internal compass – it just came out of me. Your internal compass, as you grow older, sets your principles of what you feel you can and cannot do in your life or your business or your organisation. As a conscious leader, you can go a long distance with your internal compass and never waiver. Deep, conscious leadership, in my experience, has the common feature of being a calling to a purpose."

Certainly, talking to Sally is an extraordinary experience. I felt myself being changed by the very conversation as it was taking place. The experience is of something – perhaps the same convictional energy that animates her internal compass – speaking through Sally and, being in the presence of this, it is impossible not to be touched and to be changed. I have seen Sally mesmerise a room of 500 people, not because of any ego-based action on her part, but because she was speaking about a deeper truth that some aspect of all of us in the room resonated with. It was a state of presence in her speaking to a state of presence in us, and something deep inside me recognised itself.

A conscious leader can open up the hearts of others

Such is the power that conscious leaders have and it was there again when I spoke to Sally the second time, even though this conversation took place virtually via an internet call. Distance didn't matter. Separation in physical space didn't count. The very being of a conscious leader can open up the hearts of others and uplift them. It does the heavy lifting for you in impacting people without your having to work so hard. Suddenly we can find ourselves surrounded by possibilities rather than limitations. My worldview was forever expanded as a result.

This extraordinary ability to expand our way of seeing is also present in Bob Fishman, the founder and former CEO of Philadelphia-based RHD (Resources for Human Development). This company is a non-profit organisation providing services for people with a wide range of human needs, from the homeless to veterans to youth development. It is a remarkable success story, maintaining its yearly growth rate of 30% on average since its inception more than 40 years ago, and managing close to $2 billion in revenues during that time.[13]

Bob, whose anecdotes are liberally sprinkled throughout this book, has an excellent way of getting you to laugh at yourself – or, more specifically, to laugh at how seriously you might be taking yourself. It is this lightness of touch – the ability to see things for what they are rather than what we would like them to be, and to hold many opposing views as potentially true all at the same time – that defines a conversation with Bob.

This awakened state was with Bob from early childhood. He says: "The thing I started to see, in a metaphorical way, is that the Emperor did not have any clothes on. The rules that I was taught as a child stopped making sense to me whenever I questioned them. Even as a child, I started to realise that I needed to behave in a particular way because it was expected of me, but I didn't accept the idea that this was the right way to behave. And I started to question the authorities, but inwardly, because outwardly I wanted to do well in school. I repeatedly noticed, for some reason of awareness, that very often the authorities wanted to tell me what I should say or believe and they didn't want me to hear another idea, whether it was in school or in the environment outside. So something in me enjoys – and I must put it that way – the recognition that while I can function well in a social structure (dressing in a certain way, for example, when meeting people in a particular setting), I am in fact playing a certain game."

He describes how his ability to hold many perspectives at once was with him from a very young age: "As a child, I started to speak in at least two realities: the one that was expected of me and the one I saw. I was always interested that questions could be answered in various ways. I found myself doing very poorly on multiple-choice tests because I didn't want to give just one answer! Sometimes there were a couple of answers that looked like they could work, and I was interested in the other answers. Again, there are many paths. I did well enough at school and I have a sweet personality, so I didn't question angrily, but it was a kind of questioning that was natural to me. As a way of summing it up, I'd say I've grown to realise I'm an absolute relativist."

These kinds of life stories illustrate some of the paths to waking up and how they can show up in our lives. We often associate personal growth with pain (or what feels like pain at the time: the death of our previous selves), but a defining feature of becoming a conscious leader seems to be engaging consciously with one's own process of continuously waking up. Occasionally, this might feel like life is forcing you to wake up and evolve, or it might be a gentler process, where something within us whispers that it wants to be recognised and emerge. Remaining on the path of our development as conscious leaders means being aware of what is happening to us moment to moment and keeping ourselves evolving more on purpose than by accident.

Something within us whispers that it wants to emerge

Conscious Leadership in Action:
Laura Roberts – CEO Pantheon Enterprises

Laura is a rare breed: an ex-schoolteacher who has taken over the role of CEO of Pantheon Enterprises, a conscious chemical company. She is also distinctive because her personal purpose, linked to the company's purpose, is to revolutionise the chemical industry. She aims to establish Pantheon as a role model for the industry in how to produce chemicals in a more conscious way, by taking responsibility for the end-to-end processes and considering with care the effects on humanity and the planet.

In terms of her story of waking up, Laura is a conscious leader who combines an inner knowing about life and her purpose within it, with experiences that have taken her through different stages of awakening. "I began to wake up in my teens and early twenties. I had concerns about sustainability and I was soaking up all the information I could find about the way we were impacting the world. I became very passionate and an activist – to whatever degree you can figure out a human system when you are 22 years old!"

She identifies the next stage of awakening as occurring in her thirties, as she began to realise how important her thoughts were in determining how present she was and how much she was paying attention. "There was this moment – a turning point for me – when I realised that if the internal conversations I was automatically generating in my brain were louder than the actual conversations occurring around me, then I really wasn't being present. So I started being really conscious about my thinking, and instead of letting my mind automatically generate my thoughts, I began to be really intentional about my thoughts and focussed on what I wanted to have happen instead of what I didn't want to have happen. This is a process that is still going on, but it became a very intentional practice of mine for a dozen years."

The third layer of her awakening occurred in her role as a leader. She began to wonder how she might be able to teach and coach consciousness to others and help them in their own processes of waking up. "It moved beyond me just waking myself up and being very mindful and intentional to where I felt like the next layer of awakening was, how can I help other people to expedite their developmental journey and help them wake up faster?"

Laura learned many lessons in this process, that are described further in this book: lessons about what works as a conscious leader – and what doesn't – in helping others in your organisation along their own developmental path. Her story is a great example of a starting point that began with her own awakening and continued with her taking that awareness out to others in the wider world and on to something that has implications for the planet.

We need to allow the cement of our own personal development to settle at each stage

Endnotes

1   Hamill, Pete. 2013. *Embodied Leadership: The Somatic Approach to Developing Your Leadership by Pete Hamill*. London UK and Philadelphia USA: Kogan Page.

2   Renesch, John. 2012. *The Great Growing Up: Being Responsible for Humanity's Future*. Arizona: Hohm Press.

3   http://tinyurl.com/z3rqrnf, p. 12. ©2014 Center for Creative Leadership. All rights reserved.

4   Fisher, Dalmar; Rooke, David and Torbert, Bill. 2003. *Personal and Organisational Transformations Through Action Inquiry*. 4th Edition. Edge\Work Press.

5   PwC. 2015. The hidden talent: 10 ways to identify and retain transformational leaders. http://tinyurl.com/jfxsnhl

6   Bozesan, PhD, Mariana. 2010. *The Making of a Consciousness Leader in Business: An Integral Approach*. San Francisco & Munich: SageEra.

7   PwC, op. cit.

8   Ibid.

9   Ibid.

10 Laloux, Frederic. 2014. *Reinventing Organizations: A Guide to Creating Organizations Inspired by the Next Stage in Human Consciousness*. Belgium: Nelson Parker, p238.

11 http://tinyurl.com/lnbyfd8

12 Joiner, Bill and Josephs, Steven A. *Leadership Agility: Five Levels of Mastery for Anticipating and Initiating Change*. San Francisco: Jossey-Bass, a Wiley Imprint.

13 Laloux, op. cit.

4

MASTERING
OUR EGO

I t is said that the journey of a thousand miles begins with the first step, and the first step on our journey to awakening is to begin mastering our ego. We start this with the action of understanding the ego for what it is, recognising how we are fused with our ego and learning to disidentify from it. Ego and being conscious inhabit two rather different planes, and one has to be left in order to gain entry to the other.

There are other practices we can engage in as leaders, such as practising mindfulness, developing our authentic leadership or building our systems intelligence, but without waking up to our fundamental nature as human beings and the way our ego can run our lives, we are forever destined to become caught up in automatic pilot and its patterns and habits, and this keeps us from becoming a conscious leader.

In this chapter, we'll take a closer look at our ego in order to begin the practice of mastering it. We'll look at what it is, why it's relevant for business, how it operates and some strategies for mastering it. We'll also look at how conscious leaders can work successfully with the effects of ego in their organisations. The concepts outlined in this chapter may at first seem a little theoretical, but they set the scene for being brought alive by the examples of conscious leaders throughout this book.

UNDERSTANDING OUR EGO

Most of us are familiar with the notion of an ego. Ego is the process by which we create and maintain a small, separate identity from others. It has been described as the 'finite, encapsulating skin' that defines 'me' as 'me'.[1] Cindy Wigglesworth, a recognised leader in the field of spiritual intelligence, describes ego as: "Our separated sense of self as a personality in a body who ultimately sees him or herself as disconnected from the rest of life."[2] While we may not feel ourselves to be disconnected from others, we definitely see ourselves as distinct from others.

The first step on our journey is mastering our ego

Our ego is distinct from the state of being egotistical, which is when our self-orientation is taken too far. This can lead to self-inflated opinions and behaviours that we notice in ourselves and others. For our purposes here, and in order to explore the ways in which we can master our ego and become more conscious, we are interested in ego insofar as it causes us to feel separate from others, with a distinct identity.

On the plus side, our ego has developed over the course of our life for some very good reasons. It has helped us to survive; it is an essential part of how we operate successfully in the world, since it creates a separate identity that provides us with a continuous and stable sense of ourselves over time and a template by which we make sense of our experiences in the world. Imagine how confusing it would be if we were completely different from one day to the next, or had to learn something anew each time we came across the same situation.

Our ego, therefore, is concerned with three useful things:

» Establishing and preserving our identity;

» Keeping us safe and ensuring our survival; and

» Getting our various needs met as best it can.

There is a downside, however. The role our ego plays in establishing and preserving our identity as separate from others means that we become invested in the ways we are distinct and different. We develop a 'story of self', those things we think of as 'me' and 'mine': *my* name, *my* job, *my* relationships, *my* team, *my* home, *my* car, *my* sports team, *my* personality, *my* habits, *my* beliefs, *my* values and everything else that has 'my' in front of it. It is the story of ourselves we become most attached to and it leads to some very particular behaviours.

While our story of self gives us a frame of reference for living in the world, the labels we give ourselves can equally limit who we can become. In defining what 'I am', I also define what I am not. The ego clings to these labels about ourselves very tightly and sees them as critically important to preserve and defend in order to keep our sense of ourselves intact. It accentuates how I am the same as some people and different from everyone else. Our egos don't welcome changes to our identity. We perceive change as threatening and destabilising to our security and certainty.

Self-mastery is the work of a lifetime

When we talk about mastering our ego, we are not talking about destroying it. There are different views on this: some schools of thought believe in dissolving the ego in order to live in a fully conscious way; others believe it is important to have an ego to operate in the world, but that we need to keep this tamed. It is probably a philosophical point, because for virtually all of us the journey of mastering our ego is one that continues throughout our lifetimes and, just when we believe we have dissolved a layer of it, we discover there are more layers to work on. Self-mastery is the work of a lifetime.

Conscious leaders like Tom Chi, an inventor, innovator and founder of Prototype Thinking LLC, who has previously been head of project experience at Google X, believes: "It's fine to have an ego, just like it's fine to be attached to things. It's not that you need to eliminate ego and attachment, it's that you need to have a particular relationship to it. You can't have it own you. The suffering we experience comes from the belief that this thing we've created – our identity – is permanent for all time. We don't have to get perfectionistic about it. Ego is a tool in your psyche to serve you. The illusion we have is that our lives are there to serve it."

> "Ego is a tool in your psyche to serve you.
> The illusion is that your life is there to serve it."
> Tom Chi, Prototype Thinking LLC

Our approach to mastering the ego is therefore not about knocking the ego; it's about knowing the ego. In the words of Cindy Wigglesworth, it's about gently shifting the ego out of the driver's seat and over into the passenger seat.[3] When this happens, we become more conscious of our reactions. We are less driven to defend ourselves, react to circumstances and make ourselves right and others wrong. A space opens up for greater choice. This is the beginning of self-mastery.

THE RELEVANCE OF EGO IN BUSINESS

Recognising and managing the impact of our ego is beneficial not only to us personally, but is a necessary step in expanding our focus outwards and becoming an agent for the greater good. When the subject of what we focus on is narrowed down to the pinprick point of our own survival, it seems counterintuitive for us to consider the well-being of others. Expanding our focus is needed for the journey to becoming more conscious. One of the fundamentals on this road is recognising and dissolving the boundary between 'others' and 'self'. The more we master the ego, the more we get to practise enlightened self-interest, where the well-being of everybody is more important than the well-being of anybody.

> *The fundamental leadership challenge of our time is to shift from ego awareness [self] to eco-awareness [the whole system]*

Extending our perspective even further, into the wider system of business and the world, Otto Scharmer of MIT and the Presencing Institute, writes in *Leading from the Emerging Future: From Ego-System to Ego-System Economies*, that the fundamental leadership challenge of our time is to shift from ego awareness [self] to eco-awareness [the whole system]. "The main shortcomings of traditional economic theory," writes Scharmer, "can be summarized in two words: externalities and consciousness."[4] Capitalism, as it is currently conceived, is fundamentally ego-centred, and conventional economics pays a lot of attention to externalities, the unintended effects on third parties, but no attention to consciousness

– the mind that creates these externalities. Consequently, as we saw in Chapter 1, we have been inclined to behave in business as if our actions have no effect on the wider system other than for our own gain, and we have overlooked our responsibility for the impact of our actions.

Fortunately, this is changing. Catalysts like the global financial crisis of 2008/9 and other evolutionary drivers of our growing consciousness, like the rise of social purpose in business, are creating shifts towards the desire to act with greater care for the whole system. We are being prompted to question our unconscious beliefs and assumptions about business and how it is connected in the world around us. The question many CEOs are now asking is not whether or when we need to engage in more conscious, socially responsible forms of business, but how?

This shift from 'me' to 'we' extends our focus far beyond the boundaries of our own small encapsulated selves and our organisations, and incorporates our communities, the whole of society and the planet, including everyone involved in and touched by our business – and involves us taking responsibility for our impact on all of this. Tom Chi, when interviewed for this book, told me how he thinks in a timeframe of either two weeks (as close to the present moment as possible) or a thousand years. He is concerned with how what he and his team are working on right now in business is going to add to humanity in a thousand years' time. This is a radical shift from current thinking.

We have immense capacity to consider ourselves as part of the greater whole and to listen to what it wants from us. The first step, though, is to master what cuts us off from it and drives us to act in both unconscious and irresponsible ways.

"Conscious Leadership is an inside job."
Casey Sheahan, CEO, Patagonia

A CLOSER LOOK AT OUR CONDITIONING

Our habitual ways of seeing the world and of behaving – our conditioning – sit deep within our minds, usually outside our conscious awareness, and take the form of subconscious programmes that are uploaded whenever we have to deal with a particular situation.

Sally, a leadership coaching client, had grown up in a household where strength was revered and weakness was reviled. This was reinforced both overtly by the words of her parents ("There's no time to be sick around here,") and covertly in their behaviour (Sally never saw anyone in her family ask for help). This conditioned Sally to embrace strength and shun dependency, which she saw as 'weak'. Whenever Sally found herself in a leadership situation where she needed to ask for help, or admit that she had taken on too much, she clammed up, 'went inside', as she described it, and drew on massive internal resources to cope. Relationships suffered as her team wondered why she'd stopped communicating. Being a strong leader was very much part of Sally's identity. The problem was that with this kind of programme in the driving seat, there was no room for any other kinds of behaviour – for openness, asking for help and sharing more of her whole self with her team – which limited Sally's effectiveness as a leader. It was necessary to look at these subconscious programmes that 'ran' her in order to have choices over them.

As leaders (and as human beings), we upload our subconscious programmes automatically, every time we need to make sense of a situation. Our programmes filter life through the lenses of our beliefs and the experiences of our past. This gives us a convenient shorthand for interpreting life, but it also limits us from seeing things in a different light. At our most unconscious, life becomes a repetitive cycle of rinse-and-repeat and, as the years roll by, we find ourselves saying things like, "That's just the way things are," or, "They always behave like that."

We can take this conditioning to a collective level, too, to the fundamentalism of culture, nationality, religion or any other set of large-scale beliefs that we might have adopted wholesale without thinking too much about them. This isn't about making the beliefs themselves wrong or right. The question is rather whether we've examined them, whether we're conscious of them, and whether we've authored ourselves as opposed to having been authored by them.

"Fundamentalism is a sham created by the ego to appear as though everything is under control, that there are no loose ends and that everything has been figured out once and for all," [5] writes John Renesch on the subject in The Great Growing Up. Tom Chi agrees: "We want to apply nouns to human beings because we want to label them and stop thinking about it. This is where the greatest crimes happen. We call people this label or that label – Muslims or Christians or Republicans or Democrats – and as soon as we say that, we're done thinking about them. We need to challenge the nouns; we need to suspend assigning the nouns." [6]

Challenging and changing our ingrained conditioning, whatever this may be, involves becoming aware of it so that we can gain some choices over it.

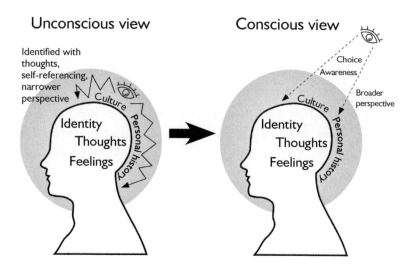

Figure 6: The unconscious and conscious view

In Figure 6, the more unconscious view is indicated by the person on the left. The sort of goldfish-bowl helmet contains this person's conditioning, everything he is identified with: his thoughts and feelings, his values, his personal history and his culture. Identifying with these parts of his conditioning becomes a self-reflexive loop. His point of view, indicated by the eye, is located within this sphere, and whatever he perceives coming in from the outside world is referenced against his own conditioning. This doesn't leave much choice for thinking or acting differently: it is simply a repeat of perceptual patterns of the past, based on what he takes as the 'truth'.

The person on the right has done some work on examining his identity. He realises that his thoughts, feelings, values, personal history and culture are merely mental constructs that make up his conditioning. He has looked into these and questioned whether he has chosen them or whether they are simply automatic, unquestioned and unconscious. This gives him a much broader perspective, an elevated point of view (as indicated by the position of the eye), from which he can sometimes see himself operating. His awareness gives him the space and options to make some different choices.

These two views, less conscious and more conscious, represent the poles of two states that we can find ourselves in. Of course, we all exist on a continuum along this dimension and find ourselves in different states of it all the time, but the act of becoming more conscious involves a purposeful move along this line, observing and questioning our conditioning and what we take for granted, and looking at where we have some choices – and the freedom to make those choices.

If we're not leading consciously, we're leading from our programmes and patterns, and they are running the show. Whatever our conditioning might be, it is affecting our choices and decisions as leaders. By becoming more conscious, we can see alternatives and begin to make decisions that have a different impact on our day-to-day businesses and on the greater good; choices that create win-win outcomes rather than win-lose ones motivated by our ego-prompted self-interest and self-preservation.

FROM FEAR TO TRUST

It would be all right if our conditioning was simply the 'bubble' that defined our way of seeing the world. The problem as we've seen is that our ego is primarily concerned with its own preservation as a separate entity, and to be successful at this we must protect, defend and guard ourselves. These are all dynamics grounded in fear. At our most unconscious, we are governed by fear and survival. We feel alone and protective, we contract and we are not at our best as people. We seek to control because life seems safer if we have control.[7]

We see the effects of this all around us in organisations. Organisations are Petri dishes for the ego. Symptoms are everywhere: whispered conversations at the watercooler after the meeting; sly glances during the meetings themselves; unhealthy team dynamics and power struggles embedded in the hierarchy, where control increases our feelings of fear. Every day in organisations, we look to increase our own power and to align with others so that we can gain control and ensure our own safety.

In their book, *egonomics: What Makes Ego Our Greatest Asset (or Most Expensive Liability)*, Marcum and Smith write: "Over half of all businesspeople estimate ego costs their company 6 to 15 percent of annual revenue; many people estimate that is far too conservative."[8] These authors also state: "Ego is the invisible line on every company's profit and loss statement." It is difficult to innovate, collaborate and create under these conditions. When we are protective, we are not engaged – with the organisation, with its purpose or with each other.

Richard Barrett, founder and chairman of Barrett Values Centre and author of several books on ego, leadership and consciousness, describes it this way in his book, *Love, Fear and the Destiny of Nations: The Impact of the Evolution of Human Consciousness on World Affairs*: "The ego-mind ... believes in scarcity and considers life to be a zero-sum game. (It) is wrapped up in the day-to-day physical experience and is totally focused on satisfying its survival, relationship, and self-esteem needs."[9]

"It doesn't care if it's being a drama queen," continues Cindy Wigglesworth. "It would rather overreact than under-react. In the logic of the ego's fight-or-flight system, overreaction is no problem at all. But under-reacting could be fatal."[10]

It is interesting to note that the sum of all of our deepest fears can be neatly summed up in three brief bullet points which are short enough to fit into a Tweet:

» I don't have enough

» I am not loved enough

» I am not enough

These three fears of the ego, identified by Phil Clothier, CEO of Barrett Values Centre, describe perfectly the deepest anxieties from which we all suffer. They can be easily activated by rejection, threat, anger or control, and we will go to great lengths to protect ourselves from feeling that, somewhere, fundamentally, who we are is not enough. Ironically, it is these same fears that unite us as human beings, since we all have them, but they cause us to defend ourselves against each another and to think of ourselves as separate, rather than as part of the same source of life.

> *"The only thing that separates me from you*
> *is my idea about myself, and when I take this away*
> *I realise that you and I are part of exactly the same*
> *process, and this makes us exactly the same."*
> Burgs, meditation teacher

The answer to how we got to be like this seems to lie as deep as the wiring in our brains. In the neuroscientific world, our brains are designed to recognise patterns in order to survive. We'd rather be dealing with the familiar than the unfamiliar, which is one of the reasons why the current VUCA (Volatile, Uncertain, Complex and Ambiguous) conditions in business are so stressful for leaders. There is no certainty and patterns are hard to recognise. We are unsure of our answers and don't have guarantees that we are making the right decisions. Even if we made the right ones for today, the world will have shifted on by tomorrow, possibly rendering our decisions obsolete. These are extremely challenging circumstances in which to be a leader.

FIGHT OR FLIGHT

From the perspective of our brains, these are ideal conditions in which to evoke our 'fight, flight or freeze' responses. Buried deep within our reptilian brains, the oldest part of our brain system, we are told by neuroscientists that these survival reactions operate 80,000 times faster than our conscious, rational and considered brain, the newest part of our brain (located in our pre-frontal cortex at the front of our heads). Within the deepest and oldest part of our brain lie the two small, almond-shaped amygdalae, whose job it is to scan the environment every five milliseconds for signs of friend or foe, risks and threats. Although our brain likes rewards, it is even more strongly wired to pick up threats – by five times as much, in fact.[11] When we feel threatened, we enter into a high-alert state and our amygdala takes over, for our own survival – something coined by Daniel Goleman, the figurehead of emotional intelligence (EQ) as an 'amygdala hijack'.

Whenever we enter into this self-preservation state, our ability to access our higher brain functions – which includes our ability to operate more consciously – is greatly impaired. It limits our capacity to be creative, to innovate, to assess risk properly and to make balanced decisions. We become caught up in a short-term mentality with little interest in considering the long-term implications or the needs of other stakeholders around us, let alone generations to come. The narrow focus on quarterly results and the analysis of the markets are just two of many examples of this kind of fear-driven response.

> "We need to trade safety and certainty for creativity
> and self-iterating blossoming and evolution.
> Because this feels less controlled, people are less willing
> to wrap their heads around it. They still want to hire the
> McKinsey's of the world and get the perfect business
> model or have the perfect quarter-to-quarter plan.
> Analysis gives us ego safety."
> Tom Chi

One of the reasons mindfulness is such a useful practice for leaders, whether to become more conscious or simply to manage stress, is that it creates some psychological distance between events and our reactions, which can help to keep our pre-frontal cortex, our front brains, in play.

The opposite of fear is love. This shows up in us as a deep and abiding trust in life. This trust prompts the conscious leader to move away from trying to control things with his or her mind towards listening quietly, inwardly, to what wants to emerge next. The conscious leader looks for the role he or she can play in this process of life. 'Me to we' is not an act of mind but an act of heart, marked by the surrender of our own egoic will in favour of being part of all of life and the generative acts that support it. The examples of the conscious leaders featured in this book show how we might go about this.

'Me to we' is not an act of mind but an act of heart

There is a great deal of trust in this way of being. Rather than needing to know all the answers in order to control the outcomes from an act of will, we still use our rational minds to work through the possibilities, but we listen too for the possibilities from somewhere else inside us – from our hearts and our intuition. We gather the insight we need from ourselves and others to sense the next steps, the bigger picture to which we are connected and the things we are in service of, that are greater than just ourselves.

At this point, in the act of surrendering our 'small self', we can find that we are part of a process in which seemingly disparate but interconnected events spontaneously occur that support what we are trying to do. I am referring here to synchronicity or, what Joseph

Jaworski in *Synchronicity: The Inner Path of Leadership* calls, "a series of reliable miracles".[12] Later on in this book, we'll explore how conscious leaders work with synchronicity.

The most important quality for this state of openness and its benefits, then, is the surrender of our ego in favour of the greater trust in life. It is the move from fear to love and trust.

In Mariana Bozesan's book, *The Making of a Consciousness Leader in Business*, she recounts the story of one of her interviewees, which beautifully describes this transformation from an ego-driven state to one of connection and serving life. Bozesan describes how surrendering and trusting was, "the most difficult element" for conscious leaders because they had achieved extraordinary success by believing that they were in control of everything, if they worked hard enough. However, many ended up experiencing how trying to control everything themselves didn't get them the outcomes they wanted and they were forced to let go. Many of the conscious leaders interviewed for this book also found how the certainty they had enjoyed was simply taken away from them, or the achievements they had attained had lost their shine, and this proved to be the crucible for the growth in their consciousness.

In Bozesan's example, the leader, who ran the marketing division of a multi-billion-dollar company, described his process of awakening and surrendering in the following way: "*At the time, I had no clue what was going on. Basically, I was being rewired. Everything I used to think was important was no longer important to me. It was me, me, me and my fabulous career and how do I help create more money for the company, so I can create more money for me and more success for me and more power for me? I was never a bad guy, but it was just a small game. It felt like a big game. I thought it was the biggest game in town. But suddenly when I was rewired, it felt like the smallest game in the universe. When you really make that shift and you start playing for an idea bigger than yourself and you start sensing into what is that divine creative impulse that's seated within me that is my gift to the planet? Within that surrendering was recognising that there's something unique within me that I was born to become and that by surrendering to that, by paying attention to that, by allowing that to emerge within myself, that I could play a much bigger game, a much more fulfilling game, a much more meaningful game in terms of being able to create from the space in service to a much deeper and broader concept."*

What could be more exciting and fulfilling than that?

THE JOURNEY FROM SEPARATION TO UNITY

We've been looking at how one of the most important journeys to becoming a conscious leader is to travel the distance between feeling separate from everyone else to experiencing how we are part of the greater human game of life. We'll turn our attention next to some ways of embarking on this journey.

Who am I?

One of my favourite exercises to do with a group of leaders (which you can follow along with here if you like) is to ask them to get out a piece of paper and write down their answers to this question: *Who am I?* Typically, they'll write down a list of fairly superficial adjectives comprising their roles and characteristics of their identity. Then I ask them to cross out everything they've just written.

This usually gets a variety of responses, from a shrug of the shoulders to a bemused or quizzical expression, to cries of outrage. I've had one horrified executive say to me, "I can't do that! I can't cross out what I've written about myself! This is me!" His attachment to the labels he had acquired for himself was so strong that it was immensely threatening to his ego to consider that what he'd written might not be permanent; that these labels might somehow be 'wrong', or even that they could be changed.

It is the process of choosing – not just our choices – that makes us who we are

---

Usually, I ask the group to go through this process a couple more times, asking the question: *Who am I?* and experimenting with crossing out the labels they come up with. What usually happens is that they drop down from the superficial labels to their deeper values and sometimes to their purpose. Our mind, upon being pressed, stops generating habitual thoughts and begins to look more deeply or allows fresh thinking to enter. It is a useful exercise to access deeper aspects of ourselves.

What fewer leaders understand, however, is the point of the exercise. It doesn't matter what we write down on the page. The point of the exercise is that we are the chooser of what we write down on the page; not the labels themselves. We are the observer, the awareness, the witness who can decide what to write. We could choose to write something else, or something different again. We are not limited by the labels that we've given ourselves unless we choose to be limited and contained by them. We could do this exercise many times over, and it wouldn't really matter what we wrote down. It is the process of choosing – not just our choices – that makes us who we are.

> *"Who is the 'I' that chooses?"*
> Cindy Wigglesworth

In effect, we are more of a process in action than a fixed state. We only get the impression that we are a fixed state because we take a snapshot of ourselves in time. Looking at ourselves over time, what we see is that who we are is constantly changing due to our process of choosing – we are much more fluid than we realise.

Who am I? can be a tricky exercise to get our heads around, and asking us to disidentify from our egos can make our minds spin. Depending on how ready we are to do this, we might experience a sense of relief, a rush of freedom or an 'A-ha!' moment. We might see a glimpse, an opening for ourselves to choose differently, or we might feel so threatened that we shut down and declare the whole exercise nonsense.

Disidentifying with the ego

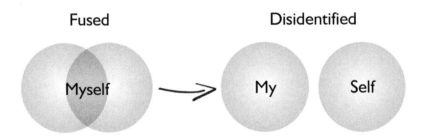

Figure 7: Disidentifying with the ego

Whatever our response, what remains is that in order to master our ego we have to develop the ability to step back from it and look at it. When we are fused with our ego, we have no choices over it. Creating some distance brings us freedom. Becoming detached from our own points of view, or holding them lightly, is also a necessary step to developing the complexity of mind we need to function as a conscious leader at the later stages of adult development, as described in Chapter 3. It enables us to hold more than one perspective at the same time, see multiple points of view and access our higher-order thinking.

Sometimes, disidentifying from the ego can take the form of an epiphany. One conscious leader I spoke to had a spontaneous experience of stark awakening that left him in a state of oneness, of pure being, for a period of weeks. At other times, disidentifying from the ego is simply a process of losing layer after layer of our conditioned ways of seeing the world. For many of us, it simply involves dedicated and ongoing practice, paying attention to the contents of our mind and how this creates a veil between us and the rest of the world.

How ready are we to engage in seeing?

My own experience of 'seeing how I was seeing' came from doing an enquiry into the question, *Who am I?* – similar to the exercise above. It wasn't particularly unsettling, but I did experience an overwhelming whoosh of freedom and creativity from the insight I had that I could choose and create my identity as I wanted it to be. In this sense, it was Damascene in the way that word describes a sudden and complete change in one's beliefs. Perhaps it came hot on the heels of several other breakdowns in my identity that I had gone through at the time. In any event, I was ready to see, and I think this is a telling point: how ready are we to engage in seeing?

Consciousness and our evolution forms a continuum, and we all have the potential to move along it. Sometimes it is through an epiphany and sometimes it is a slower process of life's prompts that causes us to move. But we are all part of this process, and we can also be *willingly* part of this process and accelerate it through our own efforts and practices.

Part of the reason an epiphany works is that the experience is often so deep that it momentarily knocks our ego out of the way, writes Jo Confino in *The Guardian* newspaper: "If you delve into the triggers for transformation among business leaders, it is often an epiphany rather than greater knowledge that leads to the raising of consciousness as well as concrete action," he says.[13]

In any of these moments of personal growth, our sense of identity itself changes. Author Jeff Carreira writes: "You do not feel that you have become an improved version of who you already were. You feel like you have become a different person altogether. You have transformed."[14]

Systems thinker Donella Meadows writes: "... there's nothing physical or expensive or even slow about paradigm change ... it can happen in a millisecond. All it takes is a click in the mind, a new way of seeing."[15]

Immersion in strange contexts opens minds and shifts paradigms

Leaders can acquire all the knowledge and information they want, but without some sort of fundamental shift at a deeper level, this knowledge will not have the same impact. We can probably engineer our own moments in becoming more conscious as leaders by immersing ourselves in unfamiliar contexts, because immersion in strange contexts opens minds and shifts paradigms. Leadership programmes that place leaders in different countries and cultures and helps them to make sense of this experience can loosen the hold their worldview has on them, making room for the development of more complex and inclusive ways of seeing the world.

Conscious leaders have therefore undertaken an outer journey and an inner journey; the outer journey being the training camp in how to run a business successfully, and the inner journey being their internal transformation.[16]

Lynda Gratton, Professor of Management Practice at the London Business School, who has chaired the World Economic Forum on Leadership, agrees that this 'inner experience' is really important: "The inner journey is really about how the leader has found their voice, their courage, their authenticity. When I've talked to leaders who I think are making a difference, they almost always tell me about their own personal journey and very often that journey includes what we might call crucible experiences, things have happened to them that have given them the courage to now stand up and say: 'I'm prepared to do that'."

Whether by stark moments of awareness or a slower process of awakening, what underpins these experiences is that they are life-long processes that require our consistent attention, as we all have the tendency to slip in and out of awareness.

Diana Chapman and her colleagues in their book, *The 15 Commitments of Conscious Leadership: A New Paradigm for Sustainable Success*, describe a useful analogy that conscious leaders can refer to, to check-in with themselves on a moment-by-moment basis. This is the analogy of whether you are 'above the line' or 'below the line' at any given time. Being above the line means you are in a state of being open, curious and committed to learning. Acting below the line is where you are being closed, defensive and committed to the rightness of your own views.

Chapman and her colleagues introduce the notion of a 'shift' as the master skill for conscious leaders. Shifting is deciding to let go of whatever we are attached to, and consciously moving from closed to open, from defensive to curious, from wanting to be right to wanting to learn, and from fighting for the survival of our ego to leading from a state of trust. Above-the-line behaviours are all higher-order behaviours that are necessary to respond to leadership challenges, since our brains, in this state, are more open and engaged rather than contracted and on high alert. In this state, we have more access to higher-order functions like creativity, innovation and collaboration that serve us in our leadership roles.[17]

The practice of asking ourselves whether we are functioning, in any moment, from above the line or below the line, is a good one.

MASTERING THE EGO'S STRATEGIES

In this section we will look at some of the strategies employed by our ego to preserve itself, which keep us acting defensively and separately. Recognising these strategies in ourselves on a moment-by-moment basis can be a very useful practice that helps us to better manage ourselves to be more conscious and to move ourselves from below the line to above the line. These are robust strategies, shared by all humans. The trick to mastering them is to catch ourselves playing one of these out. Then we get to say, "Ah, there's my ego at play again," give a wry smile and choose to do something different.

Strategy 1: Being right and making wrong

Our egos love this strategy. By making ourselves right and others wrong we are able to reinforce, if only for a moment, the certainty of our survival. We see this strategy just about anywhere we care to look: inside organisations and out. We justify our own positions and shoot holes in the views of others. We play political games, banding together with our allies and forming a defensive wall against any differences of opinion. We bond together in silos ('us'), making outsiders of others ('them'). In conflict situations, we can be guilty of stubbornly sticking to the rightness of our own views and discrediting wholesale the perspectives of others.

Sometimes, even playing the victim can be a form of being right. I can be so closely identified with how much worse life has treated me than it has treated you, that this becomes a way of subtly making myself a bit better or more special than you. In organisations, you're sure to have had several encounters with those who seem to love complaining about how bad things are, yet have no intention of, or energy for, getting into action to change it.

It can be incredibly invigorating for our egos to count the ways we have been wronged. One of my favourite coaches says we love to get our perceived wrongs out of their box and stroke them over and over again, saying, "my treasures ..." The worst thing our egos can think of is to say: "I was wrong." This literally feels like death. Saying, "I was wrong" is even worse than saying, "I am sorry".

Deciding to drop being right about something is, literally, as simple as the conscious decision to do so. Letting go of our own position and its rightness, if we choose to, is that easy – and also that hard. Our egos fight this idea because giving up our position means giving up a piece of our survival kit. Even when we know that this may end in our own demise – or the demise of our team, our company, or our marriage – at least we got to die being right. Wars are a good case in point.

Equally, we can simply let go of our position. We can detach ourselves from it. We can hold it lightly. We can recognise what we have in common with others. Getting curious about other people and their positions is a great antidote for being right about our own views. Perspective taking is a key skill in becoming more conscious as a leader. Or we can recognise that the thing we are disagreeing with in others might also exist in us. We do have a choice over our ego. It may not feel good, but we have the capacity to choose to act in spite of how we feel. We can choose to shift.

> *"When we understand, we are at the center of the circle,*
> *and there we sit while Yes and No chase each other*
> *around the circumference."*
> Chang-Tzu

Strategy 2: Looking good

We are intimately familiar with this very human tendency. 'Looking good' is kicked into play because we all want to feel special. Whereas being right and making wrong serves to protect us from fear of disintegration, looking good helps our egos to survive another day by making us feel more special than others. Looking good is our attempt at avoiding being a nobody by being a somebody.

Looking good is all around us, in every walk of life. When we drive down the road in our new convertible with the roof down, looking casual at the traffic lights, but in fact subtly watching whether people are watching, our ego is busy with looking good. When we promote our achievements at work, however subtly and artfully done, it's about being special. When we are driven to win, it's the same thing. When we make contributions in meetings simply for the sake of holding the floor and showing how much we know relative to others rather than because we have something new to say, we're looking good, too. 'Selfie' and celebrity culture is in the grips of one big movement to look good and gain admiration.

I recently had a course participant who took great pride in appearing nonchalant. All workshop long, he fiddled with his iPad or doodled in his book, or turned away from the person he was talking to as if he was slightly disinterested. I imagined he thought this might give him a sense of mystique (or perhaps he just didn't care very much about what they were saying). The effect, however, was that his air of 'specialness' got in the way of really connecting with people and gaining a lot from the conversations.

Read all this with a light heart. None of this is wrong; it's just what our egos do. We can laugh at these very human tendencies in ourselves. We are programmed to survive and protect ourselves, and this can be more easily achieved when we can be better than others, at least in our own minds.

It's useful to recognise our ego's strategies that cause us to disconnect and perhaps to suffer, especially in our relationships. As a rule of thumb, a more conscious way of being is when we are not diminishing the value or importance of others. Again, we can notice when we're engaging in this kind of behaviour, acknowledge this to be our egos at play, and shift into a different type of behaviour, one that is more choiceful or more supportive of a good outcome for all players rather than only for ourselves.

Strategy 3: Control and defence

Where do you end and others begin? From some point in the midst of our brains, from our personal sense of 'I', we draw a line around our personal space, the territory around each of us that is sensitive to being 'invaded'. Wherever we draw this boundary marks the line that our ego uses to separate everything that is 'me' from everything that is 'not-me'.

Our personal territory effectively acts as a no-man's-land between us and others, setting the limits on our willingness to engage. Our boundary line means that we can hide large parts of ourselves from others, our most vulnerable parts, and avoid being knowable and transparent. At the core is our fear of being seen by others because we might be found to be lacking; that we might not be enough. From the ego's perspective, exposure is a threat to our survival.

Hiding behind our walls has a huge price, especially for a leader. Too much control or defensiveness on the part of a leader prevents him or her from connecting to people and being available to be connected to. It limits our authenticity, our influence and our ability to inspire. The parts of ourselves that we hold back are the parts that are not present and available to others. We appear more closed, protected and distant if our ego is too strongly driven by controlling our environment or defending ourselves.

It's not only about controlling our personal space; we might also find ourselves controlling situations and people. This can be very subtle, like withholding information, withholding our participation, keeping people in suspense waiting for an answer or rebelling against the rules. I recently came across a course participant who used his personal disfigurement as a means of controlling the entire audience. Everyone, including the facilitators, were too afraid to challenge him in case they were considered insensitive. It was a subtle, and very powerful, form of control. It stemmed, of course, from his own sense of fear, which he eventually admitted – and which made him much more accessible to all of us.

Being conscious is about owning our state of being

All three of these strategies support the survival of our egos and reinforce our separation from others. They stop us from connecting authentically and openly with others.The more we practise noticing these strategies in ourselves, the better we get at mastering our egos. In doing so, we can avoid being at the knee-jerk end of our ego's drive to survive, and instead become more choiceful leaders and human beings who are conscious of the tides playing out within us at any given time, and able to make different choices in the moment.

All of this make us more response-able. Response-ability is an ability and a choice: we can choose how to respond or choose to stay in a particular state of being. This is our responsibility. Being conscious is about owning this choice, owning our state of being. Knowing the three strategies of our ego helps us to do so.

THE COST OF EGO IN ORGANISATIONS

Having the ego's survival strategies running the show on an individual level is one thing: having them collectively operating across many people in an organisation is something else entirely.

If we are all on the path of our own evolution and at various points on this journey towards waking up, it stands to reason that not everyone will be aware of – nor indeed interested in – how our egos impact our lives. As we saw in Chapter 3, around 37-43% of us have begun the process of disassociating ourselves from our egos. For others, these kinds of questions may not yet have been considered important, and conditioned patterns continue to run their lives. In reality, for these individuals this book would probably make no sense and it would seem irrelevant in their day-to-day world of getting life and work done.

In many parts of our organisations, the effects of our ego's reactions and survival strategies will be commonplace. As we've seen, this is the terrain of the watercooler conversations, of subtly undermining colleagues in meetings, of sucking up to the boss, of silo behaviour, command-and-control, disenchantment, them-and-us, and complaining whilst doing the minimum to get by. It's not a pretty place, but it's unfortunately the kind of work environment that far too many of us recognise. It is not the place where we can bring our full selves to work, with all of our potential as creative and potent human beings. The Gallup surveys on workplace engagement[18] show us that 87% of people globally report that they are disengaged and unhappy at work.

Some of the ego-based 'symptoms of separation' that conscious leaders can keep an eye out for in their organisations, and can look to facilitate a route through are:

» **Playing it safe** (people not offering viewpoints for fear of reprisal or to fit in).

» **Playing small** (not wanting to shine in case others disapprove of or reject them).

- » **Being right** (people being attached to a viewpoint and position, unwilling to consider alternatives that disagree with their own).

- » **Looking good** (posturing or building empires).

- » **Mobbing** (gathering a team of supporters in order to control outcomes in their favour).

- » **Playing the victim** (blaming others rather than taking responsibility for the outcome).

- » **Justifying and defending positions** (being right).

- » **Withholding their contributions** (to subtly punish or control).

- » **Embellishing the facts with personal interpretations** (which are defended as the truth).

- » **Assuming that their view is everyone's view** (and listening only to the information that confirms their biases).

The result of these ego-driven behaviours is that people live in a perpetual state of subtle (and sometimes not so subtle) fear. We don't communicate, and therefore information doesn't flow. The organisation becomes less like a vibrant pool teeming with life and more like a stagnant pond. Productivity suffers as people withhold themselves from contributing fully and do close to the bare minimum. Perhaps the worst knock-on effect of this kind of organisational climate is that, in a world where collective intelligence holds the answer to our success and We-Q trumps IQ, people don't generate or share ideas that can enhance creativity, growth and profit.

It's becoming increasingly important for leaders to be conscious of managing themselves and their own behaviours so that they don't contribute to this kind of negative organisational climate, and so that ideally they can ignite the enormous creativity within their organisations as people bring their potential freely and safely, and share information and their ideas.

THE ROLE THAT CONSCIOUS LEADERS CAN PLAY

I once walked into a meeting at a client's premises. Around the table were several partners of a global professional services firm and assorted employees. The atmosphere was tense and heavy. The fear and judgement felt so thick in the air that I actually stopped what I was doing and just watched people. The facilitator spoke in a whisper and seemed petrified of making a mistake. The partners sat behind their blank faces, not acknowledging anyone or showing the slightest glimmer of warmth or humanity. It was, I thought, as if they were only brains in suits.

How did we become like this? I wondered. Everybody was protecting themselves and felt dehumanised. There was no visible connection between people and the only thing apparent was the separation between the individuals around the table. I felt a nearly uncontrollable urge to tell a joke or do something reckless to break the atmosphere, but I dared not. The risk was too great.

There are three things that a conscious leader can do immediately to have a profound impact on his or her organisation. There are certainly a lot more practices of conscious leadership, but these three actions will make a remarkable difference in resetting the thermostat of an organisation.

1. Create psychological safety

Part of the responsibility of the conscious leader is to create a basic sense of psychological safety for the people in his or her organisation, so that they can speak up when there's a problem or know that it is acceptable to fail when trying new things. If people are fearful, they're not going to want to fail, and if they don't want to fail they're not going to innovate, take risks or even offer their contributions. They're going to be living in the grip of their 'fight, flight or freeze' ego-driven reactions, all of which drives a short-term, defensive mindset and does little to draw on the wisdom of the collective. This short-circuits the creativity needed to innovate or think about the future and the effects of our actions on generations to come.

Part of taking this fear away is making sure people's basic survival needs are met. Looking at it from the perspective of the theory of Maslow's hierarchy of needs, if the more basic needs of a living wage to survive, psychological safety in not feeling attacked or diminished, and a sense of belonging to a group are taken care of, this frees us up to focus on our higher-order needs of doing things that generate self-esteem, achievement and respect, and the more spontaneous and creative actions that create an experience of self-actualisation. It is much easier to grow when our basic needs are met.

Therefore, the conditions that conscious leaders set for their organisation are critical in the way their employees adapt and respond to incoming challenges. What is more, the way conscious leaders manage and master themselves and their own fear reactions is at the heart of setting this tone. Certainly, in traditional hierarchical organisations, as every leader knows, the higher you go, the more visible you are, and everybody is watching. This gives conscious leaders unparalleled opportunities to role model and influence a different way of living and leading. They can have a profound effect on the consciousness of the individuals they lead, and this can be spread to all levels in the organisation, including the way managers manage others and the way they manage themselves.

Love might be a strange word to use in a leadership or organisational context, but in fact love is mentioned more frequently now than ever before as we move towards organisations that are characterised by humanising values, purpose, meaning and inclusivity. A key consideration for conscious leaders is how to set up environments in which people feel they can be themselves and love their work.

'Love' is mentioned frequently in organisations characterised by humanising values

---

One such leader is Sudhakar Ram. A highly conscious man, Sudhakar is actively focused on creating a company that is free of fear. He has this to say about the atmosphere he is fostering in the company: "We have a highly educated, intelligent and mobile employee base and a global base of customers, so, strictly speaking, there is no reason for any of them to be insecure or anxious about their jobs and their ratings. They have the freedom to move around because there is always a demand for our kinds of services, so they are best equipped to let go of their survival instinct and come from their own aspirations. However, what inhibits them, what stops the flow of creativity and self-expression is insecurity, and that is normally self-created.

I try to come from a sense of abundance, that there are enough opportunities and enough choices. In Mastek, we'll always create a situation where there is enough work for us. Although business is ingrained to be all about the self, all about surviving and beating the competition, winning at all costs, I'm about instilling an attitude of: can we operate from a sense of abundance? As long as we get enough meaningful work for our people and we're viable as an organisation, that is good enough. We don't need to be number one in the world. That's the context we set, which hopefully creates for our people the ability to exercise choice, exercise freedom and self-expression, without being bothered that they are putting themselves at risk in any way."

> *As long as we get enough meaningful work for our people and we're viable as an organisation, that is good enough. We don't need to be number one in the world. That's the context we set which creates for our people the ability to exercise choice, freedom and self-expression.*
> Sudhakar Ram

2. Create new contexts

This links nicely to the second thing conscious leaders can do to have an immediate, positive impact on their organisations, which is to use the power of context to the advantage of themselves and everyone else.

Context deserves a special mention because there is magic in contexts that provides the highest leverage point from which we can create change, affect outcomes and make decisions. Context has transformational power, and conscious leaders are masters of context.

What do we mean by 'context'? John Renesch, who writes widely on this subject, describes context as 'the mental framework from which we think'.[19] Context has to do with the domain of purpose, of meaning and of significance. Context is distinct from content. If content is the 'what' and the 'how' of the things we do or talk about, then context is the 'why' of what we are doing.

Context has transformational power and conscious leaders are masters of context

Simon Sinek, in his idea of the the Golden Circle[20], puts 'why' at the centre of a bull's-eye. Having a clear 'why' drives the concentric outer circles of the 'what' and the 'how' of our actions. Change the why, and you change the context. Context is powerful precisely because it has the ability to shift the content associated with it.

Context also prompts us to ask, from what consciousness are we having a conversation or doing the work? We can choose a context that separates us and causes us to compete with each other, or we can choose a context that empowers us and unites us. If we truly want to shift people and realities as a conscious leader, then we need to examine the context from which we are coming and the context we are creating for our organisations, the framework that is sitting behind our individual and collective actions. When the context is energising, the actions within it are energised.

As an example, imagine an organisation where no one is connected to the impact of what they are doing. Every day, they carry out their work with no sense of what connects them to everyone else. The energy levels are understandably low and people can't wait to get home at the end of the day, and they wish away the weeks for the weekends.

Now imagine an organisation whose purpose in the world is one that inspires and invigorates its employees, and where they can clearly see the link between their efforts and the impact on the outside world. People know why they are doing what they are doing. They know why they matter. Many of the leaders featured in this book are creators of powerful contexts for their organisations, ones with which people can identify, which give them a clear sense of the value they are creating and which resonate with their personal values. Working to make other people rich does not inspire us; working to make ourselves richer, and not only in financial terms, does. We feel richer when we get to make a difference in the world and live our values through the work that we do.

One context that conscious leaders work with is to merge the separate worlds of profit and purpose by establishing a higher purpose for their organisation that transcends simply making a profit. A higher purpose creates a focus for attention outside our ego's obsession with short-termism and survival. Collectively, a higher purpose contracts our energies and attention around something we believe to be worthwhile. Giving back and contributing balances out our egotism.

A further context that conscious leaders create is one by which the maximum number of people can benefit through the actions of a business or organisation. Doing good business, while doing good for all stakeholders, is a context that energises people, from employees to suppliers to customers to investors, as well as the surrounding community and society as a whole.

Choose an attitude of generosity in a universe of possibility

Another context that conscious leaders might set is changing the organisational narrative from scarcity to abundance, as Sudhakar Ram has done. What does it mean to create a context of abundance and unity rather than scarcity and separation? Benjamin and Rosamund Zander, in their fascinating book *The Art of Possibility: Transforming Professional and Personal Life*, point out that living in this way is about choosing an attitude of generosity in a universe of possibility.[21] This is a particular context – to choose to exercise generosity of spirit and to believe in an abundance of possibilities. It creates a very different state of mind from guarding our corner jealously or believing that the worst will happen. Generative action follows from a generous attitude: we can generate new possibilities, new connections and new ideas, an infinite source of them, through an abundant attitude. Rather than focussing on how we might lose out if someone else gets a bigger slice of the pie, which drives defensive and competitive behaviour on our part, we can focus instead on growing the size of the pie.

As the Zanders point out, choosing to operate from a more abundant context doesn't guarantee results. On the whole, however, choosing to have an an attitude that there are always new customers waiting to be enrolled is more likely to result in an extension of your business than would the context that money, customers and ideas are in short supply. As Paul Monekosso Cleal mentioned in his idea of 'business karma', resources are likely to come to you in greater abundance when you are generous, inclusive and engage people in something that you are passionate about. Our context therefore generates our reality.

Moving from competition to collaboration is a context that helps with pooling our collective intelligence to the benefit of all of us, in a way that is becoming known as 'We-Q' (rather than IQ), which we will explore further in Chapter 6.

As we're becoming increasingly aware, the challenges of the world are too complex to be figured out by the minds of one or a few. We need to draw on our collective human resource – ourselves as a source of wisdom, insight and ideas – to come up with new solutions. This requires us to expand our traditional notions about competition. Typically, our context for competition is small and drawn tightly around ourselves, our team or our company. Conscious leaders are expanding this context of competition to include many others, including those we might think of as 'competitors', so that collectively they can generate a better quality of result. In short, we have to get over ourselves and our ego-driven defensiveness to exclude others, and begin collaborating with them to come up with better solutions that benefit us all.

Our context generates our reality

Collaboration features highest on the list of priorities in IBM's CEO studies, which survey thousands of global CEOs every two years. In 2008, these CEOs reported that their biggest headache was the unprecedented scale of change and the ever-increasing complexity they were consumed by and required to manage. More recently, in 2010 and 2012, they were interested in how they could capitalise on complexity and leverage their organisation's connections and relationships. In the latest studies from 2015, what is becoming ever more clear to these CEOs is the importance of leading with bold creativity and connecting with customers and a wide range of other stakeholders in imaginative ways. In fact, the watchword of the day for CEOs the world over is collaboration and they expect to collaborate even more widely in the next three to five years.

Globally, these leaders are realising that the best way to deal with complexity and create a competitive advantage is through open and collaborative cultures that drive innovation. The best leaders favour 'purposeful partnership', which is collaboration with a specific goal in mind. Collaboration might be considered as the new form of survival. The conscious leader is at an advantage not only because he or she is individually able to connect the dots by being more conscious and less fixed on a particular point of view, but also because he or she promotes collaboration and connections across the greater system. As one leader said: "If I get ten more perspectives, my IQ goes up by ten points."

3. Stay curious

This leads us to the third action that conscious leaders can do immediately to have a positive and profound impact on their organisation. This is to role model curiosity. Since our ego at its strongest loves to become fixed on particular positions and to defend these as being right, conscious leaders can role model curiosity – and later stages of adult development – by bringing various perspectives together in some kind of new way that is more useful than the previous versions.

This skill has a lot to do with adopting a 'beginner's mind'. It's a Zen Buddhist term we're probably familiar with, but it's worth reminding ourselves about. Our minds tend to stand in disbelief of anything that does not fit neatly into our current view of reality.[22] A beginner's mind is not about 'dumbing down' or abandoning hard-won wisdom. It's about suspending what you already know in order to make room for new ideas and perspectives to emerge. A large part of what makes it possible to live on the edge of our evolutionary state as human beings is to remain in a state of perpetual and profound receptivity to what has changed around us. We have to be willing to let go of all of our fixed ideas and look again. Practising the willing suspension of disbelief –otherwise known as 'living in the question' – will serve us well as conscious leaders leading our new-world organisations.

Letting go and staying curious is one of the skills developed by Lorna Davis, whom I interviewed. She had the following to say: "I'm very curious and I model curiosity really well. I was with a bunch of nutritionists alongside a group of my own people, who were very nervous, and they were all trying to look good in each other's eyes. I just said to myself, 'my only job today is to be absolutely fascinated by what these people, the nutritionists, are saying. And, at the same time, I'm modelling that for my own people.'"

Adopting a beginner's mind allows us to model curiosity and invite in many perspectives. It enables us to set the tone where people feel they can speak out, bring their own points of view and be heard, without having to argue them to the detriment of everyone else's. This creates a setting where ideas can be joined up collaboratively to create new possibilities and innovative solutions. All this can start with the leader, who shows that he or she is open to changing his or her mind.

Most importantly, being curious gives us the ability to leverage the system in which we operate, because we can transcend and even change the paradigms – the worldviews or consciousness – of the people in the room. Systems theory tells us that, in a system, a small shift can produce big changes in everything else. As leaders, if we can manage to intervene in our system at the level of paradigm or worldview – in other words, how people are thinking – we can hit a leverage point that could completely transform an entire organisation. Popular examples of leaders who have done this are Gandhi, whose worldview and interventions shifted and unified the mindset of a country, or Mandela, whose actions brought together the disparate paradigms within the South African system.

However, we don't have to be a leader like Gandhi or Mandela to have the same effect in our own organisations. Looking to bring to light the different ways everyone in the room is seeing the world, and linking these together through common threads, can create a shift in the room and allow something new to emerge. Asking a question that enables people to release their assumptions of how they see the world, and to ask themselves questions about seeing it differently, can also be a huge leverage point.

It requires a conscious leader to stay curious and not become attached to or automatically fight for his or her own small point of view. I love the comments of Donella Meadows, who was an expert and author on systems thinking, about remembering not to take our own viewpoints too seriously: *"Sorry, but to be truthful and complete, I have to add this kicker: the highest leverage of all is to keep oneself unattached in the arena of paradigms, to realize that NO paradigm is 'true', that even the one that sweetly shapes one's comfortable worldview is a tremendously limited understanding of an immense and amazing universe. It is to 'get' at a gut level the paradigm that there are paradigms, and to see that that itself is a paradigm, and to regard that whole realization as devastatingly funny. It is to let go into Not Knowing.*

People who cling to paradigms (just about all of us) take one look at the spacious possibility that everything we think is guaranteed to be nonsense and pedal rapidly in the opposite direction. Surely there is no power, no control, not even a reason for being, much less acting, in the experience that there is no certainty in any worldview.

But everyone who has managed to entertain that idea, for a moment or for a lifetime, has found it a basis for radical empowerment. If no paradigm is right, you can choose one that will help achieve your purpose. If you have no idea where to get a purpose, you can listen to the universe (or put in the name of your favorite deity here) and do his, her, its will, which is a lot better informed than your will."[23]

What Meadows is so articulately describing here is the radical freedom of the conscious leader (or indeed, anyone on Earth) to be the process of life and choose a context that is different from the one we currently hold; perhaps one that leverages the highest good in the system. This context can change; it is created. In terms of being a conscious leader, it seems that letting go of one's worldview, layer by layer, and creating something else in its place that better serves the world, and doing this as an ongoing process, is part of the way they approach leadership. Practising the art of staying curious helps us all in doing this.

Circling back to the beginning of this chapter, we've been exploring the topic of mastering our egos. We've followed a winding path, taking a closer look at our ego, how it works and how it impacts us personally and in our organisations. We've looked at mastering the ego's strategies and considered three things conscious leaders can do – safety, curiosity, context – to create a different climate in their organisations which can counteract the effects of the ego.

The ability to see our ego and our conditioned identity in action for the first time – to 'see how we have been seeing' – is probably the most important step to becoming a conscious leader. It facilitates a rise in our self-awareness and initiates a process of waking up because we realise that we are not limited to who we thought we were; our collection of thoughts, feelings, reactions, automatic responses and the stories we tell ourselves about who we are. Being able to notice when we are being run by our ego patterns, to observe ourselves in action from a higher vantage point, grants us the grace to step outside our own conditioning and creates the possibility of operating at a higher level of consciousness. It gives us the choice to play in a space of infinitely more freedom and to create a different version of ourselves. By mastering our ego, we get to step outside our habitual selves, and this affords us the opportunity to develop our personality based on choice and not fear.

Here are some context-setting questions that can help us with this creation process:

» *What would you use your life for if it were no longer about security and survival?* [24]

» *What would you choose to create and who would you choose to be?*

» *What would you use your role of leadership for?*

» *What would you create in and as your organisation?*

» *What purpose would you ascribe to your business?*

» *What would your role be for others?*

» *And how do you want to make this a reality?*

I want to end this chapter with two stories from conscious

leaders I interviewed, who describe how they see their roles and themselves beyond the boundaries of their egos.

Sudhakar Ram, whom we met earlier in this chapter, writes: *"The biggest stumbling block to leadership is ego – where our self-importance grows – fanned by feedback from people around us. As leaders, we start enjoying the fruits of our position, and grow our positional power instead of our personal power. As we have seen in the past, positional power is corrupting – a feeling of superiority, a need to compete, the obsession to dominate others... all these come out of an increase in positional power.*

How do we avoid feeding our ego? A good way is to hold all leadership as leading oneself rather than leading others. In reality, we never lead anyone else, apart from ourselves. People follow us when it benefits them and stop when it doesn't. When we want to bring real change, the only effective way is to be the change we want to see. Therefore, transformational leadership always involves leading ourselves to be a role model of the new world we want to create.

The Connected Age will see more leaders focussing on leading themselves rather than leading others ... there will be no room for a power-trip – people deluding themselves that they make a difference to a band of followers. At best, they will see themselves as a role model [for] others as their equals."

And Tom Chi, founder of Prototype Thinking LLC and a wise and prolific inventor with a universal point of view, has this beautiful and inspiring way of describing a consciousness that unites us all: *"Most people walk around incredibly afraid of death for their entire lives. When you get that close to death,"* (Chi had a near-death experience several years ago) *"then you're not afraid of it any more because you've basically experienced it and the actual experience of it was not a fearful one. The experience of it was a sense of returning – whatever the hell that means! My thought process on what it might mean is we're these particular instances of consciousness, but these instances of consciousness come from a universe that can't help but create consciousness.*

So we're kind of the apples on the apple tree, and even if your apple falls to the ground, it nourishes the tree and the tree can't help but make more apples. It doesn't really end, no matter how much you think it ends. There's just this temporary time period where you take the form of an apple and you get to be able to see through a particular window of the universal consciousness.

We see a lot better through everybody's eyes than anybody's eyes. The whole idea of 'my viewpoint is so much better than yours' or 'I'm going to beat you down and I'm going to defeat you' or even the concept of 'I'm absolutely right and you're definitely wrong' – these are such normal concepts that we don't even consider them to be a choice.

We don't recognise that the choice of labelling things in this way is a form of insanity. What is actually happening is a smaller consciousness is rallying against the larger consciousness of which it is part.

If we were to pause for a second and expand the scope of our perception to 10,000 people instead of just ourselves, or to 1,000 years of culture instead of the next quarter, we'd realise that by taking this smaller viewpoint we're doing something really moronic!"

> *"We see a lot better through everybody's eyes than anybody's eyes."*
>
> Tom Chi

In the next chapters in this Zone of Self-Mastery, we'll turn our attention to some of the other qualities of self that define conscious leaders, from their practice of authentic leadership to how they keep a relative point of view, to how they take courageous stands and create, articulate and shape a different future.

Endnotes

1   Wilber, Ken & Gafini, Marc. 2012. Center for Integral Wisdom, Unique Self Dialogue. http://www.ievolve.org/ unique-self-dialogue-ken-wilber-marc-gafni-part-1/

2   Wigglesworth, Cindy. 2014. *SQ21: The Twenty-One Skills of Spiritual Intelligence*. New York: SelectBooks, p58.

3   Ibid., p13.

4   Scharmer, Otto. September 2013. 'From ego-system to eco-system economies.' *openDemocracy* (Transformation page). www.opendemocracy.net

5   Renesch, John. 2012. *The Great Growing Up: Being Responsible for Humanity's Future*. Arizona: Hohm Press, p58.

6   https://www.youtube.com/watch?v=25fUDjMtkuI

7   Renesch, op. cit.

8   Marcum, David and Smith, Steven. 2007. *egonomics: What Makes Ego Our Greatest Asset (or Most Expensive Liability)*. New York: Simon & Schuster, p2.

9   Barrett, Richard. 2012. *Love, Fear and the Destiny of Nations: The Impact of the Evolution of Human Consciousness on World Affairs*. Bath UK: Fulfilling Books, p68.

10 Wigglesworth, Cindy. 2014. *SQ21: The Twenty-One Skills of Spiritual Intelligence*. New York: SelectBooks, p138-139.

11 Rock, David. 2009. *Your Brain at Work*. New York: HarperCollins.

12 Jaworski, Joseph. 2011. *Synchronicity: The Inner Path of Leadership*. San Francisco USA: Berrett-Koehler Publishers, Inc., p14.

13   Confino, Jo. November 2012. 'Moments of revelation trigger the biggest transformations'. https://www.theguardian.com/ sustainable-business/ epiphany-transform-corporate-sustainability

14   Carreira, Jeff. http://jeffcarreira.com/ self-truth-reality-and-language-part-4-a-model-for-human-transformation/

15   Meadows, Donella. http://integraljournal.typepad.com/ integraljournal/meadows-donella/

16   Confino, Jo. November 2012. 'Moments of revelation trigger the biggest transformations'. https://www.theguardian.com/ sustainable-business/ epiphany-transform-corporate-sustainability

17   Chapman, Diana, Dethmer, Jim and Warner Klemp, Kaley. 2014. *The 15 Commitments of Conscious Leadership: A New Paradigm for Sustainable Success.*

18   Gallup®, 2016. http://www.gallup.com/ businessjournal/188033/worldwide-employee-engagement-crisis.aspx

19   Renesch, John. 2012. *The Great Growing Up: Being Responsible for Humanity's Future.* Arizona: Hohm Press.

20   Sinek, Simon. https://gumroad.com/l/GoldenCircle

21   Zander, Rosamund and Zander, Benjamin. 2000. *The Art of Possibility: Transforming Professional and Personal Life.* Boston USA: Harvard Business School Press.

22   Carreira, Jeff. 2014. *Radical Inclusivity: Expanding our Minds Beyond Dualistic Thinking.* Philadelphia USA: Emerging Education.

23 Meadows, Donella. Winter 1997. 'Understanding Whole
    Systems'. *The Whole Earth* Catalog. http://www.wholeearth.
    com/issue/2091/article/27/places.to.intervene.in.a.system

24 Creative Consciousness International,
    http://creativeconsciousness.com

5

LEADING AUTHENTICALLY FROM OUR WHOLE SELVES

One of the most exciting memes that is emerging in our world which is ever more focussed on meaning, purpose and values, is the importance of bringing your whole self to work. As we'll see in Chapter 21, having your individuality recognised at work and being able to express yourself in your work through your ideas and values, as well as having some kind of connection to a social purpose, is especially high on the priority list for the Millennial generation.

It is not just Millennials, however, who think this is important. In most of the organisations my colleagues and I work with, purpose, meaning and values are beginning to frame the work we do on leadership on a regular basis. It seems that people are asking more questions around 'what is this all for?' and organisations are being required to provide answers.

This brings to the table the idea of the 'whole leader', a theme which is appearing in some of the largest organisations in the world.

WHAT DO WE MEAN BY A WHOLE LEADER?

Whole leaders integrate all aspects of themselves, and this is naturally channelled into their leadership style. By 'all aspects', we mean the mental, emotional, physical and spiritual parts of ourselves. Tony Schwartz and his colleagues at the Energy Project, who have done excellent work around the idea of managing your energy and not your time, regard these four domains as very useful and relevant lenses through which we can examine our own energy sources and better manage ourselves as leaders.[1] Conscious leaders pay close attention to all four of these dimensions within themselves. They look to integrate these parts into the whole of their leadership, and they also check in with themselves frequently to stay in tune with what is happening in each of these arenas.

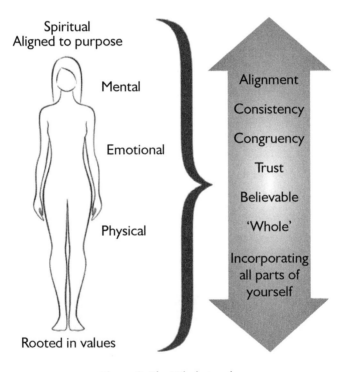

Figure 8: The Whole Leader

One way of thinking about ourselves as whole leaders is by using the metaphor of a tree. Like trees, we are steadied and grounded by the roots of our values, which give us strength and a strong and consistent moral compass to refer to when we make our decisions or face a dilemma. At the treetops, we are connected to something bigger and more expansive than our individual selves. This could be described as our higher self or the purpose in our lives. It is often linked to our spiritual selves. Our purpose provides us with a 'north star' that guides our actions and choices.

Whole leaders, therefore, are aware of their values and rooted in them; they are in tune with and take care of the physical, the emotional, the mental and the spiritual parts of themselves; and they are connected to a sense of their purpose in the world, a stand that they take or a contribution they want to make. In conscious leaders leading conscious organisations, their personal higher purpose is ideally connected to their organisation's higher purpose, meaning the reason that company exists in the world over and above making a profit.

Fully human leaders encourage full humanity in others

Bringing into one's conscious awareness as a leader all these aspects of oneself creates a tremendous sense of alignment. There are many benefits to this: leaders appear more authentic and inspirational, because they are connected to their values and their larger vision for the world and their role in this; they enjoy better relationships because they take into account not just the mental world of the mind, but also the emotional world of the heart; there is usually greater transparency and congruence, because these kinds of leaders know who they are and what they stand for in the world, and they are willing to bring this out consistently in their ways of living and leading. Others experience these leaders as being less hidden from view and more available for full engagement. The positive effects are that others are encouraged to bring more of themselves as well. Fully human leaders encourage full humanity in others.

ROOTED IN VALUES

Steve Hall, CEO of driversselect, a second-hand car company operating on the four pillars of Conscious Capitalism (*see Chapter 2*), is a leader whose own journey towards uncovering his values has led to these being closely played out in the values of his company. Steve says: "I haven't found a way to be an entrepreneur and separate business from my personal life, because I'm with me all the time. If I'm going to live a life that is true to myself, then I have to be able to align my business with my personal values. I want to be a role model for transparency, to just be who I really am and be happy."

Steve sees himself as a lifelong learner who loves to grow personally. This became the 'Learn to earn' value that was implemented at driversselect. This company value promotes the ethic that the more you learn, the more you earn the right to new opportunities.

Next, Steve looked at what frustrated him and realised he hated it when people pointed fingers at others in blame or didn't deliver on their word. That led to the company value of 'Take ownership'. Steve continues: "And then, I love to celebrate people and celebrate things, and so I said, 'why do we wait for the annual sales or the big events to happen before we celebrate? Why don't we find something each day, no matter how small, for someone to celebrate?'" This led to the 'Celebrate the small successes' value, which looks for the opportunities that arise for celebration every single day.

Steve's story is a good example of how conscious leaders can weave their personal values into their organisational values as entrepreneurs starting a new venture.

ARE OUR VALUES INHERENT OR LEARNED?

When we take a closer look at the values of conscious leaders, in truth these leaders don't so much discover and uncover their values as, to some degree, construct them through conscious choice. This is of course not limited to conscious leaders; we all have this capacity.

What do we mean by 'constructing our values'? Are we born with values and then just need to find out what they are? Or, do we somehow develop them during our lifetime? It's interesting to take a closer look at this. Cast your mind back to the *Who am I?* exercise in Chapter 3. There, we explored how the different aspects of our identity – and these include our values – are part of our conditioning. Our conditioning consists of those beliefs, thoughts, habits and values that we have come to understand as 'me', that make up our identity and that we accept as true, often without thinking about it. At our most conscious, however, we become highly aware of these different parts of ourselves and we realise that we are the chooser of the things we describe ourselves as, rather than the sum total of these descriptions. Conscious leaders may have discovered what their values are, but they are also conscious to the degree that they are not too attached to them. They recognise that their values don't make up the entirety of who they are and that these are not necessarily their 'core'. As a result, they hold themselves lightly, rather than getting insistent about their values. One of my favourite coaches of conscious leaders has a saying: "We are mostly empty space with a few stories attached."

> "We are mostly empty space with
> a few stories attached."
> GD, coach

This hints at our huge degree of freedom as human beings. The stories that we tell ourselves about who we are tend to become 'the truth' about us, but we are also capable of authoring ourselves and even transforming ourselves.

We are capable of authoring ourselves and of transforming ourselves

---

Harvard Professor Robert Kegan's work in this regard is a wonderful source of insight.[2] He describes the *self-authoring mind* as the stage in our development at which we start to loosen the reins of other's expectations on us and decide for ourselves who we want to be. One step further along, adults with a *self-transforming mind* are equally self-authoring, but they have also learned the limits of their own worldview, and the limits of having a worldview itself. As a result of this insight, they have an elevated viewpoint and can see themselves in context, which gives them a greater degree of choice. Having a self-transforming mind enables us to ask ourselves some fundamental questions about who we want to be and provides us with some freedom about how we want to construct ourselves in the world.

Self-authoring and, especially, self-transforming minds do not have equal appeal to everyone, and developing along these dimensions of self happens alongside our own development as adults and our increasingly refined and complex ways of making meaning in the world. (See Adult Development Theory in Chapter 3.) Conscious leaders tend to see the world through the lens of a self-transforming mind.

Having said that, conscious leaders do tend to share a cluster of values around being of service in the world, integrity, authenticity, truth and truthfulness, honesty, humility and seeing the oneness in the world and in humanity – in other words, unity consciousness.[3]

BEYOND PERSONAL VALUES

Being clear about and living from our personal values, whether these are self-authored or not, is good practice for any leader who wants to be authentic, interact consistently and well with others and energise them towards particular goals. Heartfelt values bring our human relationships to life.

When our values as leaders are seen in the context of the wider, hyper-connected world, then other values tend to come into play and be important, too. It is useful for leaders to think not only about their personal values, but also the kinds of values that might be needed to succeed and lead in our complex, agile and digitally connected world.

Heartfelt values bring human relationships to life

Bob Johansen points out that in our evolving world, we are seeing new diasporas (social networks of shared values) emerging that are fuelled through social media links. The implications are that tightly knit, virtual communities of like-minded people will spring up around their shared values. These people may be geographically distant, but they have power and influence due to their connectivity and their common values. Projecting into the future, Johansen's view is that these diasporas are likely to become even more important than traditional governments, especially in the emerging economies.

Within these diasporas, innovations and ideas spring up and spread quickly because of the shared values, common beliefs and consequently high levels of trust this brings. Fuelled by social media, these innovations and ideas can take on a trajectory of their own. One recent example we've seen is the Arab Spring of 2011, where a large group of dispersed people self-organised a revolution across the region off the back of social media.

However, diasporas need not be revolutionary, they can also be evolutionary. Leaders operating in the digitally connected world need to be aware that it is not only the connection to their own values that is important to enhance their individual authenticity as leaders, but they can also consider how they reflect the values of emerging diasporas. Leaders can use their personal authenticity and values to engage with human groupings around the world and extend the range of their influence, purpose and the positive effect they can achieve.

The questions that Johansen recommends leaders ask themselves in this regard are:

» *What diasporas help define who you are as a leader?*

» *With which ones can you easily identify?*

» *Which ones could amplify your leadership?*

» *Which ones threaten you and your vision of the future?*

These are important questions for any leader looking to be a source of influence in the world. They are especially important questions for those conscious leaders who want to connect to others digitally and achieve critical mass to see some form of common good being brought about.

AUTHENTICITY

It's useful to distinguish between conscious leadership and authentic leadership. Conscious leadership is not the same as authentic leadership, or we could say it is not only authentic leadership. Being authentic is certainly a large part of being a conscious leader and there are many aspects of authentic leadership that are relevant to the conscious leader, but conscious leadership brings with it some distinct differences.

The key difference is about our ability to transform ourselves. If we look at what we know about being consciously aware, and especially our capacity to have a self-transforming mind, we can recognise that as human beings we need not be limited by the story of ourselves. You need not be the same person tomorrow as you are today or that you were yesterday. You have the capacity to choose differently. We can know the story of ourselves inside out and be very authentic about this, but to be a conscious leader we need to take this one step further by examining the stories themselves, including the values we hold dear and have come to think of as 'us', and then ask whether this is still the way we want to define ourselves. There is an enormous amount of freedom in being conscious and being able to let go of the labels we have attached to the idea of being 'me'.

You need not be the same person tomorrow as you are today

Nevertheless, it is still immensely helpful for us to explore our own authenticity because it is the platform upon which many of us move through life, and knowing the platform we're standing on can only serve us well as leaders and as human beings.

One of the most intriguing arguments for the importance of authenticity, I believe, comes from Bob Johansen's work about the leaders who will be successful in the future. Johansen links the need for authenticity to the predominance of transparency as a major emerging trend in our world. He argues that some degree of transparency will be required by all leaders, certainly more so than in the past, because with our digitally-fuelled connectivity comes expanded levels of information sharing. It will still be possible to keep some things private, he writes, but these will be limited. Where customers, consumers or the public thinks transparency is important, then leaders will need to respond by being transparent, using measures others will trust. One of these measures is the ability to be open and authentic about what matters – something which Johansen calls 'quiet transparency'.[4]

Certainly, today, most business and organisational behaviour is conducted in the public eye. It is very difficult to keep things hidden any more. With the public's increased curiosity and knowledge about how things are being made (Is it green? Is it sustainable? What were the workers' conditions?), some searching questions are being asked and will continue to be asked about the way we go about our organisational life and our business. The more we become aware of how things are being made, the more conscious we are about our impact on the world; and the more we become connected to our values and the contribution we want to make, the more important these questions become to us. There is a great deal of power in the way we are able to use connected-up information to demand more transparency from leaders in business, government and organisations.

It's not all Big Brother scrutiny, though. Johansen points out that quiet transparency and authenticity are also linked to being calm, to tuning-in to the system and to listening for the future that wants to emerge. This involves a lot of sensing, an inner activity that requires whole person listening, rather than an outer-directed activity that makes a lot of noise and involves us forcing our will. Being inwardly connected to who we are and what we choose to stand for, and outwardly connected to the system, helps us to know what to listen for.

Johansen makes one further point about how our future is being shaped and the increasing relevance of our own authenticity. This is linked to the emerging 'experience economy', a term coined by Pine and Gilmore.[5] As we travel the path from commodity products to services to experiences to personal transformations, authenticity becomes an increasingly important factor. There is no value in being inauthentic in today's context. It is more effective to be a whole leader. Moving people to action, connecting with them and inspiring human transformation requires credibility and trust, and authenticity is the entry ticket to this.

AUTHENTIC LEADERSHIP

Let's take a closer look at what we mean by authentic leadership, because there is a huge amount of useful information that conscious leaders can draw upon to develop themselves and undergo their own personal transformation. It turns out that there is a fair degree of debate and opinion on the subject, possibly because authenticity is so closely linked to who each of us is personally and we want to feel we are being fairly represented on the topic.

What authenticity isn't, and this seems a fairly widely agreed view, is 'blurting out everything in our heads to another person' or, what can equally be called, 'letting it all hang out'. Rather, there seems to be a collection of qualities that makes up authentic leadership. Here are ten qualities that we can use to develop our authenticity as leaders:

1 **Awareness of our personal strengths.** Authentic leaders know what they are good at, and use and develop their strengths to the full.

2 **Awareness of our personal weaknesses.** Strengths-based approaches help us to focus on what we are good at whilst managing what we are not so good at so that it doesn't undermine our performance. Delegating wisely to others in the areas of our weakness helps us to maximise our strengths and minimise our weaknesses.

3 **Knowing our values.** As we've seen in the previous sections on being a whole leader, authentic leaders know the values they are rooted in and are able to project their leadership through these values, whether

this is to bring to life the purpose they uphold or to guide their decision-making and navigate leadership challenges.

4 **Emotional management and self-mastery.** Self-mastery is key to being a conscious leader. It is our ability to respond rather than to react to circumstances and events. Responding requires the ability to have a mental pause between an event and the effect it has on us, so that we can choose our response instead of getting into an ego-linked reaction. This is a cornerstone of emotional intelligence.

5 **Empathy, compassion and emotional intelligence.** Another cornerstone of emotional intelligence is the ability to read others, understand where they are coming from and take an empathic stance towards them.

6 **Courage to act for what is right.** Authentic leaders know what they stand for. This often comes from their values and what Bill George, ex-CEO of Medtronic, calls 'passion for your purpose'. There are many instances where leaders need to take a stand and make an unpopular decision because it is the right thing to do. It takes courage in these moments to lead authentically. [6]

For example, Dominic Sewela, Deputy CEO at Barloworld Limited, says: "I take a step, sometimes a leap, based on my value system and the principles I stand for. People get to know that if you want to deal with Dominic, this is how Dominic does things. This is different from doing what is popular amongst people of influence or peers or colleagues. It happens a lot in organisations where you walk into an executive meeting and your group says something where you fundamentally think, 'This is not right.' It's about choosing not to keep quiet under these circumstances. For me, what I believe in is stating what I believe, even if it goes against the grain, even if it means it may cost me my job. The reason things don't change in South Africa or in the world is because we don't have enough leaders in politics who are willing to say it like that. If you look at the stands of leaders like Gandhi or Mandela, they made personal sacrifices at that time, but today we regard them as heroes or legends; they are significant. You can never achieve that highest order of significance without running the risk of people opposing you."

7 **Integrity and trust.** Integrity is a huge topic, but includes keeping to your agreements, taking responsibility for your actions and speaking your truth. Integrity is not only a felt value but an enacted value; it's not just about what we believe is important in the world, but also what we do in action, keeping our word. Doing what we say we are going to do, by when we say we are going to do it, develops our trust in ourselves and other's trust in us.

Integrity is one of those words that is bandied about a lot and we all think we know what we mean by it – but we all have different definitions. My definition of 'integrity' is an action, a behaviour – in this case doing what I said I would do – whereas authenticity is rooted in my knowledge of myself and being willing to show this to the world.

One conscious leader for whom integrity is particularly important is John Mackey, co-CEO of Whole Foods Market. Mackey is well known for taking a stand on some very public issues, such as health-care in America, which is in line with his own and Whole Foods Market's purpose of helping to support the health, wellbeing and healing of people and the planet. Not always being popular in his views is never something that deters Mackey from speaking out. He sees integrity as being fundamentally important to being a conscious leader – perhaps the most important quality – and sees that it is necessary to have moral courage and do what one believes is true to one's values, the right thing whatever the circumstances, even where this might involve personal cost. Mackey is a fierce critic of spin. "Spinning is not truth telling," he said at a recent conference. "You can't trust people who don't tell you the truth. If you want integrity in your organisation, you need to role model it."

These seven qualities of authentic leadership are all part of what is required to be a 'whole leader'. They combine our values – the mental, emotional, physical and spiritual dimensions of ourselves – and include our personal purpose, and possibly also our organisation's purpose, into one aligned, unified and cohesive whole. The remaining three qualities of authentic leadership have to do with how we express this whole of ourselves to the outside world.

8   **Genuine, congruent and consistent.** Because they know themselves as well as they do, authentic leaders appear genuine (unpretentious and real), congruent (aligned in their values, words and deeds) and consistent (stable in character over time). There is a minimal gap between their being and their doing. This amplifies the trust that they are able to engender in others and in the world, especially as we become ever more fixated with transparency. The value of consistency and alignment can be seen in the following story.

Ramesh Kacholia is an Indian philanthropist and fundraiser who is involved in numerous charitable causes that have a social impact under the banner of the Caring Friends organisation. This is an informal group of friends that has come together to act as a bridge between outstanding NGOs and donors. Ramesh is a quiet and unassuming, though very effective, conscious leader. When I asked him the secret to his success – he succeeds in getting people to donate money to NGOs without being at all pushy or manipulative – he told me: "The best way to lead, especially in this humanitarian system, is by your own example. People ask me how I get such a good response when

I talk to others about donating. Personally, I feel it is for the simple reason that, before all else, I myself support that cause and only after I have supported the cause in a good or big way, I finally talk to others and I request the same from them. It is an unwritten principle that unless I do something first myself, I do not approach others."

Ramesh is an influential leader not by ego or by design, but because when he sees something he cares about and when he talks to people in his network, they see this coming alive in him through the genuine care and consistency that he has. This influences them to be curious and to take a further look at the opportunity and potentially become involved themselves.

9 **Knowing your life story.** In their research on how 125 successful leaders developed their authentic leadership abilities, Bill George and his colleagues found that one characteristic these leaders all shared was that their leadership style emerged from their life story. This is an extraordinary finding. It suggests that our values may differ from leader to leader, but it is the examination of these values through the experiences of our own lives that counts towards being authentic as a leader. Knowing and sharing the important lessons from our life story also develops openness and trust in a world seeking transparency and connection. This leads to a tenth important quality of authentic leadership.

10 **Willingness to be knowable.** There is one other characteristic that is shared by leaders who are authentic – the 'secret sauce' as it were – and this is our willingness to share our stories, to be knowable to others and not to hide behind a front of stiff professionalism or wary self-protection. There is a reason Brené Brown's TED talk[7] on vulnerability is one of the most viewed talks of all time: at some level we all

have the yearning to connect, to be who we truly are
with each other and to feel safe while doing so. As
authentic leaders, we not only deeply know ourselves,
but we are also willing to be known by others, to be
seen, to be real and not hide our vulnerability and our
humanity. Partly this is about letting our 'inner
compass' shine through our lived life purpose. Our own
inspiration can inspire others. We also let our values
shine through our life experiences as leaders. We
become the humans that other people want to connect
to. As we drop more of our pretence and cover up, we
become more relatable, which raises the level of
our connection.

Our own inspiration can inspire others

There is a saying about being authentic: that it is like the sun
shining through from behind the clouds we use as cover-up and
protection. The more we remove these clouds, for example by practising the qualities of authenticity described above, the more our
essential authenticity can shine through and be experienced by
others. This is often described not as a 'head thing' but as a 'heart
thing' which connects us to other people. We know it when we see
it. At a deeper level still, the conscious presence that is our life force
sits still and watchful within us all, unaffected, unmoved by time,
or markets, the growth and demise of companies, the cut and thrust
of board meetings. It is often called the observer or the witness of
life. The more we can be in touch with its quiet presence, the more
we are able to let our authenticity shine through.

FINDING YOUR PERSONAL PURPOSE

So far, in exploring what it means to be authentic, we've looked at the values that form our roots and the alignment this brings to our authenticity as a conscious leader. The third part relates to the purpose we are connected to and invested in. This part asks the question: *What is our authenticity in service of?*

Conscious leaders are keen, as far as possible, to marry up their personal purpose in the world with their organisation's purpose. This is not always possible if you are working in a company that you didn't create, but at the very least these leaders tend to look for a marriage of values between themselves and their organisation.

In for-profit organisations, and especially where leaders have some control over the reason for the company's existence, they establish a higher purpose for the company over and above making a profit. Naturally, profit is essential to be operationally successful, but it is not the reason for the existence of a company in the same way that red blood cells are necessary for health but are not the purpose of life.[8] We are in the midst of seeing the traditional relationship between profit and purpose being reversed, as we ask of ourselves not just that we make a profit, but how we are making it.

Aligning the energy behind our individual purpose and our organisational purpose provides a 'why' that creates a massive injection of energy that simply can't be matched by the prospect of doing more things and working harder. People don't get up in the mornings excited to be making more money for the shareholders that day. Something else has to be in place. As we've seen in previous chapters, context is a powerful catalyst for igniting effort, and our actions make much more sense to us when we have a clear 'why'. Having a purpose provides that 'why'.

The Three Bricklayers story illustrates this:

A man sees three other men laying bricks. He approaches the first and asks,

"What are you doing?"

Annoyed, the man answers, "What does it look like I'm doing? I'm laying bricks!"

The man walks over to the second bricklayer and asks the same question.

The second man responds, "Oh, I'm making a living."

He asks the third bricklayer the question.

This man looks up, smiles with a glint in his eye, and says, "I'm building a cathedral."

This story is instructive not only because it illustrates the power that context holds for us, but also how our work can be infused with energy under the right circumstances of a strong purpose.

Sometimes an organisation's purpose is lost in the mists of time. I have worked with several companies where, when I ask the senior team the purpose behind the company's existence, I was met with people glancing around uncomfortably. In the absence of a clear purpose, we tend to lean on organisational values and mission statements and strategy. But let's be honest: an organisation's purpose is its reason for existing; its 'why' in a world of 'how' and 'what'; the thing that would be lost if the organisation ceased to exist. This purpose is most alive when it is lived through the conversations and ideas of many, rather than being mounted on a plaque by the door like some kind of hunting trophy.

EXAMPLES OF PERSONAL PURPOSE

Conscious leaders endeavour to bring purpose alive for themselves and everyone in their organisation by tapping into the resonance between people's values and their personal purpose on the one hand, and the organisation's values and purpose on the other. To illustrate this, here is a collection of first-hand accounts of conscious leaders' personal purposes and how this plays out in their organisations.

Frederic Desbrosses, General Manager Mars Turkey: "I think the purpose, for me, is to positively impact my environment, either as a leader or as a human being. Even in my daily life I am trying not to impact people negatively. Whether with my kids, my family, my business or my environment, I look to bring something, to make a positive contribution, to share maybe, to give something, to leave something behind, to help. My definition of success is to make a positive impact in all areas of the world and to operate with a reciprocal mindset, with mutuality in my business."

Jean-François Zobrist, CEO, FAVI, France: "The purpose of our business beyond profit is happiness. Profit is the result of happiness. There is no performance without happiness. The search is for the happiness of all our stakeholders. Where others have an objective of profit, they get mixed up between the objective and the results, but to have obtaining results or numbers as an objective is madness. The objective is to be happy, then the results follow."

FAVI has two fundamental purposes to create this happiness: one, to provide meaningful work for those in the rural area where the company is based, and secondly, to give and receive love from clients.[9]

Steve Hall, CEO, driversselect, USA: "Our purpose is to serve as a model for how businesses can impact the lives of their people through creating a sense of fulfilment. You have people either in your workplace or thinking about your workplace for 40 to 50 hours a week, and you have the opportunity to create a sense of fulfilment for them or you have the ability to create a sense of failure, blame or defeat. A lot of companies are really trying to push metrics, but at the expense of people, and sometimes you have to grow and invest in people at the expense of metrics. We've only been doing this for five years and we think it's at least a decade of investment, rather than expecting immediate results. Nevertheless, I want to make a meaningful, significant impact. We want to show the impact of how our people can leave our business and go home to their family and friends. How do you want them to be feeling when they get home?"

Dominic Sewela, Deputy CEO Barloworld Limited, South Africa: "There is more purpose to us than just achieving day-to-day goals. We need to look at the issue of our significance. We need to think consciously: what is my purpose, do I have a purpose being here and what might that be? And then we get to a point where we say: how do I impact people? How do I really transform them and am I helping people to achieve their significance as well? To me, you become significant because you're touching people's lives in different ways and you operate far beyond just the day-to-day. You actually understand what could happen with the people you are impacting. It's more difficult because you might have to take a stand which might be contrary to the people who are cheering you on. Or you might need to challenge the establishment. People start asking questions like, why do you want to do that when you're so successful? However, I think the higher order of success is enabling this significance in others."

Neal Gandhi, Angel Investor, UK: "I invest in socially conscious businesses, which have a clear purpose to make a positive impact. One of our businesses, Farmflo, a farmer-friendly farm management software company, has the purpose to sustainably feed nine billion people. Another company I've just invested in, called Playmob, connects the online actions we naturally take, to contribute to causes that matter to you. We believe online actions can make a meaningful difference to lives globally and our purpose is to transform consumer engagement through charitable giving."

Lorna Davis, Executive Board Member, Danone (Global): "I'm a weaver, like Joseph and his technicolour dreamcoat. I really know it when I see it and I know how to put it together with other people. I weave amazing things by putting other people and things together. And I love that. I don't want to be famous. I don't want to be powerful as an individual. I want to be a weaver. That's what I'm good at."

Ramesh Kacholia, Philanthropist and Founder, Caring Friends, India: "You can have tonnes of money, but that money doesn't satisfy you because you're always thinking how you can make more money. I do keep track of my investments to try to see how best I can increase them and get more returns, but my purpose is only this: if I get more, I can give more. That is my basic purpose and I really enjoy it."

What is common in all these leaders' accounts of their own and their organisations' purposes are the themes of contribution, positive impact and taking responsibility. In this regard, I like Benjamin Zander's notion, in his co-written book, *The Art of Possibility*, of inventing oneself as a contribution.[10] There are two basic steps to inventing ourselves as a contribution, says Zander, which ultimately forms the biggest context for our lives:

1   Declare yourself to be a contribution.

2   Throw yourself into life as someone who makes a difference, accepting that you may not understand how things are going to turn out.

In typical Zander style, doing this is both simple and paradoxically complex at the same time.

There are plentiful tools to help you find your purpose, but doing so essentially boils down to asking yourself Two Big Questions:

Who am I?

What am I here to do?

How you choose to make your contribution, is up to you. The scope is endless.

Endnotes

1   http://tinyurl.com/zvr6j5h

2   Kegan, Robert and Lahey, Lisa. 2009. *Immunity to Change:
     How to Overcome It and Unlock the Potential in Yourself and
     Your Organization (Leadership for the Common Good)*. USA:
     Harvard Business School Publishing Corporation.

3   Bozesan, Ph.D., Mariana. 2010. *The Making of a Consciousness
     Leader in Business: An Integral Approach*. San Francisco &
     Munich: SageEra.

4   Johansen, Bob. 2012. *Leaders Make The Future: Ten New
     Leadership Skills for an Uncertain World*. San Francisco. Berrett-
     Koehler Publishers, Inc., *a BK Business Book.*

5   Pine, B. Joseph & Gilmore, James H. 2011. *The Experience
     Economy*. USA. Harvard Business School Publishing Corporation.

6   Bill George http://tinyurl.com/zl4dg5e and George, Bill. 2015.
     Discover Your True North. New Jersey: John Wiley & Sons, Inc.

7   Brown, Brené. 2010. 'The power of Vulnerability. TEDxHouston.
     https://www.ted.com/talks/brene_brown_on_vulnerability

8   Freeman, Ed. May 2012. 'Edward Freeman: Businesses Should
     Be Driven By Purpose'. *Forbes India*. http://tinyurl.com/zd8f3hh

9   Laloux, Frederic. 2014. *Reinventing Organizations: A Guide to
     Creating Organizations Inspired by the Next Stage in Human
     Consciousness*. Belgium: Nelson Parker.

10   Zander, Rosamund and Zander, Benjamin. 2000. *The Art of
     Possibility: Transforming Professional and Personal Life*. Boston
     USA: Harvard Business School Press.

6

RADICALLY RELATIVE AND THE VALUE OF WE-Q

A few years ago, I arrived in Basel airport, Switzerland, and exited through the wrong door, on the French side rather than the Swiss side, where my client was based. The airport is operated via a state treaty, established in 1946, whereby both the Swiss and the French are granted access to the same airport. A very nice gentleman, probably a security guard or immigration official, politely told me that I needed to go back into the airport, walk 100 metres down through the building and exit on the other side of the chicken-wire fence. He pointed to the fence next to us, a flimsy thing about 5ft high, effectively separating us humans beings onto either side of an imaginary border.

> "The test of a first-rate intelligence is to hold
> two opposed ideas in mind at the same time
> and still retain the ability to function."
> F. Scott Fitzgerald

As I amicably walked back into the airport, along the corridor, and out the other side, I was struck by how ridiculous it was that this see-through fence demarcated one type of human being from another when we were all, in reality, exactly the same. There is even less to distinguish people from each other in that part of the world, especially living as they do in such close proximity in this small, closely-knit country, and yet this fence was a symbol separating humanity into smaller boxes of difference. It was nothing more than a made-up border in people's minds, which had everyone sorting themselves into this worldview or that worldview in a very civilised way. I would've liked to simply step over the fence.

Of course, in other parts of the world, the same fences have become great big walls, sometimes curving around people's houses, for example in Palestine. They nevertheless all represent our attachment to our own made-up belief systems that are more or less consciously held, and that separate us out into different ways of being human.

Conscious leaders dissolve the walls that separate the world into 'us' and 'them'

To be a conscious leader requires us to look at these beliefs that underpin our worldviews and to become more curious about the worldviews of others. It requires us to move from being binary in our mindset to becoming much more nuanced. In effect, it asks us to dissolve the walls that seem to separate the world into 'us' and 'them', and to think instead in terms of the interconnectedness of 'we'. Global problems require solutions best generated by the thinking of a million minds, and conscious leaders are suited to help weave together these perspectives in the interests of creating new thinking.

MOVING FROM 'I' TO 'WE'

Enter the value of We-Q. We-Q tracks a new social megatrend away from the 'I society' towards the 'We society'. The central focus is on connection, the creation of synergies, working on joint solutions and the sharing of goods and products. It is a counter movement to egocentric thinking.[1] Open systems, open source, crowdfunding and co-working hubs epitomise these social shifts, and we are seeing more of them every day in the way people like to live and work. We can see them taking shape in goals as ambitious and urgent as the United Nations Sustainable Development Goals. The new world is very much about 'we'.

WHAT ROLES CAN CONSCIOUS LEADERS PLAY IN THE EMERGENCE OF 'WE-Q'?

The answer is: everything. We-Q requires us to think past our mind-generated boundaries. It requires us to think beyond what separates us and demands we recognise that when we extend our perception beyond our own minds, beyond our country borders, beyond our societies and continents, we are really left with one planet and one human race. Conscious leaders role model this way of thinking, for themselves and for everyone else.

This is as true for business as it is for life. The ability of conscious leaders to see multiple perspectives, think in systems and look to integrate a variety of viewpoints is of great advantage in business, not only, as we'll see, in pursuing new forms of competition – ones by which we all win – but to release the power of business to have an impact for the greater good. These same abilities apply equally to political leaders, leaders in education and – simply – to everyone, including ourselves.

The leaders I interviewed for this book were either born with this capacity to think in relative terms so that it showed up early in their lives, or developed it through life experiences. It is highly unusual for us to have this capacity early on, since, as children, we tend first to have to develop a sense of ourselves as a separate entity before the long journey begins to join others as being part of a single humanity. But whether it's a leader like Bob Fishman, who describes how even as a child he was aware of at least two realities, or other leaders who have discovered this as they went along, moving away from an absolute viewpoint and towards a relative one is part of the journey.

When we extend our perception beyond our own minds, beyond our country borders, our societies and continents, we are left with one planet, one human race

---

Lorna Davis describes how, now living in her seventh country, she has learned about, "this whole question of relativity. You learn that there is no absolute good or bad, including yourself."

Paul Monekosso Cleal, who grew up with his mother, shares a British and a Cameroonian heritage. He recently added in his father's surname, Monekosso, to his own name. "I like the fact that I now use both of their names rather than having to choose one," he says. "There is a tendency for people to want someone like me from a dual heritage to choose one or the other. Well, you don't have to have one, you can have two. You can be both British and Cameroonian. You can support X and Y sports teams, and I don't see the conflict between the two. Most people can't understand that at all because their idea of identity is more one-dimensional, whereas mine is more multi-dimensional."

Being a conscious leader requires us to notice when we fall into either-or thinking traps and to keep an eye on the assumptions and filters that we are seeing through. "Rather than having a filter and trying to match the world to your own definition," says Frederic Desbrosses, "I open my senses to learn. I understand the point of view of the other. The extreme views of others help me to find my balance."

LOOSENING OUR ATTACHMENT TO OUR WORLDVIEWS

In terms of their perspectives, conscious leaders have walked a good few miles down the road from seeing the world through their personal lens, towards seeing the world from the viewpoints of others. This most fundamental shift in thinking and the way we make meaning of the world, brings with it all kinds of benefits. Loosening our attachment to our own point of view lessens the urge to be right and make others wrong, or to stamp our perspective on the world as 'the truth'. It creates space for a lot more fluidity and variety of perspectives, multiple answers and for 'it depends' thinking to enter into the discussion. Those who are most prone to fundamentalist thinking are emotionally and intellectually attached to their beliefs about how things are supposed to be and this leaves little room for movement as new information becomes available. A more fluid perspective is of service to a leader looking to cope and flourish in a constantly changing and complex world, since agile thinking and the ability to flick quickly between perspectives will give you the advantage as you respond to challenges as they emerge.

Ken Wilber is fond of saying that our tendency towards fundamentalist thinking is partly what keeps us, as humans, at earlier stages of our own evolution. It precludes us from seeing more of the whole picture which is where, ultimately, the best solutions lie. "I take my part and I make it my whole," says Wilber, which leads us, collectively, to having broken or partial worldviews. "Ignorance is a partial view of reality, and if you take a broken, partial view of the problem, you get broken, partial solutions."

Chapter 3 walked us through some ways in which we can develop our minds as adults, make them more malleable, and grow to be more conscious, complex and inclusive in our worldviews. We saw that we are capable of transitioning through a series of stages, from more egocentric ('I') to less egocentric ('We') thinking. We-centric thinking that is more complex and nuanced allows us to recapture more of the whole and means we are less inclined to cut off a part and make it our whole (whilst arguing with others about the parts they have cut off and made their wholes).

It is not a requirement of adulthood to be on this journey. There are plenty of us who will happily choose to remain at the end of the spectrum that champions our own perspective over others'. To become a more conscious leader, however, we need to invest in loosening our attachment to our viewpoints and see them for what they are – mere mental constructs – which opens the door towards a more conscious way of being and leading.

One of the greatest advantages of doing this in organisations is the ability to harvest the collective intelligence of everyone. As we saw in Chapter 1, CEOs the world over are recognising that collaboration is the factor that leads to innovation and competitive advantage. Collaboration accesses collective intelligence. Rather than landing quickly on the side of one solution, conscious leaders are able, quite frankly, to get out of the way and to avoid making the conversation, the results and the organisation about themselves – because that is simply a play of ego. One facilitator I know who is skilled in hosting these kinds of emergent conversations says, "If they're applauding you at the end as the facilitator, then you've done something wrong." What she means is that we've made it about us, rather than about holding the space open for different perspectives to be heard.

Sometimes the leadership of others from this perspective can be quite radical. Jean-François Zobrist (FAVI) started off his career in the traditional 'boss-role' of this company by telling everyone: "You work for the customer. I don't pay you. They do."[2] Eliminating hierarchy and flattening out the structure in a single stroke, Jean-François gives ultimate accountability to the employees who, in turn, are accountable to the customers, not the boss. As a result, they are free to experiment and innovate, highly successfully, supplying more than 50% of the European automotive market. All of his approach is rooted in his radical relativism.

"There is no model," Jean-François told me. "Each person follows his own path, which is different to everybody else's. What we all have in common at FAVI (and on which trust is built) is little ego, we are instinctive beings; we take a long-term perspective and we are good guys. No other approach or method is necessary."

It goes without saying that Jean-François does not directly lead. When I asked him about how he goes about this, he simply said: "There is no method, no example to achieve free enterprise. One to three times a week I share my perspective that conscious leadership exists, that it is possible, and then people either do what they need to do or they don't do it. I don't feel I have to convince people. I am not a missionary."

It seems that the key requirement to lead in this way is to give up the need to control things and bend the world to our point of view. Traditional organisations have as their core operating principle that some people at the top need to make the decisions on behalf of everyone else, and then follow the faintly ridiculous practice of filtering down that information through the ranks to the nerve endings of the organisation. By the time it has reached the points at which action needs be taken, the world has usually moved on and the organisation is at risk of being out of date. This makes savvy organisational evolution extraordinarily difficult and causes all kinds of problems with scaling from a successful startup to an established business.

An alternative is to practise radical trust and radical relativity, more about which is covered throughout this book.

I was curious to ask Bob Fishman what enables leaders to let go of control. In Bob's view, "If you're aware that ideas regarding what we could do next could come from anywhere in your organisation, then how we get people to feel safe enough to contribute ideas is paramount. This still leaves the leader in the position of having to make the difficult choices, not because they know the future better than anyone else, but because it's their role to decide in which direction to go. The leader's role can still be to pull together diverse ideas and explain, transparently, that from the various resources and viewpoints, this is their best judgement on where we should put our efforts in the future. That is a more humble leadership than one that acts as though the leader knows the future and pretends to listen to others, but has the 'right' answer."

This ability to seek out multiple perspectives is also present in Eileen Fisher, founder of Eileen Fisher, Inc, the highly successful fashion company. She has always been willing to say, 'I don't know.' "This leads to radical participation," says Fisher. "People feel safe to explore their own ideas instead of feeling like they just need to do what you tell them to do." She is, by all accounts, a conscious leader who is able to be humble, present and authentic.[3]

Knowing is the enemy of learning

Perhaps the most radically perspective-changing experience I underwent in talking to the conscious leaders I interviewed for this book was with Tom Chi. Tom is a force of nature: a genius mind who is also deeply humble and conscious, and who has worked in roles as wide-ranging as astrophysical researcher to corporate executive. He has played leading roles in projects such as Microsoft Outlook, various Google X projects such as the self-driving car, and delves into human development issues with social entrepreneurs around the globe. His hallmark is a unique approach to rapid prototyping, visioning and leadership that can jumpstart innovation and he lives and breathes the ideas of opening up multiple viewpoints with humility and, in his case, rapid speed.

One of Tom's angles is the creation of 'mental debugs' – ways of getting around those sticking points in our consciousness that stop us from stepping outside our own viewpoints and leveraging our collective intelligence. One of Tom's mental debugs is: 'Knowing is the enemy of learning.'[4] Knowing something makes learning impossible, he says, because knowing holds in place the current frame of our knowledge. Letting go of our need to know and being open to not knowing, to learning, expands the scope of our knowledge with new data and new possibilities. Being willing not to know grants our minds a permeable membrane through which ongoing learning – and innovation and growth – can happen.

"Don't bring all the experts on stage," cautions Tom. "Experts are paid to be in a state of knowing." Instead, bring the new thinking on board, the fresh thinking, through the left fielders, the new generation, the non-experts and the non-leaders.

Benjamin Zander, conductor of the Boston Philharmonic Youth Orchestra and a renowned leadership speaker, talks about this kind of humble leadership: "Something happened to me when I was 45," he recounts. "I realised that the conductor doesn't make a sound. He depends for his power on his ability to make other people powerful. And when I realised that it had an overwhelming effect on me, so much so that the members of my orchestra began to ask me, 'what happened?' And what had happened was that I realised that my job was to awaken possibility in other people. You get to see whether you're doing this by looking at the eyes of the other people: if you are doing it, their eyes light up. If you're not doing it, you get to ask yourself a question: Who am I being that the eyes of my people are not shining?"[5]

Whenever I show this video clip of Benjamin Zander to leadership groups, there is a hush in the room as leaders recognise that it is their job to ask themselves whether they are being the kind of leader people want to follow, the kind of leader who gets out of the way and makes it all about the other person, about collective gain and collaborative intelligence, rather than about themselves. It is a great moment. "A monumental question for leaders in any organisation to consider," Ben continues in his co-authored book, *The Art of Possibility*, "is: how much greatness are we willing to grant people?"[6]

This kind of egoless leadership is possible as we become more conscious and as we notice when we are being driven by our ego-based needs to look special, to secure our survival, to be better than others or to win at all costs. All these things drive a one-perspective leadership style. Self-management is the key to being the kind of leader who is willing to let go of control and harness the collective intelligence across their organisation and the multiple viewpoints that enrich it.

CONTINUOUS FEEDBACK LOOPS

Once we've developed a more radical mindset, what actions can we take to help harvest the value in We-Q? One thing is to get constant feedback about how a course of action is playing out. Bob Fishman describes this as a, "shifting back and forth". The approach he takes is to say to others: "Let's tentatively take this road, but get constant feedback about the conditions because we really don't know what the future is." Conscious leaders need a lot of people giving feedback on how something is or is not working, based very much on the reality of the situation. It is the antithesis of the common practice of a small group of strategic leaders going down a road they've decided on and expecting everyone else to go down that road too despite the fact that other people might know that this is the wrong direction.

KEEPING COMMUNICATION CHANNELS OPEN

Paul Monekosso Cleal of PwC says: "I spend some time thinking through and making sense of things for myself, but increasingly by talking to other people we all learn more and we all get further together. Trying to create an environment where people can be comfortable raising their fears or ideas and discussing these openly, rather than keeping them to themselves, is important. A lot of it comes down to communication: getting people to communicate with each other and then giving them the confidence that they can actually say what they think and raise concerns so that you can start helping them to deal with issues."

It might seem unwieldy for a leader to manage such an apparently complex and chaotic process of communication amongst many voices. Enter the wonderfully practical, agile and light touch example of Buurtzorg's CEO Jos de Blok, who heads up a large network of home-care nurses in the Netherlands. This example is described much more fully in Laloux's *Reinventing Organizations*, but some of the highlights are worth mentioning here.[7]

De Blok has skilfully used technology to his advantage by directing his blog on Buurtzorg's intranet into a powerful leadership instrument for collecting multiple perspectives and turning everyone into organisational sensors. He writes posts from the heart and without PR spin, and reaches an audience of 7,000 nurses, and dozens or even hundreds of these nurses respond to his thoughts.

He addresses all sorts of organisational issues in his blogs: the direction the company could take, decisions he feels are needed, or simply examples and encounters that underpin what the company is about. Within a few hours, de Blok can sense the direction the company wants to take depending on the responses, comments and suggestions he gets.

This begs the question: Why would we, as leaders, employ people with perfectly good sensory intelligence, who have solid points of view and on-the-ground insights, and then ignore this in the name of our predetermined organisational structure? It makes no sense at all.

Laloux goes on to describe how, rather than harvesting collective intelligence in this way resulting in chaos (which most people coming across the idea of this kind of leadership and self-organisation instinctively fear the most), people in these kinds of sensing companies hold a very clear idea of the organisation's purpose and a broad commitment to where the organisation might want to go. "With the purpose as a guiding light," writes Laloux, "everyone, individually and collectively, is empowered to sense what might be called for ... The organization evolves, morphs, expands, or contracts, in response to a process of collective intelligence. Reality is the great referee, not the CEO, the board or a committee."[8] Strategy then becomes a live and organic process.

This collective intelligence extends to decision-making in the organisation. As we'll see in Chapter 8, conscious leaders are willing to let go of control in favour of the intelligence of the system – that is to say, the collective intelligence of everyone within it – speaking and determining the direction through decision-making. The source of power and decision-making doesn't lie with the leader but with everybody. It is not, however, an invitation to free-for-all chaos. There are simple, light, though rigorous, processes that are put in place to guide everyone's actions. One such approach is called the Advice Process.

The Advice Process

When leaders themselves are no longer entirely in charge, how do decisions get made? Leveraging the collective intelligence of an organisation through people's multiple viewpoints is not the same as aiming for consensus or compromise. Trying to replace a centralised control model with consulting absolutely everybody is a recipe for disaster, slowing down decisions to a virtual standstill.

The alternative is something called the Advice Process, used in companies such as AES, FAVI, Buurtzorg and others, the Advice Process is simple: decisions can be taken by anyone. This removes the need for everyone to agree or for one person to force a decision on to everyone else. However, two things need to happen before making a decision. First, the decision maker must seek advice from those people who will be affected by the decision, and second, the decision maker must seek advice from people with the relevant expertise before making the decision. The more far reaching the decision, the wider the pool of people from whom advice is sought needs to be.

Ultimately, the advice process, or any similar process, is about trust — trusting yourself, trusting your employees and trusting the process.[9]

What is becoming clear is that part of a conscious leader's role is to tune into and to use the power of your people as on-the-ground sensors for how your organisation can evolve. Done well, this can turn your organisation into an agile sensing organism that responds quickly to the changing needs of the environment, which has distinct commercial advantages and positive knock-on effects for innovation and engagement.

ADVICE FOR DEVELOPING RELATIVE VIEWPOINTS

Other than learning from life's experiences, leaders interested in becoming more conscious can try to loosen up the grip of their worldviews through some of the following practices:

» **Immersion experiences.** Immersing yourself in other cultures, taking secondments in other countries and travelling widely, especially in countries where your home language is not spoken, tend to open up the eyes and the mind as it forces us to try on for size the perspectives of others

» **Staying curious.** In conversations, avoid deciding on 'the answer' too quickly based on your well-worn thinking patterns. Try living with the question for longer. Ask about and explore the thinking that lies behind others' points of view. What led them to their particular conclusions? How do they see the world differently from you?

» **Resist converging too quickly.** Emergent conversations have three elements to them: the divergent, where everyone's viewpoints are being aired and differences are exaggerated; the 'groan zone' where conversations feel messy, difficult and even stuck; and the convergent, where new breakthroughs occur and an answer develops out of the chaos or confusion.[10] The conscious leader's role in this is to see what emerges. It is useful to leave things open beyond the point of discomfort, beyond the point where you might normally be tempted to close things down to avoid everything feeling 'too uncomfortable'. Trusting the process, that something will emerge out of the chaos, is the skill that's required and this involves knowing that you don't have to control the discussion, especially not too early.

» **Peer learning.** Engaging in peer learning opportunities with others who see the world differently from you and who feel they have the right to challenge your assumptions can be extremely helpful. Depending on what kind of leader you are, this may not be your staff members. Examine your assumptions. Get others to challenge them. If what you think is not true, what could be instead?

» **Seeking out what you don't know.** Consciously look for other perspectives that are different from yours.

» **Noticing your rules.** Keep an eye out for all your 'shoulds' and 'oughts' that naturally play out in your automatic thinking, for therein lie our unexamined worldviews.

» **Knowing is the enemy of learning.** Take a leaf out of Tom Chi's book: nouns, fixed points of view and labels are just a quick way for us to stop thinking about something. "A good time for employing 'knowing' is when you've already done the thing one hundred times and you just want to do it one more time," advises Tom. "A good time for 'not knowing' is when you're facing challenges that no one has solved yet. A good question to ask is: what else is there still to learn about it? Your mind becomes malleable again," says Tom. "All these things that have become stable and hard, become fluid again."[11]

"To be honest with you, I don't even have a lot of respect or consideration about my own opinion... because, you know, they're like noses – everybody has one."
Lawrence Koh, CEO International Diversified Products

Endnotes

1   http://www.young-germany.de/topic/live/life-style/
     weq-more-than-iq

2   May, E. Matthew. May 2012. 'Mastering The Art of
     Bosslessness'. *Fast Company* magazine. http://www.
     fastcompany.com/3001574/mastering-art-bosslessness

3   Tenney, Matt. May 2015. 'Be a 'Don't Knower': One of Eileen
     Fisher's Secrets to Success'. *HuffPost Business*. http://www.
     huffingtonpost.com/matt-tenney/be-a-dont-knower-one-of-
     e_b_7242468.html

4   https://www.youtube.com/watch?v=25fUDjMtkuI

5   Zander, Benjamin. https://www.youtube.com/watch?v=zrGAJ7h
     Vh1o&list=PL496B2B683BBE0D2F

6   Zander, Rosamund and Zander, Benjamin. 2000. *The Art of
     Possibility: Transforming Professional and Personal Life*. Boston
     USA: Harvard Business School Press.

7   Laloux, Frederic. 2014. *Reinventing Organizations: A Guide to
     Creating Organizations Inspired by the Next Stage in Human
     Consciousness*. Belgium: Nelson Parker.

8   Ibid., p207

9   Ibid., pp99–107

10   Model shared by The Art of Hosting.
     http://www.artofhosting.org

11   https://www.youtube.com/watch?v=25fUDjMtkuI

7

TAKING COURAGEOUS STANDS

What do you do once you've found your purpose as a leader and know what you want to contribute? You take courageous stands to bring it to life in the world.

A leader I once knew, a Managing Director of a freight company, was confronted by a typical leadership dilemma. An instinctive conscious leader, Mark found himself face-to-face in his office one day with an enthusiastic Sales Director who had secured a sizeable delivery deal. It presented the opportunity to make a significant profit, which would have made the company, its shareholders, and Mark, very happy. Mark had the good sense to ask what the shipment contained.

"Arms," said the Sales Director.

"Arms?" asked Mark. He was incredulous. "In that case, we're not doing the deal."

"What?" cried the Sales Director, equally incredulous. "But just think of the profit! Think of the company! Think of the shareholders!"

Nonetheless, Mark was resolute. Better, he reasoned, to refuse the deal that was so obviously against what he and the company stood for, than to sell out for profit. He was prepared to take a courageous stand despite pressure from others, including the company's owners, who weren't as committed as he was to doing business more consciously, and he did this despite the backlash it might bring him.

As it turned out, Mark made the right decision and he was supported in walking away from the deal. Conscious leaders, however, will often have to face the heat in the decisions they make and the stands they take for what is ethical, sustainable and responsible. This is especially so in business, where as we know, the dominant narrative is still to favour profit at virtually any cost. Even though this narrative is changing as sustainability concerns and the demand for trust and transparency grow, conscious leaders are the outliers who will need to hold the line in finding a different way of working; one that promotes the long term over the short term and benefit to the majority over benefit to the minority.

Let's take a deeper look at what we mean by taking a stand.

CONSCIOUS LEADERSHIP STANDS

When a conscious leader decides to impact the world, it begins with that person saying: "I believe in this and I want this to happen."

"Conscious leadership is about being spiritually courageous," says John Renesch, himself a conscious leader who has shaped the field for decades. "Spiritual courage is very quiet, but very powerful. It leads to people taking stands that they wouldn't ordinarily take."[1]

There is a deep conviction in taking a stand from your place in the world. It comes from something within yourself that is undeniable. It is about your sense of purpose and the role you feel called to play – in whatever arena that might be. The desire to see something greater be achieved or the desire to release suffering becomes the fuel for a stand, one that creates benefits not just for you, but for the world as a whole.

One such leader taking a stand is Lynne Twist, co-founder of The Pachamama Alliance (which promotes sustainable and just living) and author of the book series, *The Soul of Money*. Lynne is a global philanthropist who is dedicated to alleviating poverty and hunger, and to supporting social justice and sustainability. When Lynne speaks, for example about The Pachamama Alliance, you are struck by how she is one with this ideal she is representing in the world. She is not talking about it from her head, from her intellectual understanding of it, but from her whole being, and it is this authenticity that resonates with audiences far and wide and gains their support. They recognise there is a different fire burning in leaders like Lynne apart from just the flame of their individual will.

Conscious leadership is about being spiritually courageous

I heard someone at a conference recently asking Lynne where she found the power to stand as irrevocably and as vulnerably as she does for what she is representing. Lynne replied simply: "I am the stand I have taken. I've surrendered to that and the power comes from the stand and my commitment to this calling. It makes life so simple."

She has been described as saying: "Taking a stand is the way of living and being that draws on ... the very heart of you are. When you take a stand ... you have the capacity to move the world."[2] At its best, taking a stand is about being good for the world. It is about surrendering your small will, driven by your ego for personal gain and survival, to being in service of the larger will of life itself. You may not have the answers, but you trust that you are on the right path because it resonates with you, and resources find you to make this come alive. This is what makes these kinds of conscious leaders compelling and magnetic.

Taking a stand doesn't have to be all about acting on a global scale, however. We are familiar with the kinds of leaders who have taken clear and courageous stands about what they want to see happening in the world: Aung San Suu Kyi and Malala Yousafzai being but two examples. Equally, in all kinds of organisations, conscious leaders take stands every day that require courage and moral conviction, motivated from a place of wanting to see a difference around them or challenging something out of their sense of personal integrity, authenticity and care for the wider system. It is about the courage to do this even in the face of opposition.

Sudhakar Ram told me about the transformation of his company from a traditional hierarchy to a self-organising system, something he deeply believes in and which is in line with his principles and his own development as a conscious leader. "There was a set of shareholders who used to be particularly nasty. I kept telling them that this is what was needed, this is what I'm committed to. In the end, we went through a demerger, which unlocked a lot of value for the shareholders and, in the process, those who had some very quaint notions about shareholder value all got what they needed and have exited the company. So if you're very clear about who you are and you don't get obsessed or anxious about a shareholder or a customer or a board member, but rather include them in the changes you're looking to make, this can turn out positively. These people are now all doing things that are probably more rewarding for them and there's no negative feeling either way."

Even the smallest actions on the part of conscious leaders can represent stands they take to create some kind of positive impact. Leaders like Lorna Davis takes a stand for the culture she believes in and wants to create in the company. While Lorna's role as the chief catalyst for bringing Danone's sustainable growth manifesto to life gives her the opportunity to make a positive impact on the world every day, she also takes smaller actions at a very local level to create her desired culture: "I'll push it a bit if I get the chance," she told me. "For example, I start some of my meetings with a five-minute meditation. I could feel the surprise of people the first time I did this, but now I have enough credibility – I ran a $7 billion business in my last job – and I will push it more."

Another of her stands is on the topic of recruitment: "I refuse to make any appointments without having seen at least one woman and one person from an emerging market and I'm not interested in talking further about it until I've seen those two candidates." For her assistant, she has taken on a Vietnamese-Indian born woman because this person really believes in the company's manifesto to become a more responsible business. "I'm sure there are other people out there who may be better assistants in the short term, but this woman is diverse in her history and in her experience, and she believes in what we're doing, so through me appointing her I'm saying that this is where I'm going to take a stand. I can do more of this the more credibility I gain by making these kinds of decisions."

Bringing to life the stand we've taken is best done through clean action. What counts are the facts of the impact we've made. We are inclined, as human beings, to attach stories to the events of our lives and then to use these stories to explain away whatever effects are undesirable. "I tried my best, but the reason I couldn't do it is because..." or, "I would have done it differently, but the other team..." are examples we are probably very familiar with and have either heard multiple times, or even used ourselves.

> "There is only the present moment
> and the stories that we tell."
> Nithya Shanti

We can be tempted to live our lives like the commentator of a game. We can live in the grandstands of life, throwing in comments about how the game is being played, but none of these comments has the slightest impact on the game itself. To have an impact on the game, we have to get on to the field and take action – sometimes courageous action – for what we wish to see in the world. At the end of the day, it's about continued action in service of the result we wish to create or the purpose we wish to serve. As Jim Collins described in his notion of Level 5 leaders, "The key sign – the litmus test – is whether you begin to explain away the brutal facts rather than confront the brutal facts head on. That's sort of the pivot point."[3]

To have an impact on the game, we have to get on to the field and take action

---

When conscious leaders role model this courageous, reality-based action in their behaviour it can create a kind of incorruptible culture in which people are less inclined to bring their story or excuses to the conversation. When everyone is dealing in the reality of what is being created and the facts of moving towards it, our ego has less opportunity to get into justifications, explanations and excuses. The results can be shorter, more efficient team meetings that get back in line with the desired result, rather than raking over the past. Performance conversations become about desired future reality, rather than about history. Some of the emerging methodologies of self-managing organisations, such as Holacracy, are specifically designed around processes that stick to the facts and avoid the stories. These processes help to bypass the emotional 'drag' that is characteristic of the ego playing out in organisations, which shows up as endless, politically fuelled meetings that go over old ground but never seem to get to an outcome.

In developing yourself as a conscious leader, here are four questions to build the muscle of taking stands:

» What are the stands you are most inspired to take?

» How does this relate to your personal purpose and
   what you want to see becoming a reality in your
   organisation or in the world?

» What are the qualities of the stories you are telling and
   encouraging to be told in your organisation?

» What practices are you putting in place in your
   organisation to support reality-based action free from
   limiting stories?

Endnotes

1   Renesch, John. 2012. *The Great Growing Up: Being Responsible for Humanity's Future*. Arizona: Hohm Press.

2   Ibid., p142.

3   http://archive.fortune.com/magazines/fortune/fortune_archive/2002/05/27/323712/index.htm

8

CREATING THE FUTURE

As we've seen, being more conscious as a leader has a lot to do with moving away from ego-based living and leading towards collective, inclusive leadership that achieves results by harvesting the intelligence of multiple stakeholders and having a positive effect on the wider system. Conscious leaders think in terms of 'we' rather than 'me'. They bring their whole, integrated selves to their leadership and give as much importance to their leadership being as they do to their leadership doing. They feel inspired to take a stand in the world about something they believe is important and they take courageous action to support this. They move away from getting stuck in stories about the past and they get into action for creating a different future, one that is of benefit to the wider system and sometimes to humanity at large. This way of living and leading is about creating the future and pulling it into the present. It is not about reacting to the future as it rushes towards us, but about making it.

This is probably one of the most exciting canvasses that leaders can create on. As we'll see from the leaders featured in this chapter, they take joy in playing with life and creating outcomes that benefit the many, while being relatively free from the limitations of the ego such as a mindset of scarcity, the need to protect their own interests or excessive self-doubt. They are acting for something valuable for all that they see in their mind's eye and feel drawn to contribute towards.

LEADING IN AN UNCERTAIN FUTURE

The future, of course, isn't as clear nor as simple as we might like it to be. We are no strangers to the narrative that the future will be more complex, more connected, more ambiguous and more unknowable than it is today. VUCA is a term derived from the US Military that is an acronym commonly used to describe the state of the world we find ourselves in today: Volatile, Uncertain, Complex and Ambiguous. Our sense of the future is that it will only become more changeable and complex as time moves on, giving the impression that the future is rushing towards us at an ever more unpredictable and unknowable rate.

Most conscious leaders are comfortable with being in a state of not-knowing. They sense into the system and what is required next. As we've seen, they tend also not to be as attached to their views or even to having 'the answer' (see Chapter 6). Because they are practising the art of self-mastery over their egos, they are less driven by self-preservation needs, such as safety and security, and are less inclined to react under conditions that threaten their safety, such as uncertainty.

Some of the conscious leaders interviewed for this book positively relish the prospect of uncertainty and a relative answer. One such leader is Bob Fishman. Bob offers an ironic challenge to leaders everywhere. "Do you really think you, as a leader, can predict the future?" he asks. "The myth that leaders are godlike and can predict the future needs to be dealt with by every individual that is asked complex questions that they know they don't have the answer to, but act as if they do. Because if as leaders we think we can predict the future better than others, then there is no need to involve anyone in any discussions. That becomes dangerous when you're trying to relate to a large group of people or to thousands of employees in a company. People look to you for the answers, saying, 'what shall we do?' and the risk is that leaders may start to believe they are able to know the future. As leaders, we need to acknowledge that despite any fortune we've had in the past, and despite any perceptions that people might think we have the answer, we cannot predict the future better than a group of people can. It's vital that, as leaders, we become aware of the differences between a gut feeling of knowing the future and realising that we can't be certain about this. This leads us to an important discussion about which group of people you should put in place to deal with the question at hand. It asks us to engage with many different people in the organisation in coming to a decision about what we should try, how we can test the market or what our customers say."

This does not necessarily imply that leaders have to make a decision via consensus, which as we've seen in the previous chapter usually results in endlessly tiring rounds of consultation and argument to get to a possible agreement. Leaders, in Bob's view, still need to be responsible for the point at which a decision is made, based on having enough information, and which can be reviewed and adapted as the situation moves on. This sense-and-respond approach is a great tool for helping leaders to manage an organisation under ever-changing conditions.

In other cases, self-managing organisations respond to uncertainty and complexity by allowing decisions to come from anywhere in the organisation. This is based on a set of robust principles and processes and there is no formal leader in the way we traditionally understand that word. The most robust self-organising mechanisms at the moment, for example Holacracy or the Advice Process (*see Chapter 6 for a description of the Advice Process*) operate by empowering any person to make any decision as long as he or she has sought advice from a) people with expertise in the matter and b) everyone who will be meaningfully affected by the decision. These kinds of processes show how initiative and personal power can increase across the organisation when these are released from the clutches of the leader.

As we change across generations and those who come after us understand the mechanisms and complexities of the future better than we do, it becomes imperative to include more voices in the way we shape the future. Paul Monekosso Cleal believes that changes in the world driven by technology signal a natural shift in knowledge and power towards the younger generation. He believes it is essential to include not only their voices, but the views of everyone at all levels.

Alongside his consultative approach and the recognition that he, as a leader, doesn't have all the answers, Paul sees his leadership role as stewarding and helping others to cope and prosper in conditions of uncertainty and ambiguity. He explains: "People tend to like things simple and clear, but life isn't like that. So as a leader, my role is to help people make sense of what's going on and be able to function effectively, despite the fact that the world isn't as simple as they would like."

With their ability to hold multiple perspectives and not to be wedded to specific outcomes, conscious leaders are well-equipped to navigate complexity and shape the future by communicating that they are seeking alternative answers from others because there is no one right answer.

What these leaders do instead is set up the conditions for the best thinking in the room to emerge. (We'll look at how they do this in Chapter 12). Decision points may rest with leaders (sometimes), but it seems that with conscious leaders a great deal of leading and shaping the future in a VUCA world is about giving up the need for being in control and having to be the source of direction. This begins with being aware of the limitations of our own perspective and the self-management to know that others have an equal part to play in the way forward. It extends to a willingness and the skills to open up the discussion and, to a greater or lesser extent, to get out of the way while the answer evolves.

ACTS OF CREATING THE FUTURE

It is one thing as a conscious leader to have the qualities that help you cope with an uncertain and unknowable future; it is another thing entirely to act into that future and create new and fresh outcomes in a universe of possibilities.

In his highly insightful book, *Synchronicity: The Inner Path of Leadership*, Joseph Jaworski writes: "The deepest assumption that we human beings hold [is] that we cannot change things, so we must live our lives reacting to forces outside our control ... If individuals and organizations operate from the generative orientation, from possibility rather than resignation, we can create the future into which we are living, as opposed to merely reacting to it when we get there."[1]

Rather than controlling the present through the rear view of the past, or trying to tame the future into something that is simple and manageable, conscious leaders can do what Bob Johansen calls 'forecast rather than predict'. "A forecast is a story from the future that provokes insight and invokes action in the present,"[2] explains Johansen. This is a key skill in articulating and creating the future and pulling it into the present.

A very good example of a leader who epitomises this way of operating is Tom Chi, whom we've met in earlier chapters. He has an exciting approach to articulating and creating the future fuelled by a multifaceted perspective on life and a deep insight into the value of using these acts of creation to be in service of humanity.

Tom Chi: Creating for 1,000 years

I believe there's analysis and there's creation. A lot of people get stuck in analysis because they want the safety of having the provably best answer before they do anything and the assurance that this is definitely going to work – and that doesn't exist, especially in creation.

Creation really is something that is new, that is added to the world. Eight thousand years ago it was impossible to be a concert pianist because a piano had not yet been invented. At some point along the timeline, 500 years ago, someone made a harpsichord and people could build on that, and nowadays there are people with a good chunk of their brain constructed around being a concert pianist. This type of creation was truly not possible before and I don't even believe it was in the universe and somebody just found it.

There are these conscious acts of bringing things together in service and in new combinations of service that have never been seen before in the universe, that all conscious beings have access to as a tool. We get to choose what percentage of our lives is spent on that tool and what percentage doesn't get anywhere near it. We also get to choose when we apply these tools of creativity, and at what scope of compassion and consciousness we do it. Do we try to do it for seven billion people for 1,000 years, or do we do it for ourselves or for a smaller set (for example for our company for this quarter – a very micro perspective). It's actually even more micro – most people do it to serve just a subset of their ego, not even their full ego. Our normal operating size is usually smaller than one person!

I like to do things very practically. Currently, I'm interested in how you could practically construct an organisation with the incentives and ways for people to societally interact within it. We just created a company that launches a new company every 10

weeks. Every one of those companies has alterations in the DNA
of how it operates, how it's legally structured, how the team
members are recruited and incentivised, etc. Each of these is
an experimental vehicle that allows us to see whether the types
of tweaks in companies' DNA lead to better, more constructive
behaviour in the company and in the relationship between the
company and society.

We are taking the results of those experiments and publishing
them out every six months, because every six months we will
have a good roundup, about 30 to 40 experiments, and then
we're open-sourcing the legal documents, the operational
playbooks and some open-source codes to help people to
duplicate this. We're publishing a new approach to ownership.
Normally, if you work for a company, everything you think,
do and say related to that company, and sometimes not even
related to it, gets to belong to that company during the time you
are employed by them. There is something about that which
didn't strike me as correct. Our new approach to ownership is
one where we don't own anything you've done. You've granted us
an unlimited license to use what you've created and you retain
the ability to do whatever you want with the things you created.

As soon as you share that, investors say: what happens if one
of your employees does something brilliant while working for you,
then leaves your company and starts their own company with that
brilliant idea? Would that be allowable? I would say absolutely.
If they beat us to market or capture the market share or get their
idea out of society faster, then the net effect is that society benefits
faster, right? That's the point of entrepreneurship. This small
tweak actually changes a lot of things. If we're not going to do
something with an idea, I would actually encourage employees to
leave and make a company that uses that intellectual property.
If this experiment works, then we are trading off benefit to the
company with benefit to the individual and society.

This example from Tom Chi illustrates a whole range of qualities in the way that conscious leaders act to create the future. There is his willingness to experiment powered by an evolutionary mindset, through which he can see how one experiment has the potential to build on previous human achievements. There is his heightened service orientation and how these conscious acts of creation he and his teams are involved in might be of service to humanity as a whole. There is the recognition that many of us think about what's in it for us personally, but we have the potential and scope to contribute to the entire world, both for now and for future generations. There is the openness and willingness to share discoveries for the greater common good, rather than hold them close to his chest. This belies an attitude of abundance rather than scarcity. And there is the ability to draw the context of competition as broadly and widely as possible, seeing past barriers of you-vs-me and thinking instead about how everyone can benefit. This is open flow of information, for everyone. And for everyone along a timeline of a thousand years.

This is possibly the most exciting application of conscious leadership for the world. It is not so much about managing the current state in a more conscious way, it is about creating a future state that is more aligned to what we'd like to see. Those who are engaged in the sustainability movement will recognise the need to create a future that can benefit all of humanity for all of time to come, or at least as much of this as we can influence.

THE MAKER INSTINCT

What Tom Chi's example also demonstrates, between the lines, is the capacity of the conscious leader to tap into the 'maker instinct' of other people and to work with them as co-creators of products, services and realities that serve the common good and that future-proof us. The notion of 'maker instinct' is taken from Johansen's book, *Leaders Make the Future* mentioned previously.[3] Johansen pinpoints the maker instinct as the number one quality of successful leaders of the future. He defines this as 'the ability to exploit your inner drive to build and grow things, as well as to connect with others in the making.'

Our maker instinct is a universal urge, and therefore by definition something we all have as human beings. It is built into our language, our histories and our ways of seeing the world. We see the maker instinct arising in the way we have built tools and technologies, the way we speak ('make sense'; 'make money'; 'make friends') and the way we reach for the future. The challenge, as Johansen points out, is to turn our urge to make into a leadership skill, to synchronise the maker instinct of leaders with the maker instinct of others, just as Tom Chi has done.

Exploit your inner drive to build and grow things and connect with others in the making

---

Here is a crucial question for conscious leaders the world over: How can you, as a conscious leader, enable people in your organisation to tap into their profound capacity for creating and, in so doing, climb out of a feeling of being trapped by current circumstances and climb into a future of our own making?

This is a choice we all have. Some of us choose to continue playing the victim role, because we cannot see an alternative for ourselves. It is within the conscious leader's potential, however, to wake people up to the possibility of expressing their creative maker instinct, rather than letting it lie dormant. "It must be recognised, valued, and nurtured if it is to become a leadership skill for the future. The maker instinct is key to making the future," declares Johansen.[3]

In turn, Mackey says: "Managers do not make history; conscious leaders do. They imagine bringing into existence that which did not exist before and which most thought could not be done."[4]

By harnessing the collective intelligence of everyone to make, innovate and collaborate, conscious leaders help to create a future that we all want to live in.

A helpful tool to encourage the maker instinct within us and others is taken from the work of Dr Fernando Flores, recognised leader of ontology[5] on how our use of language becomes the driver of how we act in the world. "Language is like the chisel of the carver; it shapes our world," says Mike Griffiths from the Centre for Strategy Implementation, speaking of Flores' approach. We can use language to create breakthroughs in performance depending on where we place our focus. On the one hand, we can focus on the domain of the past – analysis, explanation, stories about what happened – which fundamentally changes nothing about the situation, but it does inform what we do in the present and thereby creates our future. Living from the assumptions and conditioning of our past – especially our unexamined past – shapes who we are and what we see as possible for our future.

Or, we can choose to live from our future. This involves making a declaration or a commitment about what we want the future to be like (a 'speech act'). Speech acts have power. Rather than just speaking, they are the *intentional* use of words with commitments behind them. We declare who we will become in the future, and that informs what we do in our present, giving us the results we have as this moves into our past. The idea of taking stands lives in the domain of the future which is shaped by design, not just inherited from the past.

"We don't want to be limited by our past; we want to really be informed by the best of our past, but then we want to reference our actions from a different future," says Mike.

Performance based on tradition

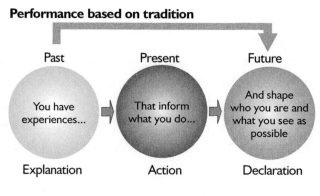

Performance based on the future

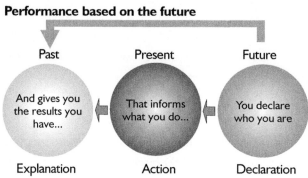

Figure 9: Speech Act
(Ref: Mike Griffiths at CSI Centre for Strategy Implementation)[6]

This choice is one that we all have and this frame can guide conscious leaders' conversations with others. It has the potential to prompt a different kind of conversation, moving from 'business as usual' – where much of the time is spent in a dissatisfying post-mortem of the past in which nothing much changes – to break-throughs about imagined futures and desired results.

"Most organisations look at what they did last year and then add another ten percent. It's like living your life through your rear view mirror," says Mike. Conversely, organisational purpose lives in the future. Layers of hierarchy and organisational sediment live in the past. The idea of decluttering this and getting people together with some simple rules that hold them in formation, that bind them together loosely around a common purpose, can help people to be in action of their commitment to the future and create it.

Absolutely key in creating the future is to do so collaboratively with others. As we can see in the examples of the leaders throughout this book, they see beyond the typical boundaries of self and others, beyond boundaries of 'us' and 'them', and into the possibilities for the future of the collective 'we'. They recognise that it is the collaboration of many minds and diversities of perspective and effort that give us the greatest possibility to not only survive but to flourish into the future. We all become collectively responsible in making our future. "Leaders are nodes," said Johansen, "and the best ones are hubs that form, nurture, and grow networks that stretch far beyond themselves. Leading is making."[7]

> *"Leaders are nodes and the best ones are hubs that*
> *form, nurture, and grow networks that stretch far*
> *beyond themselves. Leading is making."*
> Bob Johansen

The maker instinct is amplified by connectivity and the greatest possibility for conscious leaders to leverage this in business is through the higher purpose of their company. When an organisation's higher purpose is aligned with its values and with the values of employees who work for it, this ignites and energises the maker instinct throughout the organisation. When this happens, employees get to bring their whole selves to work, rather than only having the option of finding avenues for their maker instinct and creativity in their hobbies and lives outside of work.

The maker instinct is particularly relevant for the Millennial generation, and it would be unsurprising if it didn't feature even more prominently in the generation of Digital Natives and beyond. Bethany Hilton, a conscious Millennial featured in Chapter 21 of this book, describes it as follows: "Being comfortable isn't living.

We are creative pioneers. We need competition and growth to pioneer and become who we were destined to be. We have it within us, we can't fight it; it's who we actually are. Rather than saying, 'let's grow our volume target,' let's rather ask how do we change the way things are done, how do we improve society in some way?"

> *"The 21st century is the age of the unfinished work."*
> DJ Spooky

What are the ways other conscious leaders are bringing this quality to life in their work and in their lives? Neal Gandhi is a successful serial entrepreneur who has woken up to the way in which he can create the future without the stresses and strains that in his previous life cost him his motivation and his marriages.

These days, Gandhi is an angel investor in purpose-driven start-ups that have a social impact. He has a distinctly relaxed and unhurried style of life, and his entire way of being is one of calm and maximum creativity. He even underwent Alpha brainwave training to generate the well-being of Alpha brain waves at will.

Gandhi exudes a tangible sense of abundance, whether this is abundance of time or of resources. He uses his gut instinct to tap into synchronicity to find himself in the right place at the right time. If it looks and feels like an interesting and right involvement, he always has the time for you, but without this taking away from his quality of life. He lives in the moment, creating from his sense of abundance and positive intent, and without being attached to the outcome. This is a common theme amongst conscious leaders.

"I don't feel stressed for time at all, about anything," says Neal. "I don't feel the need to run around and be a crazy person, because it doesn't serve to do that. I'm lucky because one of my businesses is a cash generator which gives me an ability to do all I do without worrying about generating income. Maybe I built that in such a way. However, trusting in life is really important. It's really easy to let go.

It's all about energy and the energy you put out. You can put out a bunch of negative energy and that energy will come back to you. It's basic physics, really."

Gandhi creates the future by choosing to become involved in businesses that contribute socially, do good and give back. One of his investments is Playmob, a technology-based platform for voluntary giving that makes a business out of the act of doing good. Playmob connects businesses and causes, customers and communities, actions and impact. Its purpose is to put 'doing good and feeling good' at the core of every online interaction that counts in your business. In so doing, Gandhi foresees and intends Playmob to be the platform that drives $1 billion of giving.

What Gandhi shares with other conscious leaders is the tendency for:

» Focussing on intentions rather than forcing outcomes;

» Acting to create, while letting go of control and accepting what is;

» Being open, curious and creative; and

» Practising a mindset of positivity and abundance.

Gandhi says of this approach: "I do go for goals and I am on top of my businesses, though I am unattached at the same time. I came across this quote by Deepak Chopra that describes how it is for me: *intention and desire married together with detachment.*"

Paul Cleal describes his approach in similar ways: "I'm ambitious in a non-specific way. I'm not wedded to a specific outcome that I'm trying to achieve. There are a number of possible outcomes that I'd like to achieve and I'm comfortable with all of them. My leadership is about trying to get people to see that there is not one single definition of success, it is much broader than that, and there are multiple right answers."

The four qualities above are mirrored in the research of Mariana Bozesan, who studied the inner worlds of conscious leaders. The conscious leaders she interviewed went about the act of making and creating their future along very similar lines. They realised that they became even more successful if they let go of their goals, of the need to control people and situations, and stopped working so hard. They got rid of their 'outcomes', 'life plans' and even 'personal careers', and got into the flow of life.[8]

As they set intentions (instead of setting outcomes), they became more open and so were able to see more opportunities which presented themselves than they had previously. Their curiosity and open focus meant that they got out of the way and were able to spot more circumstances and could take advantage of synchronistic events that had the potential to fulfil their intentions and turn those into reality.

Set intentions instead of setting outcomes

The more willing they were to let go of control, the more success they had. This is certainly echoed in the examples of Neal Gandhi and Tom Chi. Starting from a base position of accepting life, rather than fighting to control it, they can meet people where they are at and enjoy an inner state of knowing that everything is perfect as it is and that they are enough as they are.

When we look at the state of the world and of business today, or even at our developmental centre of gravity as human beings, we suffer from the perception gap between where we are compared with how we would like things to be. This causes immense suffering, something which the Buddha identified 2,500 years ago.

Somehow, in relaxing into life as it is, this seems to put us in a better position to create the future through intention, desire and non-attachment.

TOOLS FOR CREATION:
INTENTION AND ATTENTION

Earlier we met Nithya Shanti, a former Buddhist monk who now works with corporates to develop their levels of consciousness. He talks about his view of acts of creation. He sees that our intention to create forms two sides of the same coin, both equally and simultaneously true.

One approach is to look at what we want to create, what it would look and feel like, what it would take to create this and, as we start treating it in this way, we start energising the intention of what we want to create. "This," says Nithya, "is a very 'yang' or masculine approach: one of giving energy to your intention by visualising it, vocalising it, emotionalising it, acting upon it and actualising it. Doing so changes our thinking process, our feelings around it and then brings it into being through changing our behaviour."

Nithya continues: "The other way of looking at intention is by accepting that the universe is completely sacred, just, and an expression of God, where nothing is out of place. This breeds an approach and attitude of 'allowing', the 'yin' or more feminine approach. This is much more about recognising what's already right, what's already good, paying attention to the magic and miracles that are already happening and, by trusting and allowing, everything falls into place, everything moves by itself.

I think both of these approaches are actually very complementary, so the word I use for the first one is intention and the word I use for the second one is attention. Intention and attention. Intention refers to the thoughts and feelings that create what we want in the world; attention is being conscious and aware of events that are already happening. Creation is both of these. A simpler way of saying this is: there is only the present moment and the stories that we tell. Live in the present moment, which is attention, and tell higher quality stories, which is intention. This is the way we create."

> *"There is only the present moment and the stories that we tell. Live in the present moment, which is attention, and tell higher quality stories, which is intention. This is the way we create."*
> Nithya Shanti

While conscious leaders may be using all of the tools covered so far in their role as leaders, there is one action that they are continuously taking and which is, in effect, a never-ending act, namely the ongoing practice of their own self-mastery. It is this that we will turn our attention to next in the final section in the zone of Self-Mastery.

Endnotes

1   Jaworski, Joseph. 2011. *Synchronicity: The Inner Path of Leadership*. San Francisco: Berrett-Koehler, p.182.

2   Johansen, Bob. 2012. *Leaders Make The Future: Ten New Leadership Skills for an Uncertain World*. San Francisco. Berrett-Koehler Publishers, Inc., *a BK Business Book.*

3   Ibid. p28.

4   Mackey, John and Sisodia, Raj. 2014. *Conscious Capitalism: Liberating the Heroic Spirit of Business*. USA: Harvard Business School Publishing Corporation.

5   http://www.talkingabout.com.au/FernandoFlores

6   Mike Griffiths at CSI Centre for Strategy Implementation, http://www.csistrategy.com

7   Johansen, Bob. 2012. *Leaders Make The Future: Ten New Leadership Skills for an Uncertain World*. San Francisco. Berrett-Koehler Publishers, Inc., *a BK Business Book.* p29, 41.

8   Bozesan, Ph.D., Mariana. 2010. *The Making of a Consciousness Leader in Business: An Integral Approach*. San Francisco & Munich: SageEra.

9

PRACTISING CONTINUOUS SELF-MASTERY

When we are engaged in the journey of becoming more conscious and leading more consciously, it is just this: a journey. It is not a destination we reach but a process we are living, daily, and adapting through the practices of conscious leadership. We are never a finished article.

More than anything else, what distinguishes a conscious leader from an emotionally intelligent leader or an excellent transformational leader, are two things:

» Conscious leaders have realised that they are not the sum total of their egos. They work at consciously choosing their reactions and responses outside of their automatic, habitual conditioning.

» Conscious leaders are actively engaged in self-mastery. They are on an evolutionary path – consciously – and they do things that help them to move along this path.

It might sound as if this makes life a whole lot easier and, in some respects, it does, but it also takes courage to face up to yourself and to keep confronting your ego and choose the shift to opening up rather than closing up.

I heard John Mackey tell an audience at a conference that

self-mastery is at the heart of becoming a conscious leader. "It's not easy," he said. "Being a conscious leader is hard work. You have to become a master of yourself." I agree with Mackey, along with anyone who is doing this work. In my personal experience, this kind of learning can feel like root canal for the soul, combined with regular bouts of exfoliation of our ego, peppered with moments of hilarity and laughter at the human condition and our own failings. It's not for the faint-hearted. Developing as a conscious leader requires you to have the courage to look at yourself completely naked with none of your usual defences to hide behind and no one to rescue you.

Mackey also goes on to say: "As a conscious leader, you have an ethical imperative to grow and evolve."[1] How is it that our commitment to personal growth and self-mastery is an ethical imperative?

All of the conscious leaders I spoke to while researching this book, and especially the Millennials, recognised that how we conduct ourselves as leaders sets the tone for what goes on in the rest of the organisation. This thinking is not new, but in the case of conscious leaders it is not merely that they are managing themselves well by attempting to avoid outbursts and reactions or role modelling particular leadership behaviours. They are actually involved with role modelling to the rest of their organisations what it means to be more conscious. They are examples of a particular way of being.

Conscious leaders have an ethical imperative to grow and evolve

An organisation can only evolve to the level of consciousness of its leader[2]. In my experience, and I'm sure in yours, great teams have fallen when a new leader has entered the arena. In traditional, hierarchical organisations, the tone of corporate culture and what is acceptable or what is not is directly set by the leader who is in charge at the time. It stands to reason that if a leader who is operating at a later stage of meaning-making (for example a Strategist, with the desire to integrate many diverse viewpoints) is replaced by a leader whose centre of gravity is at an earlier stage of meaning-making (for example an Achiever, which is focussed on finding the quickest route to goals and driving through obstacles), this will have a profound effect on the example the leader sets and on the culture which is created around him or her. There are multiple examples of companies that, having reached a particular level of operating consciously, have found themselves sliding back to earlier, more mechanistic forms of operating under the gaze of a new, and less conscious, leader.

Equally, conscious leaders see it as part of their role to provide the right kind of developmental environment for people in their organisation, and this is not only in their personal development, but also in how they are evolving in their own levels of consciousness. These leaders recognise this can never be forced and that personal evolution is the choice of every individual; it has to be voluntary. Nevertheless, they see it as important to do what they can to provide the right sort of environment in which personal evolution might occur and they do what they can to enable this in a sensitive, non-prescriptive way.

John Renesch says: "What we can do is be a role model. You can't be an inspiration because you choose to be an inspiration, but if you're leading your life and living your values and other people are aware of it, they might be inspired by it; they might not. If they are inspired, they might seek you out, and, if they do, you have an opening where somebody is asking you for something. Evangelism doesn't go over well."

BEING PRESENT WITH ACCEPTANCE

When it comes down to it, the self-mastery of conscious leaders is about building their relationship with the present moment and practising as much acceptance as possible about what's going on in that moment. These leaders try to avoid getting caught up in concerns about the future or hankering after the past. As a result, they are fairly free of fear and anxiety (about the future) and guilt (about the past).

"The biggest shift for me," recounts Sudhakar Ram, "was acceptance. I saw that if I accept everything that happens as something that is positive and good – including an irate shareholder or a board member who is being tough – then I get to take the approach that everything is right and perfect. There must be a reason why they are being this way and I just need to discover that reason and find a way to address it."

Accepting everything as it is, is therefore a key practice of the conscious leader as part of their ongoing self-mastery. Frederic Desbrosses agrees: "What happens, happens. It's how you deal with it that matters. Every day something happens, for the good, for the bad. Sometimes, on two different days you'll see the same event in two different lights. The point is: are you going to learn, are you going to take the right action and optimise whatever has happened? You can't fight against it. For me, self-awareness is a minimum foundation of conscious leadership."

To illustrate this, Frederic tells the fascinating story of how, on the last day of his four-year sojourn working in Africa, a civil war broke out: "I woke up from my farewell party and, there was a civil war on, and the same guys who I was partying with the day before were standing on pick-up trucks and shooting Kalashnikovs. None of this is something you can control. What happens, happens. The question is, how do you respond to it?"

Staying neutral, whether or not results are achieved, is possibly the most challenging thing of all for leaders to do, precisely because they are measured, promoted and paid on how well they achieve results. Being a conscious leader does not mean that you suddenly give up caring about whether or not results are achieved – it means not getting caught up in whether or not results are achieved. There is a subtle but important difference.

Accepting everything as it is, is a key practice of the conscious leader

---

Results remain important to the business, but as a conscious leader one's personal barometer of value is less set by the fluctuations of achievement. Instead, it requires staying in the moment with things as they are, and at the same time remaining attentive to what you want to create in the business. It's about coming from a less needy place in yourself, where you are not simply trying to fill a void or chasing the tail of something that promises goal fulfilment. It's a state where, rather than struggling, you are whole, complete and happy; where you are able to hold yourself in a way of being where you don't need anything to be different from how it is, yet where you can still be effective in creating results and outcomes.

From this place, even your identification with being 'the leader' loosens and you have less of a fixed point of view about your own identity. It becomes more about your being than about your doing, more about sensing and less about controlling.

Steve Hall, CEO of driversselect, describes how this process works for him: "Often, when I focus only on results, I hone in on short-term gratification and I just don't allow enough time. When I'm not attached to the results, but rather to the process, I'm happy. The times when I'm happiest and fulfilled, there is no metric in my mind; it's all about just experiencing the process and myself in action."

Being a conscious leader is therefore often about achieving more with less effort. Because these leaders release their fixation on outcomes and controlling them or forcing them in a particular direction, less resistance is created. Instead, by accepting their current reality, staying present and slowing down, they become more attuned to more possibilities of what might happen next. Patterns emerge, systems are clearer, possible next steps stand out in greater relief, and their responsiveness to what is most important is heightened. Mackey talks about how the attentive mind is capable of noticing more about the relationship between things and seeing the larger system. And, according to Bob Johansen, all leaders must filter and learn how to see patterns as they emerge. It's important to be able to listen through all the noise in a VUCA world. "You cannot listen for the future if you are deafened by the present or stuck in the past,"[3] says Johansen. Therefore, being present with acceptance is a key practice of the conscious leader.

What gets in the way of being present with acceptance?

Fear is the biggest factor in determining whether we stay conscious in the moment or clam up with the need to control circumstances and protect ourselves. We know from popular neuroscience that our threat-detection centre in our brains, the amygdalae, are hypersensitive to any signs that we might be in danger or might lose out in some way, even when these threats are not particularly real. Becoming a more conscious leader is partly about figuring out how to uncouple yourself from your fight-or-flight reactions.

"You are not going to be able to remove this part of yourself completely," says Sudhakar Ram, "but as you keep reflecting on it and you gain awareness, you react less and are able to create more. It's good if the larger percentage of your responses can come from abundance rather than from fear, out of love and actually being able to contribute."

What helps to develop this capacity?

Mindfulness, certainly. The mindfulness revolution is filled with leaders attesting to the benefits of practising mindfulness meditation or *metta bhavana* (loving kindness) meditation, as a way of creating some sort of space between events and their reaction to these events, or spreading love and goodwill rather than fear and anger. Mindfulness helps to cultivate presence and strengthens the muscle of being the observer of your life, rather than the soap opera star.

Laura Roberts, CEO of Arizona-based conscious chemical company Pantheon Enterprises, says: "Part of expediting the journey is to figure out how to spend less time in fight or flight. I recognised that fight or flight was an intellectual handicap – as soon as you're triggered, you don't have your full faculties around you. I wanted to be able to find ways to reboot when I was triggered and I started using meditation as a way of exercising that interruption muscle. Now I get to interrupt what's happening in real time and reboot, rather than being stuck in a loop of negativity."

A great example of self-management in action comes from conscious leader, Lorna Davis. She recounts how she was once preparing to give a very important presentation alongside a colleague, and found herself annoyed at being swamped by his huge personality and being micromanaged at the same time. All of this began leading to an inner monologue that wasn't helping her nerves or her performance.

She caught herself in the thick of her reaction: "I said to myself, 'How interesting. I'm telling myself a story about this.'" She made some space for herself during the evening before the presentation and, instead of fretting about it, planning her approach or going over her notes, she read some inspirational text completely unrelated to the subject of her talk. She went to bed and woke in the morning with absolute clarity about what she needed to do: make one small change to her position on stage and one larger change to her attitude. Rather than making it about herself and her colleague, she realised she needed to connect to her audience from her own authenticity. "This isn't about me," she thought, "this is about the message, and the message needs air to breathe, and it doesn't need my small-minded inner monologue."

All the work Lorna has done on herself over the years to become more conscious – on her self-awareness and self-management – allowed her to sidestep her ego and her pride and defensiveness, and enabled her to find enough space in that moment to lead differently.

Sometimes, developing this capacity for being present with acceptance is done through the simple practice of gratitude. Neal Gandhi says: "I reckon I must say to myself, 'I am so lucky' at least 20 times a day. I see something or I experience something and say, 'Wow! That is so cool', at least 20 times a day; probably more."

Or in Paul Monekosso Cleal's case, it is about calmness: "You can spread calmness and goodwill," says Paul, "or you can spread anger and confrontation, and you'll probably get back roughly what you spread. You can't control life's outcomes too much, but there's a lot you can do, like help to create an environment that is more likely to lend itself to being successful."

As conscious leaders continue to practice self-mastery, they recognise that this is something that happens through the medium of their own leadership actions. Rather than seeing their personal development as something that sits separately outside their leadership role, they tend to see life itself as their teacher.

Sudhakar Ram describes it in the following way: "The whole idea of lifelong learning is that it's not any extra effort. On a daily basis, the encounters that you have and what life brings you are all learning opportunities. Either way you can remain in autopilot mode and ignore it or treat it as another weird incident that happened to you, or you can pay conscious attention to it and see what it is that you are being asked to pick up from this specific incident. What is your contribution? How are you being contributed to at this point in time? It's not about reading more books; it's just being present to what is happening on a daily basis."

A LIGHT TOUCH

Ultimately, conscious leaders seem to master the art of holding life lightly and employ a sense of play and creativity in the way they interact with what is happening around them. Playing with it rather than getting bogged down by it requires a certain shift of mindset, one which Diana Chapman of The Conscious Leadership Group and her colleagues know well and teach leaders.

This exercise, taken from their book, *The 15 Commitments of Conscious Leadership*, helps:
What if there is no way the world should be and no way the world shouldn't be?
What if the world just shows up the way the world shows up?
What if the great opportunity of life isn't in trying to get the world to be a certain way, but rather in learning from whatever the world gives us?
What if curiosity and learning are really the big game, not being right about how things should be?
Can you see how this would radically change the way we see and live our lives?

The practice of 'what if' and curiosity moves us away from heavy and burdensome expectations to something which is lighter and more free.

A final word on playing lightly with life comes from GD (Gyandev), an India-based spiritual teacher and leadership coach who likes to distinguish between Mastery and Transcendence. Mastery, he says, is all about handling the dream of life, improving how it is playing out day by day. You might get really good at creating results or excelling in meetings or accumulating money, and this is all part of mastering the dream of existence. Transcendence, on the other hand, is when you realise that this is all a dream and that ultimately, none of this really matters. So you don't take anything too seriously. Instead of running around like a ferret in a cage trying to make life better and better and more successful and more abundant, you playfully engage with life... more like a lighthearted explorer. For GD, conscious leaders need to have awareness of both these dimensions. They need to have the knowledge of Mastery and they've also got to have some measure of Transcendence. Without Transcendence, there is danger of getting fully sucked into this temporary drama. Holding ourselves lightly in life, we can say that we might as well choose to invent something that brightens our lives and the lives of those around us.[4]

IN CONCLUSION

This concludes this section on Self-mastery, in which we have looked at the various ways conscious leaders become conscious or wake up and detach themselves from their egos, how they bring their whole selves to their leadership role to underpin their authenticity, how they hold their own views lightly so as to capitalise on 'We-Q', the collective intelligence in their organisations and stakeholders, and how they take courageous stands to articulate and create a future that benefits others as widely as possible. All these practices relate to the zone of 'Self-mastery' in our model of conscious leader-ship. In the next section on Conscious Relating, we'll explore some of the ways in which these leaders engage with people to get the best out of everyone.

Endnotes

1 Mackey, John and Sisodia, Raj. 2014. *Conscious Capitalism: Liberating the Heroic Spirit of Business*. USA: Harvard Business School Publishing Corporation.

2 Ibid.

3 Johansen, Bob. 2012. *Leaders Make The Future: Ten New Leadership Skills for an Uncertain World*. San Francisco. Berrett-Koehler Publishers, Inc., *a BK Business Book*, p21.

4 Zander, Rosamund and Zander, Benjamin. 2000. *The Art of Possibility: Transforming Professional and Personal Life*. Boston USA: Harvard Business School Press.

ZONE 2: CONSCIOUS RELATING

10

RELATIONSHIPS AND CONNECTION

A few months ago, I was working with a non-profit in a workshop on how they told the story of their organisation to the outside world. As part of this, we invited each person to tell the story of why they had joined the organisation and what was important enough to them about what they did to make them stay.

At first, the room was icy with defences. People stared straight ahead, dreading their turn and worried about revealing themselves and what others would think of them. But then, something magical happened. As person after person joined in and everyone listened, the atmosphere warmed up and people started seeing behind the masks they all wore to work every day. They began to identify with others and hear their own values echoed in what their colleagues were saying. Before we knew it, the room was buzzing with conversation and laughter, and people were saying things like: "We had no idea that we had so much in common about why we joined, because we never speak about it." The rest of the day went brilliantly. More importantly, those people connected at the level of their authentic selves, over what was most important to them, which can never be erased and which now serves them in the way they work together.

Conscious leaders value connection and they promote it at many different levels. This is not simply because better human relationships make for a more pleasant workplace; it's also because fostering connections creates possibilities for new and innovative thinking to occur. Conscious leaders see it as a key part of their role to get people talking to each other and they actively encourage these connections.

"Relationships, stakeholder management, and a keen appreciation for values and purpose are essential for effective leadership in the complex world of the twenty-first century," writes Mackey, "and analytical intelligence by itself does not equip leaders to handle these challenges."[1]

Fostering connections creates possibilities for new and innovative thinking to occur

---

In Section 2 on Conscious Relating, we will explore the ways in which conscious leaders promote connection. We'll look at how they reframe competition, practical ways in which they use connections to jumpstart innovation, and their views on power and how they approach decision-making. We'll gain insights from them on how they nurture the quality of their relationships, the tone they are looking to establish, and what this means for the human environment they help build in their organisations.

KEY FEATURES OF CONSCIOUS RELATING

Below are five key features of the ways that conscious leaders relate to others, to set the scene. We'll explore these features in more detail in the further chapters of this section.

1 Placing connections before hierarchy

The quality of the connection and dialogue is what counts when leading consciously. In essence, amplifying connection replaces hierarchy. Many of the conscious leaders interviewed for this book follow a flat structure or self-organising approach in their organisations and try to encourage as many connections as possible between as diverse parts of the organisation as they can. As we saw in the previous section on Self-mastery, these leaders avoid becoming too attached to their points of view or arguing over the rightness of their perspective compared with others. They recognise that all perspectives are relative and valuable, and that the best solutions often come from a combination of these. Part of their role is to encourage these viewpoints to come forward.

Many people's voices are brought into the room and melody arises out of these different notes

---

Bob Fishman advises that talking to employees about their ideas is an 'emotionally relative space'. People are emotionally invested in their views of, for example, where and how the organisation should spend its money. Playing his role as a listener and convener respectfully, he told me: "I've always walked into a room and never wanted to sit at the head of the table – and I've told people why this is."

Frederic Desbrosses continues: "Everything plays a role and everyone has a point of view. I don't start every conversation like this, but an interesting provocation is first to assume that the other person might be right. Sometimes I find myself in combat because

I'm a human being. I'm swept away by the time pressures or other demands, and it's difficult to step back. But that's the time for conscious leadership, to help you reflect, take a break, and ask whether this is the right thing you're doing."

Gathering multiple perspectives brings a richness to the organisation. Instead of a leader enforcing his or her opinion, or employees looking to the leader for the 'right answer', many people's voices are brought into the room and melody arises out of these different notes. The leader's role becomes the conductor of this orchestra of connections.

2 *Role modelling connectedness*

Business is a human adventure. The leaders interviewed in this book connect people to people to create something new. Human connection is the foundation of trust and of learning, as well as innovation.

In this kind of setting, these leaders de-layer themselves and their own importance in order to foster connections. For example, Frederic Desbrosses was prepared to load containers in the factory when they were short of staff, while he was dealing with the president of the company at the same time.

Dominic Sewela told me: "People don't interact with you in a normal way when you're in this role, so it becomes incumbent on me to take off those layers and make sure they know I'm a normal human being. Since I realised the power that I have, I will now consciously walk over to an employee I can see is shy and trying to avoid me, and I just go to them and talk to them in a nice way. And you see them melt, literally, and become easy and comfortable."

At its peak, this kind of connection can be considered a form of stewardship. "Leadership is the stewardship of the lives entrusted to you," says Bob Chapman, CEO of the $1.7 billion manufacturing company Barry-Wehmiller. He accepts that lives are influenced by his leadership, and he takes responsibility for this, right down to the way his employees are treated and the way this has a knock-on impact on their families. During times of financial pressure, he is inclined to ask, "How can we keep our friends?" rather than "Where can we cut jobs?"

"The more people you lead; the more people you serve."
Tom Chi

Studies in human development and neuroscience underline the importance of human connection for us. At the end of the day, what we all long for is to be connected, to see and be seen by others, to transcend what separates us. Facilitating connections as a leader enables positive effects to occur. Your own transparency and authenticity is an essential component for doing this, since allowing yourself to be seen and related to encourages others to do the same.

3 Consciously creating ripple effects

We've heard how Paul Monekosso Cleal refers to this as 'business karma'. "If you are positive and helpful, then people will help you. I see this happening all the time, both at an individual level and also at a collective business level. The people who go out of their way to be helpful find it easier to get help from others. I've paid a lot into my relationship bank account over the years and that means I get to make withdrawals sometimes as well. It's amazing how it comes back around, sometimes even on the same day! Or sometimes A helps B, B helps C and C helps A. It's strange how that happens too."

Cleal is describing the way in which conscious leaders take responsibility for the ripple effects they create in the pool of humanity surrounding them. Another way of looking at this is that the medium of leadership is these very moments of engagement. This is where leadership shows up, in the connection points between you as a leader and those you are interacting with. Creating the right ripple effects in these moments produces opportunities for others to see themselves in the future you are looking to create, and to engage with this future in a way that contributes towards it. It helps them to deal with the present situation, too, in more effective ways.

How do you stay in the moment and stay in the medium of leadership? By being conscious that everything you do, and everything you say, and every way you're being, is impacting those around you and rippling out to create a reality for others. Although it's not realistic to expect us to manage ourselves in every moment, it's about the development of the skill to do this more frequently. Such is the responsibility – and the potential – of great conscious leadership.

> *"Leadership is just the act of creating shared value."*
> Tom Chi

4 Moving from brokenness to wholeness

Bob Fishman, who is also a marriage and family counsellor in addition to former CEO of RHD, sees many similarities between dysfunctional human relationships and corporate life. "This," he says, "originates in the rigidity of roles and authority over others that exists in typical corporates. If you want to destroy a young person's sense of themselves, continue telling them that what they are doing is wrong but that you are the one providing them with food and shelter. This is what's done in autocratic organisations all over the world. People think that the way to run a company is only to look at how to direct people towards making more and more money, while ignoring all the other factors, including severe disturbance of our environment. People sense this and speak out, saying, 'Hey, we're doing something wrong!' but the corporation says, 'No, no; we are making more money. It's okay; don't worry.' This leads to a complete splitting of our experience."

This brokenness is what causes us to bring only some of ourselves to work while frequently leaving the best parts outside in the car park. Not engaging with the whole person means that leaders are only getting a portion of their full contribution and potential.

What does moving from brokenness to wholeness look like? It's captured in the shift from 'me-versus-you' thinking to 'me-and-you' thinking. It shows up when it becomes less important for us to enforce our own views, to destroy the competition or to find a common enemy. It's part of recognising that we are all intercon- nected. Tom Chi describes this interconnectedness not from a spiritual but from a scientific perspective. "Whenever I hear people mention this phrase that we're all connected," he says, "they do so in such a way as if it's something they believe was true, as if it's something that's abstract, esoteric and unprovable, that they really just wish that the universe was like that."[2] In reality, Tom explains how the very elements in our cells can be traced back to the galactic movements of the universe; the iron in our blood originated as part of the original supernovas. When looked at from the vastness of this perspective, wholeness and interconnection are not just clichés, but a truth of our existence.

As we recognise this more, we begin to see that everything is more interconnected than we had seen before, and this affects the way we conduct our relationships and act as leaders. "... it dawns on us that we are just one expression of something larger, an inter- connected web of life and consciousness ... We strive to repair [the brokenness of] that relationship ... knowing that we are not separate from but one with nature," writes Laloux.[3]

"We've been given this amazing gift of consciousness," continues Tom Chi, "and because of this we've been able to deeply understand our connectedness. Over time as a society, this deepens our levels of consideration, expression and understanding for each other."

On an everyday level, conscious leaders can foster wholeness by amplifying strengths and acceptance of differences, and dialling down behaviours that break things up, like judgement, destructive criticism and unhelpful comparisons. They can prompt others to think about the important questions, such as: how do we make our work more meaningful? What is our purpose and how do we bring it to life? How can we bring more of ourselves to work? How can we contribute in a fulfilling way? How can we foster pride in what we are doing?

Of course, human relationships are not only about harmony. Developing as a conscious leader is not tantamount to having an effortless life, free from human conflict. Rather, it is about the way we respond to these incidents and how we choose to manage ourselves in these moments.

Peter Matthies believes the question should be how we build relationships with others when we're all under pressure or when we find ourselves in conflict. "Partly it's about how we create openness and transparency to allow other people to see us, and to help us to see them. Intimacy – into-me-see – creates trust."

In the tough conversations that leaders need to carry out in business, it's easy to become defensive and shut down, shut out and separate. I asked Sally Ann Ranney, whom we met in Chapter 3, how she helps people to talk collectively about important planetary issues in the various conversations she participates in. "Ask questions," advises Sally. "Bulldozing and accusations don't work, but being firm, having the facts and asking questions helps. It doesn't guarantee results, but when you ask really pertinent questions that go deeper and then deeper, what this does is firmly and gently expose that their approach may not be working, or it highlights the assumptions they are holding."

5 Convening for innovation

Good human relationships bring multiple perspectives to the table and weave together the human intelligence that can lead to new outcomes. We are human creative sources and this 'maker instinct' is becoming more amplified through technology. "Leaders will know how to tap into that maker energy as a force for change," says Bob Johansen.[4]

In sum, conscious leaders are in an ideal position to take advantage of the perfect storm of factors emerging on the horizon of our humanity right now: the mobilising power of purpose; the resonating role of values; the liberating force of technology; and the social power of the sharing meme. They can use their willingness to tap into multiple perspectives, and to collate and collaborate around these, to call us all towards an image of our highest potential future. They can use their relationship skills to convene communities, both real and virtual, that address the most important and complex challenges, and innovate some of our most admirable solutions.

Endnotes

1   Mackey, John and Sisodia, Raj. 2014. *Conscious Capitalism:*
     Liberating the Heroic Spirit of Business. USA: Harvard Business
     School Publishing Corporation.

2   https://www.youtube.com/watch?v=25fUDjMtkuI

3   Laloux, Frederic. 2014. *Reinventing Organizations: A Guide to*
     Creating Organizations Inspired by the Next Stage in Human
     Consciousness. Belgium: Nelson Parker, p49.

4   Johansen, Bob. 2012. *Leaders Make The Future: Ten New*
     Leadership Skills for an Uncertain World. San Francisco. Berrett-
     Koehler Publishers, Inc., *a BK Business Book,* p34.

11

REDEFINING COMPETITION, REFRAMING INNOVATION

I believe it's important to discuss this subject before we dive into the relationship practices of conscious leaders because, in effect, it describes the bigger context that shapes all other relational behaviour. With this context in mind, it is not possible to act within the constraints of our former, smaller selves.

REDEFINING COMPETITION

As we've seen in previous chapters, conscious leaders move beyond the traditional boundaries of competition. In a typical marketplace, businesses vie for the attention of customers and the entire cycle of activity is powered by the engine of scarcity. In the traditional world of leadership and business, the size of the pie is finite. If you get a larger slice than I do, this means I am losing out on my share. Therefore, businesses do whatever they can to secure their corner.

I was recently listening to the territory head of a large professional services firm, who was relating a story about how virtually an entire team had upped sticks and gone off to a much smaller competitor. Rather than displaying any curiosity about why this might be the case and what may have caused this valuable team to leave his organisation, this particular leader demonstrated scorn towards the competitive firm. "We will crush them!" he admonished, in a single stroke dismissing that they might have anything different to bring to the marketplace based on his standards of what was important. We never did find out why all of those team members had left, nor what was more appealing to them at the smaller competitor. And, in the process, this leader did not learn anything from his competitors that could improve the game of his own organisation.

His story is not atypical, and this kind of battle-talk is part of the mainstream narrative of business and leadership. Conscious leaders, on the other hand, draw a much bigger boundary around the game, whether this be business, politics, education, non-profit, society, the environment or anything else.

As we saw in the previous chapters on self-mastery, these leaders have progressed along the spectrum of adult development, leaving behind earlier attachments to 'me-versus-you' and evolving further towards an updated mindset of 'me-and-you'. They are less ego-driven, less likely to be triggered in the face of competition, and more likely to identify the connections that exist between different viewpoints. They are inclined to look at how we all can win, rather than how only they or their companies can win.

Tom Chi, whom we met in previous chapters, is highly invested in the practical application of intelligence and the creation of new ideas and products that both serve humanity as a whole and which unlock the genius in all of us. He has a huge and expansive mind and the experience in conversation with him is of being pulled to the outer reaches of your perceptions towards the really big picture. Tom has this to say about collaboration compared with competition: "Collaboration versus competition is a false dichotomy. People often say the natural state of nature is competition, but that's not so. Every living thing, through its life cycle, improves the viability of life of every other thing in the ecosystem in the process of living its own life. The fact that we consider competition and collaboration to be opposites is a completely human construct. This is us just identifying two attributes of the natural world and pretending that they're in opposition. In truth, both of these things coexist effortlessly as part of a single thing, but this single thing is harder for us to identify. Because it has so much nuance and dimensionality to it, our perceptual models to understand it do not fit very cleanly."

What Tom is saying, in effect, is that the unity that is life is beyond many of our mental constructs to make sense of it. He is not alone in saying this. Though he comes from a scientific more than a spiritual perspective (although even this is a false dichotomy based on the notion that these two things are somehow separate), his words echo the great spiritual traditions, especially of the East, where we are encouraged to see and experience unity consciousness for ourselves, and to suspend our mind-generated dogmas of difference.

This tendency towards unifying permeates the mindsets of all conscious leaders. They think far less in competitive terms and will often partner with so-called 'competitors' to come up with new solutions and innovations that serve the greater good. With a higher purpose held firmly in mind, especially one that contributes to the whole of society or to the planet, it suddenly doesn't make sense any longer to be fighting for scraps on the ground. Better, for the benefit of all, these leaders reason, to think about what we all need for the prosperity of everyone.

In *Reinventing Organizations*, Laloux quotes Jos de Blok, founder of Buurtzorg ('Neighbourhood Care'), a supplier of community nursing services that has captured 80% of the market share in the Netherlands without actually striving too hard to do so. Their purpose is so clear and the way they run themselves so aligned around the needs and aspirations of their community nurses, that they naturally attract talent, grow and deliver excellent service to their customers. De Blok says: "In my perspective, the whole notion of competition is idiotic. It really makes no sense. You try to figure out how you can best organise things to provide the best care. If you then share the knowledge and the information, things will change more quickly."[1]

So simple and profound – yet requiring such a stretch of mind for so many people. De Blok's view shows how he holds in mind a much bigger context about how high-quality nursing care can positively impact the communities in Holland. His aim is that society benefits from great healthcare. He is not obsessing about how he is doing in relation to the competition. In fact, the story goes, he frequently gives presentations to competitors without charging them for it, to share the methodologies of his organisation.

The role of conscious leaders is to watch for moments where our scarcity mindset prompts us to play small

---

To anyone who is programmed for traditional competition, this seems like a nonsense strategy upon which to run a business. Why would you give away your trade secrets to the competition? However, this is only a question that occurs if the boundaries of our perspective remain narrow. When we connect to a higher purpose and bigger possibilities, we begin acting in the interests of that purpose alongside others, including competitors. As counter-intuitive as it appears to the parts of our minds concerned with scarcity, this kind of approach can actually grow the business exponentially as more talent and customers want to become associated with such an aligned and energised organisation. It can result in increased abundance for everyone. The role of conscious leaders is to watch for moments where our scarcity mindset (triggered by our ego), prompts us to play small.

Broadening the field of competition in this way tends to bring distinct evolutionary advantages. By sharing the best ideas, we create a new context where pooled resources enable us to achieve unprecedented innovations. In fact, creating radical partnerships with those outside our normal boundaries gives us a direct line to innovation in a world where collaboration can provide us with better answers to bigger and more complex challenges.

Is there really any other way to go than this?

REFRAMING INNOVATION

The way for all of us to benefit from the inexhaustible source that is human potential and human imagination is for us to think together, rather than to think separately. Joining up different parts of the system becomes the means by which human potential can be realised. Conscious leaders who see this will find that they have the advantages and benefits of a diverse range of viewpoints and ideas available to them that are outside the reach of those leaders who think more about their own gains and their immediate circle, or what they can get their arms around.

> *"Imagination is the new currency. Imagination is the ultimate renewable resource."*
> DJ Spooky

> *"We need all the gifts from all the people."*
> Raj Sisodia

This is typical of what Bob Johansen calls 'reciprocity-based innovation'. This kind of innovation is founded in collaboration and is derived from leaders asking themselves: what is the value that can be created for the widest possible range of stakeholders

– and how do we need to collaborate to get there? "There is a leap of faith involved in reciprocity-based innovation," says Johansen. "There are no guarantees. The trust that is required is a kind of faith."[2]

It is impossible to keep this kind of faith or to promote radical partnerships across previous divides if we are operating from a mindset of scarcity, fear and self-protection. Reciprocity-based innovation requires us to trust that together we can create more than we can create separately; that a win for all is better than a win for some. This is a radical mindset shift for many.

In addition to promoting new kinds of radical partnering, it is also important for leaders to encourage innovation by reducing fear and allowing people to 'fail fast and fail forward'. Nothing stops the flow of innovation more quickly than the spectre of blame for getting something wrong. Conscious leaders can help by setting the right kind of tone, one that celebrates iterative gains of experimentation, hypotheses and small discoveries.

Ownership is the terrain of the ego

The essential ingredient is rapid prototyping. This involves quick cycles of trying, learning and trying again, on an ongoing platform of practical experience. "Rapid prototyping is the 'maker instinct' (which we heard about in Chapter 8) applied to innovation," says Bob Johansen.[3] Timelines are short. Tom Chi has created a company that launches a new company variant every ten weeks to experimentally tweak the DNA of company structures. The team has 30 to 40 experiments to report out on after six months. They are not caught up in cumbersome reporting or spreadsheet analysis. They are engaged with the practical application of human genius and imagination.

Bob Johansen also goes on to describe how the next generation of innovation will be driven by 'do-it-ourselves' leaders who don't get stuck on the idea of ownership. In the process of rapid prototyping, people's ideas get mixed quickly and it is often impossible to sort out who thought what. Nor does it matter. Ownership is the terrain of the ego.

Laura Roberts embodies all of these conscious leadership qualities in the way she goes about her business. In addition to looking for ways to collaborate across the original enemy lines, Laura also talks about the new mental game of the revised competition model.

Laura is ultimately driven by her higher purpose of changing how the chemical industry operates, from generating chemicals that are pumped into the ground and the atmosphere with little regard for what happens next, to planning for and producing chemicals in ways that are more conscious, responsible and sustainable. Her purpose provides the bigger context for her to draw on as she makes her decisions about who to collaborate with, what it means to compete, and how this drives innovation. "There might be a competitor out there trying to do the same thing we are, and maybe they have more traditional chemistry and our chemistry is better in that it's more innovative and disruptive," says Laura. "And they might have held the marketplace for a long time and we represent to them a potential loss in the market share. We'll all have wins and losses and it's about the way we respond. If we have a temporary loss of, say, a customer, then it's about not being angry about it, it's showing us to think about how we can potentially partner with the competitor."

This new form of competition, which is essentially collaboration, makes the most of the vast possibilities available to us. "We live in a world of possibility," says Laura. "We can ask ourselves: what is still possible even though the current circumstances look like this today? Oftentimes I find that people who are more conscious can hold bigger containers for possibility. It shows up in ways where someone says, 'We can't do that because of XYZ', and then it's up

to me to say 'What would it take to make this other thing be true?'
You're just trying to have bigger conversations because really you
can make just about anything happen. Granted, resources can get
in the way, but if you push 'possibility conversations' more often,
and you role model it, too, that helps."

> *You're just trying to have bigger conversations because*
> *really you can make just about anything happen.*
> Laura Roberts

One of the practices in Pantheon is the creation of a really large
stakeholder map. They are embedding a stakeholder orientation
and stakeholder nurturing as part of their DNA. It is very clear to
everyone who their stakeholders are, and one branch on the map
lists what would traditionally be competitors, except this branch is
called 'future potential partners'. "I want everyone inside the
company to understand that even though someone might look and
feel like a competitor in a traditional sense, they really are all future
partners and customers," says Laura. "But even then, I'm still trying
to figure out a way we can collaborate and partner together, even
though they might be out there trying to vigorously pound us into
the ground."

COLLABORATIVE INTELLIGENCE

In our ever more hyper-connected world, the intelligence that will
enable us to reach higher possibilities and thrive is collaborative
intelligence. Our ability to leave behind ego-driven fears and scarcity
mindsets, and to know how to partner with those who we previously
construed as 'the enemy', will be essential for us to find new answers
to unchartered challenges and to flourish, not only to survive.

In this, conscious leaders lead the way. As we've seen, they have natural collaborative intelligence because they have evolved beyond the small ego self and they are pulled towards contributing to the greater whole of life in which we all participate. "Together," says Renesch, "we can do what we cannot do separately. Our challenges are beyond the heroic actions of the few. This means that collaboration is essential to make the shift to consciousness a new reality."[4]

Bob Johansen agrees. He has identified the skill of Commons Creating as critically important for successful leaders of the future to have. Commons Creating is the ability to nurture and grow shared assets with others for greater benefit. What is it that we have in common that could help to make the world a better place for more people? We can see this skill coming through clearly in the mindsets and approaches of the conscious leaders featured in this book.

Technology is consciousness externalised

Future leaders will be called upon to create new commons, says Johansen, new opportunities where collaboration and mutual successes can occur, but it will take genuinely creative thinking for leaders to identify these potential new commons opportunities both within and outside their own organisations. This kind of creative thinking is only possible if we master the tendencies of our ego to play it small and close to our own chests.

All this is powered by our technical revolution. Digital connectivity simply increases the number of touch points for exchanging value. As writer Patricia Aburdene says, 'technology is consciousness externalised.'[5]

Bob Johansen has the last word: "Reciprocity-based innovation will be, I think, the biggest innovation opportunity in history," he says. "In an increasingly open world, connected by cloud-served supercomputing, the opportunity to create a new commons (new forms of collaboration) will be everywhere – and available to everyone."[6] Already we are seeing this with Airbnb as one current example; Uber as another. Digitalisation is revolutionising the way we think about progress, learning and ownership. The currency of the Cloud is reciprocity.

The currency of the Cloud is reciprocity

It goes without saying that rethinking what we mean by competition is essential to unlocking our future. The leaders featured in this book are well-practised in how to reach beyond the boundaries of where their counterparts might be inclined to go. This allows for competition to take place at much higher levels and, with so many stakeholders in the mix, for multiple wins to take place in parallel for multiple stakeholders. There really can be no other way forward to our future.

Endnotes

1   Laloux, Frederic. 2014. *Reinventing Organizations: A Guide to Creating Organizations Inspired by the Next Stage in Human Consciousness.* Belgium: Nelson Parker, 195.

2   Johansen, Bob. 2012. *Leaders Make The Future: Ten New Leadership Skills for an Uncertain World.* San Francisco. Berrett-Koehler Publishers, Inc., *a BK Business Book.* p178.

3   Ibid., p141.

4   Renesch, John. 2011. *The Great Growing Up: Being Responsible for Humanity's Future.* Arizona: Hohm Press, p9.

5   Aburdene, Patricia. 2007. *Megatrends 2010: The Rise of Conscious Capitalism. Charlottesville: Hampton Roads,* pxvi.

6   Johansen, Bob. 2012. *Leaders Make The Future: Ten New Leadership Skills for an Uncertain World.* San Francisco. Berrett-Koehler Publishers, Inc., *a BK Business Book.* p180.

12

CREATING
THE RIGHT
ENVIRONMENT

The old-fashioned way of seeing an organisation as mechanical – a set of moving parts that can be manipulated, chopped off and stuck on somewhere else – is fast disappearing. This view is giving way to something much more organic and fluid in the minds and approaches of conscious leaders. Because they think in terms of the whole system and look at the relationship between the parts, they take into account the natural ebb and flow of their organisations, just like breathing. In fact, for many of these leaders, the organisation is a living entity, the same as any of the individuals within it. To a conscious leader, organisations are dynamic places, teeming with life.

In this book so far we have covered a number of ways in which conscious leaders focus on creating the right type of environment which brings out the best of human potential. These ways are summarised here, and we'll also look at some of the other ways that these leaders shape their organisational setting.

THE POWER OF PURPOSE

In Chapter 4 we read how conscious leaders are masters of setting contexts. Context has transformational power because it has a higher leverage point, which shapes our attitudes, thoughts, emotions and behaviours. These contexts include uniting different positions; the importance of the way you achieve profit; of benefitting the greatest number of stakeholders; of abundance rather than scarcity; and of larger-scale collaboration over small-scale competition, thereby driving different organisational behaviours and creating different kinds of environments.

One of the most powerful contexts conscious leaders have at their disposal to create the right environment is their organisation's purpose. As we've seen, this has to do with why an organisation exists in the world and the difference it is making. If it is profit-making, purpose has to do with why it exists over and above the need to make a profit. Purpose paints a compelling picture of something that people can resonate with and feel they belong to.

Consider the difference in your reaction to a purpose statement such as: 'We look to increase value for our stakeholders and customers' (a generic purpose) compared with a purpose statement such as: 'Improving the health of people, the food system and the planet' (Whole Foods Market) or 'Reconnecting people with nature' (from outdoor apparel company, REI). The latter two evoke images of something we can feel part of, that resonate with our values and fire us into action.

The power of purpose, and creating compelling contexts in general, is one of the major currencies that conscious leaders have in shaping the right environment to enrol people and capitalise on their engagement. The more linkages they can create between what people are inspired by, what their values are and what they love to do, the more powerful will be the results. The work of a conscious leader is to create many such linkages.

> *"The best conscious leaders are merchants*
> *of hope and entrepreneurs of meaning."*
> John Mackey

REMOVING FEAR

We've seen that another way conscious leaders create the right environment is by minimising people's needs for self-protection. As we saw in Chapter 4, we are hardwired to protect ourselves against any form of perceived threat, and social threats count for a disproportionate amount of our protective behaviour in power- and hierarchy-driven organisational settings.

In organisations where fear is ingrained (for example, where blame is readily thrown around or fear of failure is rife), this agitates our brains into states of high alert. In such environments, creativity, innovation, collaboration, dialogue, risk-taking and decision-making are all negatively affected. As Mackey says, "Fear is the opposite of love. An organisation suffused with fear is inherently less capable of real creativity and innovation. Fearful people are hypervigilant, defensive, and purely self-interested."[1]

Neuroscientist Srivi Pillay explains that there are two brain-based reasons for creating a culture based on love rather than fear. The first is that we feel more rewarded and motivated when we find ourselves in a culture of care and appreciation. This encourages us to bring our best selves and best efforts to doing our work. The second reason is that when our brain's fear centres, the amygdala, are deactivated, we have the ability to make decisions that are less impulsive and reactive – and so are able to make superior decisions. More motivation and better decisions: just two of the reasons why it's important for leaders to create the right environment by minimising fear.

I asked Tom Chi how he sets the right conditions for his astonishing track record of creating fast iterations and project launches. I wondered whether he actively strove to raise the levels of consciousness in his teams. Actually, he does this through a mixture of very pragmatic leadership and his perspectives on what it means to be conscious. "I don't push strong concepts of right and wrong," says

Tom. "Whether something went awesomely well or terribly, the question is always the same: what did we learn and how does it change what we do now?" There is no blame or failure – there is only learning. People become attuned to this value of learning over time.

There is no blame or failure
– there is only learning

Driving fear out of organisations can be as simple as encouraging innovation and ideas to come forward, and allowing mistakes. As conscious leaders, we can role model the attitude that mistakes are not only allowable but expected as part of learning.

Sometimes Tom will set a very concrete challenge to eradicate fear. "For example, I'll set our marketing teams the task of going out and doing all our marketing without employing the themes of fear, scarcity or shame. They go and work it out. They'll look at what it means to go to market and speak to people in a way which doesn't invite those three things, which is 95% of marketing today."

Conscious leaders intentionally create a culture in their teams of no fear, no shame and no scarcity. Sometimes it's about a sense of abundance. "There are occasions where you need to go out and hustle to make something happen," says Tom, "but that's not because things are scarce. If there's anything that's scarce, it's that you only have so much life to live in this form in this universe. This is a very different kind of scarcity to 'I'm going to get it and you're not going to get it.'"

Sometimes conscious leaders promote love rather than fear simply by the attitude they take towards people in general, which infuses how they lead. Jean-François Zobrist of FAVI has created an environment of high motivation and ownership based on three key assumptions about people: that people are considered to be fundamentally good; that performance follows if there is happiness, motivation, responsibility and freedom; and that value is created on the shop floor not in the corridors of the executives.

I asked Jean-François how he keeps people connected to the vision and values of FAVI: "By walking every day into the factory and saying, 'Hello, how are you?' to 600 people and knowing the names of all their children," was his reply.

GIVING AN A

Jean-François' approach is reminiscent of world-renowned conductor Benjamin Zander, who starts off his teaching year by giving all of his students an 'A' grade. This takes away the pressures of performance and failure. All Zander asks them to do is to write a letter to him dated one year into the future, describing the musical genius they have become that warrants their A grade. This changes the relationship of the music student to him or herself, and Zander's relationship as a leader to the student. Giving an A is a practice that any leader can employ with any of his or her teams. It is a quintessentially conscious practice because it looks for the best in people, rather than the worst. It trusts people, rather than waiting for them to reveal reasons why they should be trusted or why trust will be broken. And it promotes an attitude of love and acceptance, rather than fear.

The practice of Giving an A is incomprehensible to more traditional or command-and-control leaders who work in the usual environments of measurement, critique, analysing gaps and fixing problems. Under the wrong kind of leadership, this critical mindset can be the very thing that drives fear into our organisations and makes people afraid to bring ideas and take risks in case they fail and are blamed. Virtually every leader to whom I show this practice of Giving an A, however, experiences a palpable sense of relief at the possibility that they can let down their guard and trust people. Few of us enjoy having to be in a state of continuous high alert.

"How leaders see people is a powerful concept," agrees Nithya Shanti, the former Buddhist monk who now develops consciousness in organisations. "If the leader sees people as not inherently motivated, as just there to do a job, as not really being conscious, then that's going to create that particular outcome and people will live up to it. Once you start thinking differently, you get a different result. If you feel that everyone, deep down, wants to contribute, then you create alignment around that particular way of seeing the world. That's how we inspire: we change the story we are telling ourselves and which we are telling others."

MAKING LEARNING DIGESTIBLE

Here is another one of a conscious leader's powerful tools for creating the right environment: translate all that you see into the next step that enables others to get it. Another way of describing this is: don't scare the horses.

The difficulty with conscious leaders is that they are further along the line of adult development and, as we saw in Chapter 3, they tend to see the world in much more complex, evolved and nuanced ways. They are able to hold multiple perspectives as true at the same time, something which others, at earlier stages of adult development and therefore more inclined to see the world in black-and-white terms, can find confusing and downright unsettling. Yet, the conscious leader can encourage the development of levels of consciousness across the organisation without telling people what to do. The leaders interviewed in this book agree that it is not their role to force people to grow and evolve, but rather to create the right environments for them to do so, if they choose.

So how to translate what you see as a conscious leader into digestible chunks that makes it easy for other people to get it? Tom Chi follows a mental rule that 'Metabolizability is more important than truth.' What he means by this is that it's no good if you have a PhD in a topic and want to convey the whole body of knowledge to others who haven't even got their first degree yet. "It doesn't serve others at all if they are not ready to hear what you have to say. Being able to translate what you see as the next step for them enables their learning to be metabolized, and this is what moves people forward. Metabolizability, not truth, is what is important and of service to the person in front of you."[2]

This is the most humane and compassionate thing conscious leaders can do in trying to uplift their environments: to give their insights in digestible chunks. Tom's views are shared by another conscious leader, Laura Roberts. She deeply believes that everyone in the world and everyone who has come to Pantheon is exactly where they are on their developmental journey and their worldview is what it is. This needs to be accepted. Her view also gives other conscious leaders some good advice. "In the early days" she recounts, "I would speak to a certain consciousness or worldview and not be heard as intended. Sometimes speaking about consciousness is a little too 'woo-woo' for some worldviews, and so instead you make it about emotional maturity. I find it has a better impact with a broader population in the company if I use words that don't sound too 'out there' for them. You can use words like 'enlightenment' and 'consciousness' sometimes – 'mindful-ness' tends to work a little better – but if we frame it in the context of being mindful of your emotional state and working to reboot yourself, we're teaching increased consciousness but not neces-sarily using the words."

Timing is everything and, in her own way, Laura Roberts is also thinking about the metabolisability of truth. "When I first started working like this on a daily basis, there was a part of me that defaulted to being impatient – why don't they just get it! Now I realise people get it when they get it; we just have to keep investing in them. Sometimes it's about holding their feet to the fire of their commitment to their own development and sometimes people opt out because it's too hard for them at that point in their life. And sometimes conscious leaders have to realise that, although they support and even love the person, the investment in that person isn't going to manifest itself anytime soon. If someone has engaged with the work and they're now aware of their thoughts, they realise we're expecting them to really pay attention to their thoughts and their habitual ways of responding. We coach each other to really push ourselves beyond that. Again, you see people having big breakthroughs and then you have others who just aren't ready for that level of self-responsibility."

Nithya Shanti continues: "As conscious leaders, this is the wisdom we have to have. Once people trust you, at that point you can use any language and any words; it's only the first few miles you have to walk with them in their shoes, and they have to feel that you are really with them. After that, you can use any terminology you want."

BEING THE TUNING FORK

The more you, as a conscious leader, can be in the right space yourself – in the moment, present – the greater your potential to be transformative and create the right environment. Conscious leaders describe this as happening almost by a kind of grace, rather than anything they are acting upon or enforcing from their small, ego-self. Small actions seem to have big effects. They are being the tuning fork for expanded consciousness.

How they carry themselves in day-to-day life can help this transformational effect to occur, in ways that are least likely to cause resistance in others. In Chapter 16 we'll explore further how leaders become the 'tuning forks' in their organisations for expanding the levels of consciousness.

For now, two pieces of advice come from Nithya Shanti, taken from his own practices as a forest meditation monk. "When I enter a room, I know that by being authentic and sharing from my heart, I allow others to be authentic and share from their hearts as well. The intention with which we enter any interaction makes all the difference," he says.

This resonates with other conscious leaders, who know that arriving in the room with a convincing energy is probably not going to go down well. Alongside this, Nithya advises that the way to create change is to question, understand and appreciate what they have done already.

"I ask questions like: when in your work experience have you felt most connected to what you've been doing? When have you been most satisfied with your work? What contributions do you cherish the most? When have teams really come together and achieved miraculous results? By questioning where they're already doing it, you can help them get in touch with this. At this point, you can share an idea about conscious leadership or conscious business, hitching it to what they are already doing."

There are other ways that conscious leaders help to create the right kind of environment to bring the best out in others and those mentioned above are just some of the ways. Many other ways are featured in the rest of the chapters in this book.

By way of practical example, let's finish this chapter by exploring how a conscious leader, intent on creating a whole company with the right environment, has gone about this task.

Steve Hall, CEO of driversselect

Raj Sisodia, author of *Firms of Endearment,* has a way of talking about the oft-quoted Gallup polls findings on levels of engagement in business. These show the proportion of people globally, who are 'engaged', 'not engaged' and 'actively disengaged' with their organisations. Of ten people rowing towards a finishing line in a canoe, says Sisodia, using a popular metaphor, three would be actively rowing in the right direction, five would be rowing in the opposite direction and two would be hitting each other over the head with their paddles. Such is the level of global engagement.

This is an amusing anecdote, but one which Steve Hall is keen to address by his approach of creating the right environment so that employee engagement can be turned up to its maximum.

Early on in his career, before founding driversselect and while working in other businesses, Steve was astonished by how people went to work and spent so much of their time, 50 or 60 hours a week, having different values in the workplace from those they had in their personal lives. "People often come to work to be someone they're not," says Steve, "and then they want more balance by being more of who they are and being around people with similar values." He began to see that being fulfilled is about living and being who you are in and outside work. He thought: why not make a company where work life mirrors personal life?

Success at driversselect is built upon and measured on the degree to which the company is able to create the kind of environment where people can really be themselves. Part of this is encouraging them to bring their talents and personal values to the workplace and align these with the business. "Being in retail, there are a lot of evenings and weekends that people have to work, so it's always a challenge to create work-life balance," says Steve. The company aims to bridge this divide.

I asked Steve how they measure the success of their approach and he told me they do it through the recruitment process, by measuring at which point people are entering the company. "If we're hiring at senior levels, then we're not growing our people," says Steve. Over the last two years, 95% of their hires have been at entry level, which means they've been able to grow people by investing in them. This is a significant shift from five years ago, where much more of their recruitment was done at middle-management and senior levels.

Creating the right environment extends far beyond the recruitment and employee processes, however, into the fabric of the customer ethos itself. Steve regards the brand of the company both inside and outside as one and the same. There is a high level of transparency and empowerment for the customers as well as the employees.

In the way it does business with its customers, driversselect is completely transparent, laying out all the options and putting forward their very best option. They effectively remove the negotiating process, something that is unheard of in the second-hand car sales business. "We think you don't need to waste any time haggling because you know this is our best price and we're fully transparent about it," says Steve. Customers are given all the information before they even come into the dealership – financing terms, the price of the vehicle, the price of the trade-in – which cuts down the time the customer spends sitting in the dealership. Customers are also free to take this information and use it to shop and negotiate a better deal elsewhere. It's clear from Steve's description of driversselect's business principles that the company follows a model of abundance and one where transparency and trust are key features.

Internally, the company is built along similar lines. Steve constructs his employee satisfaction around a version of Maslow's hierarchy of needs. When they are recruited, they are ensured a living wage – driversselect pays salaries, not only commissions – and a guarantee that they will earn at least the same amount in their first year as they did in the year before they joined the company. This takes the issue of money – and Maslow's first level of survival – off the table, because they can feel safe financially.

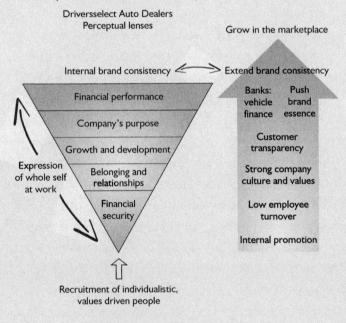

Figure 10: Perceptual lenses

At Maslow's second level, belonging, relationships with their colleagues and their boss are actively nurtured, ensuring that they feel like they're part of a team.

The third level is about personal growth and success.

"You don't come here to sell cars; you come here to grow," says Steve. They look to recruit people who are a little quirky and not afraid to be themselves, while investing heavily in the person to grow them. This investment is the same whether that person has spent two years or five years with the company. "We're not going to look only at what we can get out of you, but at what we can put into you," he says. They are unconcerned about whether people might leave the company after being heavily invested in – like most conscious companies run by conscious leaders, operating from a scarcity mindset doesn't come into it. "If you choose to leave us and go elsewhere, you'll have become a better person, with more skills and powers," explains Steve. As driversselect's growth and recruitment figures show, people aren't inclined to leave but rather to move up the ranks of the organisation.

By creating an environment where the basic levels of Maslow's hierarchy of needs have been taken care of, the company can turn its attention outside, to the customers and the industry. Since employees feel financially safe, experience that they belong and can see that they're growing and developing, they are ready to make a big impact in the market. They do this through driversselect promoting its purpose in the outside world.

Then, at the fifth level, is the financial upside for the company. This 'inside-out' approach to car trade is radically different from the rest of the industry, which puts the big potential financial upside first, but which is based on shaky foundations, without much sense of belonging, no financial security and a huge commission structure. It is everything needed to ignite a fear-and-scarcity reaction in the salespeople and their companies.

While driversselect has only been doing its deep transformational work for five years, early signs are promising. These show up in the way they recruit internally for all their middle- and senior-level hiring, which enables them to continue to grow because they have low turnover and because the culture is sustained. Steve says: "When our people are living the company's values, that shows up in the outside world. It shows up to our banks that provide the financing for the vehicles, and to our customers, where we are able to really push the essence of the brand and extend that in each car sale."

Endnotes

1   Mackey, John and Sisodia, Raj. 2014. *Conscious Capitalism:*
     Liberating the Heroic Spirit of Business. USA: Harvard Business
     School Publishing Corporation, Chapter 13.

2   https://www.youtube.com/watch?v=25fUDjMtkuI

13

GENEROUS LISTENING, GENEROUS SPEAKING

ecause leadership is an action that counts by how effectively it engages, impacts and moves others, right at these points of engagement is where the quality of contact matters. We already know that emotional intelligence counts for a large part of a leader's success, and ever more so the higher up the leadership ladder you go. Since conscious leaders put effort into developing their self-awareness and self-mastery, they have high levels of insight into how they come across to other people. They continue developing their emotional intelligence to read situations and people, and the flexibility of range and presence to adapt themselves in the moment.

In addition to emotional intelligence, conscious leaders are also interested in bringing all aspects of themselves to their relationships. They incorporate their physical, emotional, mental and spiritual sides to create a whole-person leadership experience. You won't find conscious leaders operating only from the head; all of them recognise the importance of the heart, and their intuition, in the way they live, interact and lead. Furthermore, they are connected to their values and to their individual purpose, which can be linked to the organisation's purpose as well. The experience for others, therefore, is one of authenticity: a leader who is willing to be seen and be known, who doesn't hide behind a 'leadership position' and who is consistent and congruent in his or her behaviour.

Beyond both emotional intelligence and authenticity sits aware-ness or consciousness itself, that connection to the quiet space that bears witness to one's life and to the world outside. Being connected to this stillness, to awareness, lends conscious leaders presence and gravitas. They are less rushed; they are not desperate for approval. They are willing to remain spacious to allow wisdom to reveal itself and many voices to be heard, rather than dominating the conversation.

"Speak only to improve on the silence."
Mahatma Gandhi

While being conscious, emotionally intelligent and authentic in relating to others can build your levels of engagement – which is a natural advantage in leadership – it also helps in gathering up collec-tive intelligence via the contributions of others. As we've seen throughout the qualities of conscious leadership so far, being a successful leader of an increasingly complex future demands our ability to step aside from having to be the source of all answers, and instead to tap into the views and ideas coming from all corners of the organisation and beyond. Successful future leadership hinges on being an agile learner able to navigate complex situations, and both of these demand our resilience and our openness.[1] Therefore, successful leaders need to be able to create commons with people who are willing to share their different perspectives, and these leaders need to be able to create dialogue and role model it so that these different views can sit comfortably alongside each other[2].

Under these conditions it becomes essential to communicate with clarity, but not necessarily certainty. Leaders can paint a clear picture of the challenge ahead or the context the organisation finds itself in without needing to have all the answers. To do this, Paul Monekosso Cleal advises: "You can reassure people by telling them that things are uncertain. At the very least this reassures them that they're not the only ones who think this way. Honesty is important.

If people are pretending that things are better than they are and in denial about this, that doesn't really help. Those who are worried are more worried because they think they're in the minority. If everyone is at least clear that we need to find a way out of this together, people start to point in the same direction much more quickly."

One of the ways conscious leaders can optimise their listening and their speaking is to make use of Otto Scharmer's 'Theory U' process which proposes that the results we create in any kind of social system, from a family to a company to society, arise from the quality of awareness, attention or consciousness of the participants of that system. While it is a framework and a method for thinking about how we can create change, it is also about a way of being. In particular, it is about how we bring ourselves to our conversations and connect with others from the more authentic, higher aspects of ourselves.[2]

Individually, conscious leaders who role model this way of being in their listening and their speaking create different and deeper kinds of connections with others. Collectively, a group of people operating in this way can create different future outcomes. Rather than pulling the past into the present and repeating old patterns to create the same kind of future, they can sense what is needed for an emerging future and take action towards bringing this into the present. How does this work in practice?

The Figure 11 illustrates some of the important aspects of Theory U and how the process works. Essentially, we can take the faster, more superficial road ('A') or the slower, deeper road ('B'). Given the speed of the world of work, our intensive connection to our devices, our perception that we need to be available to our clients 24/7, and that we need to answer emails as soon as they come in, this can lead us unthinkingly down the 'A' road. This road is essentially the shortest distance between two points. We feel like we are getting somewhere because we reach a destination quickly. However, in effect we are frequently simply repeating the patterns and habits of the past at speed. And what do we get? A repeat of the same solutions, applied to new situations. The future becomes a repetition of the past.

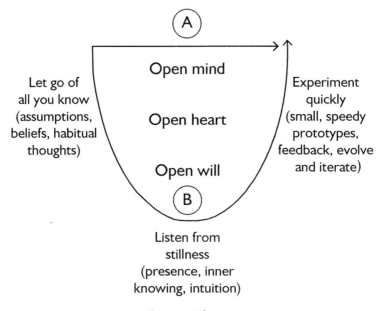

Figure 11: Theory U

The 'B' road is the slower road, but also the wiser road. This is the path towards real change, deep listening and deep connection. It is where we create a different kind of future and bring the collective voices of everyone on board.

From an individual perspective, following the U process requires us to travel down the left-hand side of the U by letting go of all of our habitual patterns of thinking, our beliefs and our assumptions. We let go of all we are in a knowing, expert mode to make room for something new and different to come through instead. In the process, we open our minds and also our hearts by connecting with others.

At the bottom of the U, the deepest point, we are in a state of being which is open and present. We listen from a state of stillness and we also listen into the stillness. This is where we put our small wills, our egos, aside, and listen internally, sensing what wants to emerge next, through us. This might be drawn from whatever we feel we are here to serve, or we might think of it as our intuition arising. It creates a deeper level of solution.

With these insights in hand, the third stage is travelling up the U on the right-hand side. This is all about quick, experimental action. We engage in prototyping, small, speedy experiments from which we can get feedback and refine and iterate our ideas. We test what we sense at the bottom of the U by bringing it into reality and testing it out for its usefulness, adapting as we go.

When Theory U is put into practice, what arises is the U-Process that works for conscious leaders in at least three ways:

1   Individually, these leaders pay greater attention to other people, staying present and making space for them in the conversation. This gives others the experience of being seen and heard, building a strong connection and a positive leadership experience.

2   Collectively, a group of people going through this kind of conversation can develop a deeper dialogue as they talk about the situation from their points of view, as they sense together what is needed and as they co-create new ideas and build prototypes to try out.

3   The quality of the collective solutions is deeper and more considered because we are not simply applying our existing knowledge from the past to the future, but conscious leaders are creating many connection points between people to find richer solutions.

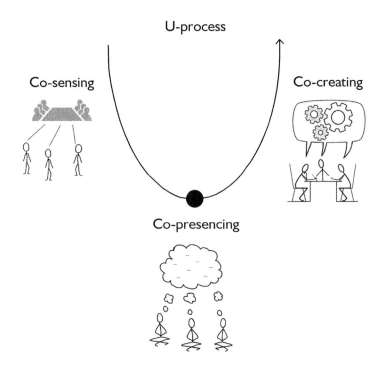

Figure 12: The U Process[3]

If leaders are to take full advantage of the collective intelligence within their organisations, they will need to marry speed of execution with deep listening for richness of perspectives. Often, because of the time pressure we're under, the point of our focus narrows to a pinprick, and we can easily fall into doing and forcing, without listening to our deeper wisdom. We can especially stop talking and start co-creating with others.

THE ART OF LISTENING

Speedy listening and speedy talking is not generous. It comes from our small self, our 'I' or ego, that is invested in moving things in the direction we want them to go. A colleague of mine handily calls this kind of listening 'pretendy listening', and the more conscious form of listening 'radical listening'. It's a good distinction to have. Pretendy listening is all of the unconscious habits we know of, like waiting to speak (listening to the first three words of someone else's sentence before we stop listening and prepare our reply, waiting only for them to draw breath before we butt in with our own views) or listening with bias (listening only to the part of what they're saying that confirms what we already know and want to believe).

Radical listening, or generous listening, is a really useful skill in becoming more conscious as a leader. In many leadership workshops I hold, there is an exercise that involves someone talking about a dilemma they have while the rest of room is divided up into listening with their heads (to what is being said, the factual storyline), with their hearts (to the feelings present, the emotional storyline) and with their intuition (to what might be going on between the lines, to what is not being said but which is still important). We often represent this as an iceberg (see Figure 13), with the results of listening with your head being placed above the surface (what we can see), while the results of listening with your heart and your gut being placed at ever deeper levels beneath the surface.

What we find time and again is that the power to truly connect with other people, to move them, to allow them to feel heard and understood, lies with the heart and, especially, with intuition. To be able, as a leader, to really hear what is not being said explicitly, but what is nevertheless so important to the other person, and to acknowledge this in a respectful, collaborative way, can move mountains in both the relationship and in that person's self-development.

Leaders are often amazed at how much rich information there actually is beneath the waterline of the iceberg, and the importance of the levers that lie there in what is not being said. They realise that by tapping into this deep well that comes from being present and putting aside our speediness and the temptation to listen only for what we know, our capacity to truly touch someone, move them or dissolve resistance, is immense. It comes from what Buddhist monk Thích Nhat Hanh calls, 'allowing the other to empty their heart'.

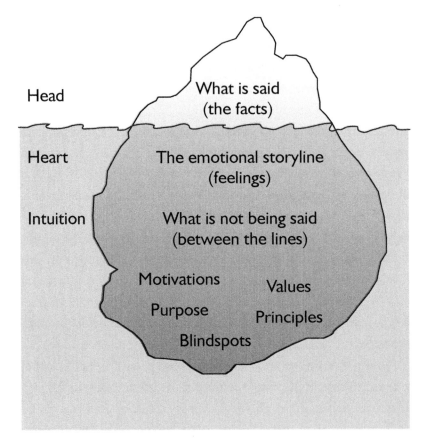

Figure 13: Radical listening

Diana Chapman and her colleagues describe in *The 15 Commitments of Conscious Leadership*, that radical listening is listening with all three centres of intelligence intact – the head, the heart and the gut. This not only allows the person to feel accurately understood at the content level of what they have said, but also helps them to get into contact with their own layers of feelings and authenticity, and their own sense of purpose and meaning. It is a profound gift that conscious leaders can offer everyone, to listen in this way and to speak from a thoughtful and compassionate heart.[3]

"People live so much in their heads and then, when you start waking up, you recognise that your heart is the primary organ," says John Renesch. "The heart knows what it wants to do, even if your head doesn't. We are a bunch of minds, and, if we are going to get into our hearts and into that compassionate place we need to be in, to be in relationship with one another, and in right relationship with our home planet, we need to pay more attention to our heart and less to our head."

Conscious leader Laura Roberts believes conscious listening and conscious speaking is essential for the difficult conversations that take place in leadership. It's important to be skilful at this and not get triggered, as well as not triggering the other person. Laura learned from her teachers this is 'generous speaking' and 'generous listening'. "It's about turning your internal conversation down and really trying to be skilful at speaking to where the other person is at so that your messages are well received. This is a tactical way to talk about someone's development. But generally how we listen and speak and how we hear each other is really an important part of the journey, and if you're doing that well as a leader, more often than not I think you're a more productive organisation."

Exercising these skills as a conscious leader and using them to inform both your deeper listening and your impactful speaking can be used in a variety of ways to manage yourself, to connect with those around you and to create potential pathways through complex challenges. What we know, is that as leaders we frequently fall from one meeting into the next, all the while thinking about the next one that is coming up. This results in us never really being fully present in the moment to pay attention to the depths of information and insight that are available to us. Part of becoming a conscious leader is to be as fully present in the here and now as possible, to be able to withdraw one's attention and energy from the past and bring it into the present, while curbing the temptation to project ourselves into the future. By being fully present, we can access the rich seams of human experience available to us, which helps us as we lead others.

Endnotes

1   Renesch, John. 2012. *The Great Growing Up: Being Responsible for Humanity's Future*. Arizona: Hohm Press.

2   Johansen, Bob. 2012. *Leaders Make the Future: Ten New Leadership Skills for an Uncertain World*. San Francisco. Berrett-Koehler Publishers, Inc. 2nd edition.

3   http://www.slideshare.net/nomadeo/a-developmental-perspective-on-theory-u

4   Presencing Institute, https://www.presencing.com

5   Chapman, Diana, Dethmer, Jim and Warner Klemp, Kaley. 2014. *The 15 Commitments of Conscious Leadership: A New Paradigm for Sustainable Success*.

14

THE CONSCIOUS
USE OF POWER

Conscious leadership requires a radical rethink of the whole arena of power and authority in relation to leadership. One of the hallmarks of conscious leaders is that they have become disenchanted with the organisational pyramid. They no longer have the need to see themselves at the apex of the triangle. They're thinking more about interconnectedness than hierarchies.

They stand for what the interconnected whole can collectively become, and therefore their attitude towards power and authority tends to be how much of it they can give away, rather than how much of it they can keep for themselves. The image that accompanies this shift is one of open hands in which the organisation rests, and for which the leader holds the space, rather than hands that puppeteer the organisation and control and orchestrate it.

A leader like Bob Fishman is a good example of this style of power. He advises that it's useful not to take ourselves or our position as a leader too seriously. Bob is keen to point out that the leader is not the most valuable person in the organisation. Leaders might get paid the most money or have the most decision-making power because the buck stops with them, but they are not the most valuable employee. They can't divine the future better than anyone else in their organisation. There is an unquestioned assumption, advises Bob, that needs to be uncovered in leadership, which is the idea that 'I think you're all valuable, but I'm the most valuable, because I'm the leader'. Conscious leaders are those who move away from this unconscious mainstream view.

The leader is not the most valuable person in the organisation

---

The position of leader also brings with it the trap of power. The minute that you have the role, others look to you to lead and take charge. It's what we expect of leaders: to have the answers. This is difficult from the perspective, as we've seen, that the more complex challenges of our world are beyond the mind of one person or a few people to solve. Yet people look to leaders to tell them what to do in times of complexity and confusion, and they want simplicity and clarity from their leaders. Doing this automatically takes power away from people and potentially works against drawing on their collective intelligence, as they look to leaders for answers. Equally, it is difficult for leaders to empower others, because it presumes that you as a leader have the power to give away which, paradoxically, puts others in a powerless situation. This power-empowerment tug-of-war is one that frequently plays itself out in the organisational system.

In *Reinventing Organizations*, Laloux deals with this question of empowerment in greater depth as he explores those organisations that have transcended the old model of hierarchy and pyramids, and have transformed themselves into self-organising structures. In these organisations (which are typically called 'Teal' organisations), Laloux describes how empowerment is not granted by the grace of the leaders, but instead is baked into the very fabric of these organisations. Traditional leadership hierarchies are done away with and people don't need to fight to get power; they simply have it. [1]

As a result, it is no longer possible to be powerless or a victim in the organisation because of your role or 'level' in it. Everyone is required to step up and take responsibility for themselves and their performance, and to make the whole organisation work together. In many respects, it does away with the parent-child dynamics associated with power and makes the issue of power much more adult-adult in nature.

At the very outer edges of those organisations that we might consider as 'evolutionary', the role of the 'leader' actually becomes defunct. In several cases, as described by Laloux and others like Brian Robertson, founder of self-managing approach Holacracy, the basic structures of these organisations are so different that there is essentially a completely new DNA for the way people come together to get work done. Leadership in the traditional sense is not needed because people lead themselves. Using specific processes and principles, they self-organise to achieve the outcomes of the organisation.

THE ROLE OF TRUST

Immediately we can see that trust plays a key role. Rather than someone in a leadership position telling others what to do, leaders need to believe that people are trustworthy enough to do what is necessary. Their role shifts from making people do things to ensuring that people have what they need, including the motivation, tools and connection to a purpose or 'why' that enables them to carry out their roles in a fulfilling way. In the more radical self-managing organisations, small and agile teams take care of all of this.

Most of us coming from a traditional mindset would shake our heads and think that this is a recipe for chaos, regardless of the fact that these types of organisations achieve very good results. Even where we find the idea enticing, many of us recognise that we still have a long way to go before these sorts of distributed organisational power structures become mainstream.

In the meantime, we have the gap of existing leaders operating in more conscious ways as their organisations evolve, becoming more whole, more valuing, with distributed power and which contribute in a greater way to the world around them.

STEP ONE: LETTING GO OF CONTROL

> *My ideal would be if everyone operates like an*
> *entrepreneur rather than as an employee.*
> Sudhakar Ram

In Chapter 4 we looked at how, especially in our less conscious moments, our ego tends to drive us towards holding on, tightening up and controlling. All these are symptoms of a way of being fuelled by scarcity and a fear of losing what we have. When leaders become more conscious, a key challenge is, how to inhabit the role of leader, and all the power that this traditionally brings, while holding it lightly – so much so that these leaders are actually letting their power go and avoiding making the situation too much about themselves.

This is extremely tricky because it takes a great deal of conscious intention and courage to walk this line between being accountable while at the same time letting go of controlling everything in the organisation.

How does this work in practice? A more in-depth look at the case study, below, of the CEO of Mastek helps to illustrate this.

Mastek is a multinational IT company headquartered in Mumbai, India, with offices in the UK, USA, Europe, Asia-Pacific, the Middle East and Malaysia. Its aspiration is to be an admired, evergreen institution, not just a successful company. Since 2014, through its Mastek 4.0 programme, it has fundamentally changed its structures and practices to empower all employees to deliver innovation and value, and enhance their engagement with clients.

Structurally, Mastek has reorganised around the principles of self-governance, which has eliminated almost all approval and control processes and replaced these with an environment of trust and freedom that drives initiative. The company has also eliminated several layers of management and now just three layers separate the CEO from the frontline developers. The entire company is organised in self-managing teams of three types who are free to set their own goals in line with the company's objectives and aspirations. With no bosses to supervise them, individual 'Mastekeers' are expected to take charge of their own development by choosing mentors for themselves, and their performance is assessed by peers in their team.

Sudhakar Ram, co-founder and CEO, picks up the story. "One of the biggest shifts of Mastek 4.0 is how I get people to experience the power that they really have and how I can create a role model company where every person is really free. My ideal would be if everyone operates like an entrepreneur rather than as an employee. If they can bring a degree of choice to what they do, even when they are employees and they have to earn a living, I think this would be a good example of a role model company I want to set up.

Especially in our business – IT – the people who actually produce the most value for the customers, who write the software and develop the code, are youngsters in their twenties. However, they don't know that they are the most powerful because there is a big hierarchy above them and there are people they presume are more powerful or knowledgeable or experienced, more in tune with the customers, who they look up to. This is especially the case with an Indian mindset, which is about an acceptance of authority and seniority.

We've realised that people at the middle-management level are not really in a position to add value to these developers. Most of the time the developers see the manager as someone who is getting in the way of doing something rather than helping them to get something done. And this is not because these managers are bad people, it's just that they've not figured out how to align and get the best out of the people below them in this kind of industry. So my question was, how can we turn the pyramid upside-down so that the hierarchy doesn't become an overwhelming thing where people don't think for themselves and are not willing to challenge?

Even just a year and a half into implementing Mastek 4.0, the changes are starting to embed in 70–75% of the project teams. They are realising they don't need to look at someone else to make their decisions; they are perfectly capable of doing it themselves. One of the teams I met recognised that usually 95% of the time their tendency was to ship the decision up the line of seniority, but in six months they had realised there was only about 4–5% of decisions which they needed to consult someone else about because they didn't know the right thing to do. This is a huge shift to 95% self-empowered decisions with only 5% needing input from people above them in the hierarchy.

The problem is the middle-management, which has not fully figured out what they're supposed to do in this kind of situation. There are two roles they can actually move into. One is to become mentors and coaches for people below them, rather than someone who is managing and driving performance. The other is to engage with the customer and be an adviser to them, helping them see the ways of getting the best out of the team of developers.

I've been paying attention to two sources of feedback for how this is working out in reality. One is the feeling I have when I speak to the teams of developers and the other is what the customers are saying. When speaking to the teams, the feeling I have is they're all getting used to it in their own way. Nobody makes this kind of transformation overnight because they've not been used to making decisions on their own, ever. It's scary sometimes for people to take that kind of responsibility, but that's why we didn't make this about individual accountability. The whole thing is about team accountability. No one is going to blame you for something that as a team – a 'scrum' team of 8 to 10 people – you get to design, deliver and assess amongst yourselves as to whether or not you've delivered it. They get feedback from others, but they determine their own fortunes in terms of how well they've done. The appraisal systems have been turned around as the team appraises itself and every individual within it.

When I speak to customers, the feedback that I'm getting is that our guys are far more enthusiastic and far more engaged than they were last year. We have long-term customers and they know how the teams typically responded to them before. Many of the customers, without even knowing what Mastek 4.0 is, are giving me this feedback. One and a half years in, we are at about 60–70% transformation – well ahead of what I thought would happen."

RESPONSIBILITY AND POWER

When you speak to somebody like Sudhakar Ram, you become aware of how much he stands by what he calls 'the sovereignty of the individual'. He really is intent on enabling all in the company to act as free, enterprising and self-actualising agents, and he holds the space for them while they are doing this.

In its essential relationship to power, conscious leadership is very much about getting out of the way of the traditional notions of the tag 'leadership'. When we look at how conscious leaders create the right kind of environment, their actions are designed to bring people together and encourage free action, rather than control them. These leaders get, at an instinctive level, that many intelligences are better than one intelligence in an organisation that is full of intelligent, living and motivated beings. As Sudhakar's example also illustrates, no matter how conscious the leader is, this doesn't necessarily mean that others will be willing to take on the levels of responsibility given to them.

Many intelligences are better than one intelligence

A case in point is the recent transition to Holacracy, the self-management system, in Zappos led by its CEO, Tony Hsieh, that saw 14% of the company choosing the paid-to-leave option when Hsieh announced in March 2015 that the company would be changing to a self-managing structure, a figure that went up to 18% in January of 2016[2]. This could be read as 18% of employees not yet ready to make the shift towards more radical levels of self-organisation and self-responsibility, or 82% of employees either ready to do so or willing to give it a go. The media has been scathing, often reporting the paid-to-leave figures out of context, whereas, in reality 82% is a large number of people willing to engage with such a radical transformation.

More recently, Zappos reports that its employee numbers have already increased with new joiners actively choosing to work for the company under the self-management system. It's worth noting that Hseih's paid-to-leave policy meant that leavers could use their severance pay to start their own businesses and still had an open door to return to Zappos in a year's time if they chose to.

Zappos' – and in particular Hseih's – position is interesting from a conscious leadership perspective because, similar to Sudhakar Ram promoting the sovereignty of the individual, Zappos promotes a high level of freedom amongst employees. It did this through the option to leave with a generous package if they didn't think the self-management way of working was for them and it offered them the chance to return if they wanted to. In the process, Hseih ensures that Zappos is staffed with willing employees who support self-management and, through this, that the company can scale effectively while maintaining its entrepreneurial culture. Hsieh has said that self-management enables Zappos to function more like a city or an ecosystem that doesn't need constant direction from the top of the organisational pyramid and which will assure the company's survival even when he's no longer CEO.

THE LADDER OF POWER

In order to encourage a more conscious relationship to power and responsibility in both themselves and in others, the question becomes: *how can conscious leaders successfully instil a different mindset to power in their organisations?*

A useful self-management and leadership tool for this is the Ladder of Power[3] (see Figure 14), which is essentially a guide for how we can choose to respond to situations. It helps us to think about how we can exercise our creative agency as powerful and responsible human beings in our own lives to bring about more of the outcomes we would like to see happen.

Whenever I use this tool in organisations, people typically recognise instantly how they fall down the ladder of power and how, conversely, they can choose to exercise more responsibility by getting into action to produce the results they want.

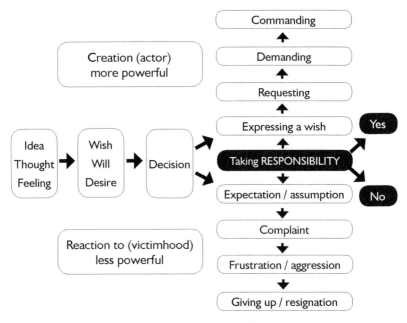

Figure 14: The Ladder of Power

We begin on the left of the horizontal line, prior to having any thoughts about what we want, and, following this line across, we experience an idea, thought or feeling that might gather some energy or force and becomes stronger, turning into a wish or a desire to see something come about.

By way of illustrating what might happen next we can follow the story of David, a senior manager in a retail bank who believed the time had come for his promotion. The idea for getting promoted occurred to David one afternoon over lunch as he sat with his colleague and friend, Ben, who was also considering his prospects. David realised that there was little that distinguished him from Ben

– he had an equally good track record and he had brought in a good chunk of revenue to his business unit over the past year. As lunch progressed, his idea about getting promoted grew in strength until, by the time they returned to the office, it had become a clear desire to be promoted the following year.

David decided to go for it. At this point he had two choices: he could get into action and start taking steps to achieve his promotion; or, he could wait for something to happen. The first is the path of creative agency; the other signals the path of ever diminishing agency towards victimhood. The difference between these two paths is the degree to which David was willing to take responsibility and get into action for the outcome he wanted to happen, rather than to complain about it.

One might well assume that as a senior manager on the path to directorship, David would be fairly skilled at self-management and achieving outcomes for himself. The truth was that despite being stoic about achieving business results, David was far less confident in himself. He worked exceedingly hard to hit his targets and constantly felt that others might overtake him. He spent a good deal of his time in a state of wary watchfulness to see if others were doing better than he was. He suffered from 'imposter syndrome' and often wondered when he would be found out. You might say his ego was in the driving seat much of the time, fuelling self-protective behaviours. He also hated what he thought was any kind of self-promotion. Good results and good manners, his ingrained conditioning told him, should speak for themselves.

David decided to achieve his promotion by securing a large piece of business with a client the bank had been courting for a while. He put in extra hours, pulled out all the stops, and after several months won the client over. On the ladder of power, his assumption was that this win would be the deal-clincher that would get the top leadership to notice his value and secure his promotion.

Three months later, no mention had been made of promotion.

David began to feel a bit resentful and, inviting another colleague to lunch, he started complaining about the bank and how the leadership didn't recognise how hard he and others worked. Before long, both men had fallen into a mutual moaning session about the bank and the way things worked. By the end of lunch, they both felt marginally better. On the ladder of power, David was at the 'complaint' stage.

As he returned to the office, he began wondering why he was putting in so much effort. The bank's leadership obviously did not appreciate the long nights he put in, the way he worked at weekends. Over the weeks his frustration began to leak out in the way he spoke up at meetings and how he dealt with his team. He was on a short fuse, irritated with demands on his time. When a new project was offered to him, he secretly thought to himself, 'Yeah, right!' and batted away the opportunity. He began going home as soon as official working hours were over and his previous discretionary effort disappeared. Soon, he began whipping up his colleagues into impromptu moaning sessions at the coffee machine where they shared their dissatisfaction about working at the bank. Without being aware of it, David had fallen down the rungs of the ladder of power and his frustration at not getting recognised was manifesting itself in subtle forms of passive aggression, creating a mob-mindset of complaining and withholding his participation from meetings.

Eventually, David concluded that his promotion was not going to happen. Worse still, a peer he thought of as 'mediocre' was successfully identified for promotion. David felt isolated, angry and helpless. He wanted to give up at the bank, unsure about what to do next. How did he fall so quickly from being a star in his own right to being in the bottom 10% of the bank?

If we look at what happened to David, we can see that he slid down the rungs of the ladder, at each point losing more of his power along the way as he failed to take responsibility for what he wanted. He failed to recognise how he was falling further and further into 'victimhood'. He expected others to see the world as he did and complained when they didn't, becoming frustrated and angry, and finally giving up. The slide down this ladder of power is inevitable for as long as we are not taking direct action for what we want to create.

You probably all know a 'David' in your organisation, and quite possibly have found yourself on some of the bottom rungs from time to time. We see this kind of behaviour in teams and in whole organisations. One particular public sector organisation I worked with had a pronounced 'bullying' sensitivity throughout the entire organisation. Anyone who took any kind of initiative, even to give some high quality, though mild, developmental feedback, was labelled a 'bully', and the only way to survive was to join the others on the lower rungs of the ladder of power, all feeling like victims of the organisation together. It's a powerful and alluring place to be in, sharing mass complaints with other people about our common lot, and it's also the most powerless we can ever be in our lives.

Champions of self-organisation, such as Laloux and Robertson, are quick to point out that the simple hierarchies of organisations contribute greatly to the loss of power experienced by individuals – and they are right. People anywhere near the 'bottom' of the organisational ladder in traditional structures feel powerless, waiting for those at the 'top' to give them clarity and instructions. As we've seen through the example of Sudhakar Ram, if conscious leaders are to be as effective as they can be in their organisations, they need to encourage not just a change of structure and an accompanying shift in distributed power and responsibility (a systemic change), but also help those who have difficulty in taking responsibility to own it (an individual change).

What does the opposite of powerlessness look like? How does being an agent of one's own effectiveness and embracing self-responsibility play out? The top half of the ladder of power represents what we might do when we are most effective. These steps are not necessarily sequential. Whereas the fall into victimhood tends to be inevitable for as long as we are not taking responsibility for our outcomes, we can equally step consciously into our agency and power as creative human beings at any point by choosing some of the conversion actions at the top of the ladder.

Taking David as our example once again, he would have exercised far more agency if he'd expressed his wish to be promoted to someone, perhaps to his business unit leader. Even this subtle shift, "I would like to be considered for promotion," is a more powerful action than expecting it to happen.

David could also have decided to take a firmer approach by making a direct request to someone. Somewhat more powerful than simply making your wishes known, a direct request has momentum by placing an expectation out in the world that you want to create a particular future for yourself. David's request might have been: "I would like to have a proper review against the promotional criteria and that we have an honest appraisal of my suitability for being promoted, within the next three months."

Stepping up another rung on the ladder, David might have decided to take a much more authoritative approach, in the form of a demand. Assertive in nature (though not aggressive), a demand is clear and powerful because it requires you to be specific about what you want. In David's case, this might have looked like: "I want to be put forward in the promotional process beginning in three months' time."

In special circumstances, we might express maximum power in the form of a command. Doing this is appropriate for some contexts but not for others. It's useful when the other person doesn't have the leeway to say no, for example in the armed forces, mining environments where safety is paramount, or the fire services. It is appropriate where clear rank is in place and where those of 'lower' rank need to carry out the instructions of those with more positional power. For most corporate environments, this expression of power probably wouldn't apply, or not without causing quite a bit of resistance in the process.

Because the higher rungs of the ladder are not necessarily sequential, David might decide to make a clear request of his business unit leader to be put into the promotional process in three months' time, without having to first express the wish for it. He might turn up the heat and make a demand if he is still not getting a sense of movement in the promotional process. In this way, he can play with his level of agency.

The truest expression of our power lies in taking action to get what we want, not in our getting it

---

When introduced to this tool, people often say that just because you make a request and take responsibility for what you want, this doesn't mean that you will get it – and they are right.

The truest expression of our power and self-responsibility lies in taking action to get what we want, not in our getting it. This is a really important distinction. Where things don't turn out as we would like, we have choices: we can take the same actions; we can take different actions; or we can decide between whether this is something we really need or we want. If it's something we want but don't necessarily need, we might decide to give it up and live with the situation as it is. If it's something we need – for example, a pay rise in order to meet our new monthly mortgage payment – then we have a choice to make: we can make the request or demand again, or we can go elsewhere to get our needs met. Either way, we are exercising our creative agency.

This tool works as well for individuals as it does for teams and whole organisations. The moment we give up, saying, "Well, I've tried everything around here and nothing works," we have fallen down the ladder of power again towards 'victimhood'. The moment we step into action about what we would like to see happening, we have regained it. It is a dynamic tool to help us stay aware of our relationship to our own power as creative beings.

Frederic Desbrosses, who has used this tool, describes how it helped in his organisation: "We had quite an extensive discussion about where each of us was as a leader during a time of change, where we were positioned on the ladder and why. If you were at the bottom part, why is that? It was a really good tool for getting in contact with the team and unlocking resistance for the guys to get on board with the change. Actually, it turned out that there was resistance to the new GM in my succession plan. The process really opened our eyes and got us to question whether this was the right decision as a team – and for each of us as individuals. Were we going to sit there and complain all our lives or were we going to make an intentional and responsible decision and get into choice, for each of us personally and for the business?"

Frederic's story illustrates how a team can hold itself accountable by using a tool such as this one and asking where we have fallen or reflecting back where others have fallen down the ladder of power. It's important not to blame people for where they are. Instead, the tool is helpful for an open enquiry to explore where people stand in relation to a decision or path of action. Sometimes just having the conversation enables them to pick up responsibility once again and make different choices. As conscious leaders, teaching others (and practising ourselves) when we have stopped exercising our power, choice and responsibility can be extremely useful for aligning people around a purpose and getting them to pull in the same direction.

FIVE LEVELS OF POWER

Viktor Frankl, a psychiatrist and Holocaust survivor, discovered the ultimate source of our power and freedom. Frankl, who was tragically caught up in Nazi concentration camps, lost everything, including his wife and his children. He came to realise there was a difference between those who survived the concentration camps (outside enforced death) and those who gave up despite being kept alive. This difference was in the mindset they managed to adopt under such extreme circumstances – specifically, their attitude towards the events that were happening to them. In the midst of such immense suffering, Frankl discovered one of life's great truths:

> "Between an event and our response, there is a space. In
> that space lies our power to choose our response.
> And in our response lies our growth and our freedom."
>
> Viktor Frankl

What Frankl realised is that our last great human freedom, which no one can take away from us, lies not in the events themselves that happen, but in our relationship to them. Things are things, events are events; yet the meaning we choose to imbue them with lies with us. With this comes our greatest freedom, and also our greatest responsibility, because if we are not responsible for our own reactions to the events of our lives, then who is?

What Frankl's story shows us is that we can be highly conscious in the way we use our power and exercise our responsibility in the way that we manage ourselves in the face of our circumstances. This is not easy, especially in extremely difficult circumstances, but we do still have this choice available to us.

Another way of looking at our relationship to the responsibility we take and power we exercise invites us to consider ourselves at five levels.[4]

Level 1

This can be thought of as: Accepting responsibility for all of my actions and my non-actions, in other words taking responsibility for everything I do and don't do. This is a fairly easy level of responsibility for us to achieve, though it does require us to give up hiding behind excuses or blaming others for what we do. 'I did it because …' or 'He made me do it' fall short of even Level 1 responsibility. To succeed at this level, we need to accept responsibility for ourselves in terms of what we have and haven't done.

Level 2

This level relates to: Accepting responsibility for being the creator of all my experiences. Following Viktor Frankl's example, this is about choosing our response to situations and our interpretation of events. It's about realising that our relationship to events is something that we own and that we can influence.

Level 3

Accepting responsibility for everything that happens to me. This level of power asks us to look at this question: how might I have contributed to what happened to me? For example, if I was involved in a car accident, what part did I have to play in being in that place at that time? Was I paying attention? Was I just in the wrong place at the wrong time? Rather than this being about apportioning blame, accepting responsibility at this level asks us to look at our own contribution to the circumstances of our lives. Buying into this level of responsibility means that we can begin to look at what we want to create in our lives, instead of feeling like a victim of our circumstances. This grants us a much more powerful position from which to operate.

Level 4

This takes the limits of our responsibility one step further: Accepting responsibility for what others do to me. At this point our ego usually starts objecting and demanding, "How can I possibly be responsible for someone else's actions?" Nevertheless, it gives us a lot of power to ask ourselves, how might I be the cause, in some way, of others' behaviour towards me? How might my actions be contributing towards this? It is exceptionally easy to blame others for what they do to us, but it is much harder to ask ourselves honestly about the role we had to play in the dynamics that have been set up. Doing so gives us a lot more power over our lives because we can make some different choices, and feel a lot less powerless or victimised.

Level 5

This furthest limit asks us to consider the possibility of accepting responsibility for what others do to others. For almost anyone, this is a very provocative statement. It seems to be outside our power and to belong in the domain of saints.

This stance is possible and has been adopted by various very famous examples of world leaders such as Gandhi, Martin Luther King, Nelson Mandela and Mother Teresa, who have taken on this context of responsibility in order to impact the world on a global scale. These kinds of conscious leaders not only take actions that create ripple effects in the system, they also see how the actions of others might be reflected in themselves.

For example, Ghandi went on a number of hunger fasts during World War II. One of these was for what he saw as his role in the uprising of violence in India against British rule. Despite the fact that he had acted in good faith and was a role model of non-violence, Gandhi saw the part he had played in the actions of how the Indian nation was retaliating against the British colonials. He saw that he was a contributor to events, even though he was not directly retaliating violently. He went on a hunger strike not as a penance towards himself or others, but as a symbol to the Indian nation that he considered himself a contributor to the problem, and as a powerful metaphor to encourage them to stop. And so we see Gandhi's most famous statement: Be the change you want to see in the world, taking shape. Taking responsibility in ourselves for what we would like to see others doing to others is the highest form of responsibility. It requires us to look at what we don't like in the world, or in our organisation, or in our team, and change anything similar that exists in ourselves. Is there complaining and dissent in our organisation? How might we also be complaining? How might we have contributed to what people are complaining about in our roles as leaders?

At the time of writing this, the world seems overwhelmed with chaotic and destructive actions. In the summer of 2016, we have encountered Brexit (the exit of the United Kingdom from the European Union), the divisive political campaign of Donald Trump, multiple terrorist attacks across France and Germany, the racial shootings across the USA, and the failed military coup in Turkey, in which at least 294 people were killed. Turkish president Recep Tayyip Erdoğan had more than 6,000 soldiers, senior military leaders and judges arrested and vowed to 'cleanse' state bodies of the 'virus' that caused the coup, ironically replicating the behaviour patterns of the coup itself.

It is incredibly easy to look at the actions of others and separate ourselves from them, making the others 'wrong' and ourselves 'right'. In many cases, we feel justifiably right to do so. However, it can also serve as a prompt to us to consider for ourselves: where might similar qualities of hatred, fear or desperation live in us, even if we don't react at such extreme levels? And, where these qualities do exist in us, how could we practise a different level of self-mastery in ourselves? This is the kind of responsibility that is available to us at the level of what others do to others; to take responsibility for what we see manifesting in the world around us.

There can perhaps be no greater need to take this kind of responsibility than there is now.

THE NEW BUSINESS MODEL OF RESPONSIBILITY

In many respects, the new style of capitalism and the growing trend towards including all stakeholders and creating value for all of them operates in this fifth domain of power and responsibility. It requires conscious leaders who extend their perception, responsibility and power far beyond the boundaries of their organisation, of profit and shareholders, to include the wider business system. Conscious leaders can use the responsibility of Level 5 (what others do to others), to ask themselves what role they have to play in how people are treating one another in their organisation – and how their organisation is treating its stakeholders and the world.

I am responsible – at all times, in all places, under all circumstances, without exception.

This is very different from having, at its worst, a corporate social responsibility department bolted on somewhere in the basement of your organisation, painting a school wall (with local media in attendance) as part of a public relations effort. This is about thinking through the implications of the impact your organisation is making on the wider world, and realising that the decisions you make and take as a leader, and the way these effects ripple through your organisation, continue to ripple out into the world as well. It is about seeing that the boundaries of your responsibility as a conscious leader do not end at the boundaries of your organisation, but in fact that the boundaries of your organisation end at the boundaries of the world.

Conscious leaders might even choose to take responsibility for the effects of their organisation on the broader field of capitalism itself. Conscious Capitalism Inc.'s vision is articulated as: 'A more complex form of capitalism that ... has the potential to enhance corporate performance AND advance the quality of life for billions of people on the planet'. That is a very broad level of responsibility indeed.

Although we each get to decide how much responsibility we wish to adopt, the opportunity is there for conscious leaders to hold as their context a very powerful and requiring stance: *I am responsible – at all times, in all places, under all circumstances, without exception*[5].

We are ultimately responsible for everything, together, since there is no separation in humanity other than that in our minds. If our urge as conscious leaders is to leave the world a better place, what could be more encompassing than to consider how we might take on this level of responsibility?

Endnotes

1   Laloux, Frederic. 2014. *Reinventing Organizations: A Guide to
     Creating Organizations Inspired by the Next Stage in Human
     Consciousness*. Belgium: Nelson Parker, 137.

2   http://uk.businessinsider.com/
     zappos-ceo-tony-hsieh-on-holacracy-transition-2016-1

3   Creative Consciousness International,
     http://creativeconsciousness.com

4   Ibid.

5   Stephen Norval.

15

DECISION-MAKING AS A CONSCIOUS LEADER

I wanted to include this brief chapter about how conscious leaders make decisions in their organisations, because although decision-making is influenced by many of the qualities of thinking and behaving already described in this book, there are some distinct features which deserve a mention.

Conscious leaders tend to make their decisions in the zone of balance that lies dynamically somewhere between the edge of waiting without over-hesitating and acting quickly without over-forcing. It is a flexible, agile and adjustable style of decision-making, one that recognises that the way the world is tomorrow might be very different from what it is today, but equally that some form of dynamic stability is needed over time.

Of course, conscious leaders in business are subject to the same pressures of markets and shareholders or stakeholders as any other leader; a pressure that tends to accelerate time and forces an ever-quicker pace of decision-making and action. The conscious leaders interviewed for this book spoke of their tendency to hold off from forcing things down a particular avenue in favour of finding the right balance. Fast and furious decision-making is not something they want to feel pressurised into; they prefer well-timed and well-considered decisions that blend inputs from a range of sources, including the organisation itself.

It's worth exploring this last comment further. By 'the organisa-tion itself', many of these leaders consider the organisation to be a living entity the same as any individual within it. The organisation is seen as a living system, not a box of parts. It is regarded as having its own energy, its own creative potential and its own sense of direc-tion.[1] These leaders tap into the intelligence of the organisational system by listening in to it, to what wants to happen next in order to serve its purpose in the world, and this influences the decisions that they make. This is an entirely different decision-making strategy from one that comes solely from the rational mind and individual will.

Rather than the traditional trade-offs, with decisions that tend to be driven solely by a profit-first mindset or a desire only to secure a bigger share of the market at virtually any cost, conscious leaders use their 'whole listening' – deeply, intuitively, systemically – to consider questions such as: "What is this organisation's creative potential as a living system? What deepest creative potential exists that is asking to be brought to life, that can contribute something energetically, valuably to the world?"[2] It is decision-making that comes from an entirely different place in the human spirit.

As we'll explore in the next chapter, there are strong links to the conscious leader's capacity to hold the space for his or her organisa-tion and to be an open and receptive tuning fork for sensing what wants to emerge next. In practice, there are certain behaviours that support this kind of decision-making style, some good examples of which are told by the conscious leaders below.

Bob Fishman describes his decision-making style as "looking for fluidity until somebody says we have to take the decision". Fishman holds the space open and does whatever he can to encourage multi-ple viewpoints to be aired, at which point he might, in his position as leader, say that in his best judgement this is the route to go, unless someone puts a strong case otherwise. He also recognises and is open about the fact that this decision is only connected to that point in time and might need to be different as new perspectives emerge: "I started having meetings with all levels of the corporation that I called a Fourth Dimension Space Meeting," he says, "where no idea during that timeframe was to be put down, no idea or topic could not be discussed. It's an attempt to create a space that doesn't have a right/wrong reaction. In that space, after a little while, people who usually don't talk or contribute feel a bit safer to say what they think. In many organisations, there is a fear that people will say the wrong thing, because there is an assumption that there is a right thing to say, and usually the answer to that starts with: 'Well, the right thing to say is what the leader wants me to say'."

Frederic Desbrosses describes his decision-making process in similar terms around timing: "I'm not as much a data-orientated leader as an intuitive leader, but I do collect data and I get a gut feel about the timing of the right decision and how we get there. I think principles and values always play a role, especially when it's a decision about people. I'm always thinking, is it fair, is it mutual, is it the right thing to do for them? Even if the first decision looks good and is the most appealing to me at first glance, I still ask myself, 'did I take the decision because it was the easiest one or because it was the good one?' Most often the good decision is the most difficult one. So that's my instinctive filter: is it an easy decision or is it the best one? Sometimes if I feel that I don't have the best decision I will take the time, even under pressure, and say to people that I cannot make the call right now, there is something missing from the story, it does not come together."

As we have seen previously, in other, even more radically self-managing organisations, there are multiple decision-makers, because decisions are not made by 'the leader' but by anyone who takes responsibility for doing something about an issue that comes up and needs a decision. This could be done via something called the 'advice process' (described in Chapter 6), which involves checking-in with the most experienced people in that area and with those who will be affected by your decision.

This kind of decision-making style is a massive driver of autonomy by naturally building empowerment into the system. People don't need the leader to make a decision; they already have the power. Using certain broadly set parameters, such as the organisation's purpose or keeping the customer happy, for example, all people get to decide how best to act to bring this principle of the organisation to life.

A conscious leader's role in this kind of evolutionary organisation is to role model upholding the organisation's values and higher purpose, and co-sensing which direction the organisation wants to go in next. When many people are co-sensing in this way, you get the exponential benefit of collective and collaborative intelligence, helping the organisation to be at its most agile, its most fit for its changing environment, and its most intelligent.

A conscious leader will also hold in mind multiple reference points outside the organisation. Taking a wide range of stakeholders into account, such as customers, suppliers, the community, society at large and the environment, provides rich intelligence to input into the decisions of the organisation.

Paul Monekosso Cleal mirrors this approach in his own leadership style: "A lot of economic theory is based on really quite drastic removals of a lot of the realities of the world by the assumptions we make. And that's the problem. You can't remove the rest of the world. You can't try to reduce your business to a simple decision. Externalities exist outside your immediate decision-making capabilities and the world's a complicated place. If you ignore the externalities you get all sorts of problems, like climate change and damage to the environment. A proper economic decision should include all the variables we talk about. For example, in relation to the community, if you decide to fire somebody you should be taking into account the economic consequences on them and the rest of the community. The taxpayers might have to pick up the bill for welfare that might end up costing more than employing them."

It is no wonder that conscious leaders are more considered and thoughtful about the decisions they make, rather than racing ahead on the basis of their individual will. There are a lot of factors and inputs to consider, and a fine balance to be struck in making the best decision possible at the most opportune time.

Following our model of conscious leadership, these leaders take into account the four 'zones' as they go about their decision-making. These equate to exercising their responsibility towards the greater whole:

» They keep their egos in check by being alert to when they are driving or forcing the situation forward based on their own egoic needs or fears (vertical development).

» They bring in multiple viewpoints by including many others as sources of wisdom in decisions and encouraging a diversity of views (perspective taking).

» They think in terms of the system and the wider implications of their decisions, and they look to create value and contribution to the widest possible range of stakeholders (systems and stakeholder thinking).

One of the conscious leaders we've heard from in this book, Sudkahar Ram, has written a book called *The Connected Age: Being the Best You Can by Reinventing Your World*, in which he has outlined a set of ideas and principles for leading consciously. These form a good set of guidelines for any leader wanting to make decisions more consciously. They are slightly adapted here and are recommended for sticking up on your office wall, in full view, to prompt your reflections.

Sudhakar asks:

» Does this decision promote and protect the sovereignty of the individual?

» Does this decision foster compassionate coexistence?

» Is it good for the planet and all life on the planet?

» Does it empower the lowest possible level to make decisions?

» Does it require a market mechanism or deep individual engagement? If it requires a market, does the mechanism embody and promote the principles of free markets?

» Does the decision foster governance that balances individual freedom and the common good?[3]

With these principles as a guide, any leader can develop the practice of more conscious decision-making.

DEVELOPING YOUR DECISION MAKING CAPACITIES AS A CONSCIOUS LEADER

Whether it's the flexible timing of Bob Fishman, the stakeholder mutuality of Frederic Desbrosses or bringing communities together to make decisions (like the advice process), your decision making capacities as a conscious leader can be developed through a more formal and systematic approach.

Decision making in the increasingly complex VUCA environment, where there are few clear right-wrong answers, requires leaders to focus on developing their decision making capabilities as a core strength. They must be able to anticipate issues, think through potential consequences, prepare alternatives and appreciate the interdependencies of multiple factors and diverse stakeholders. They also need to be agile in adjusting their decision making style: sometimes problems need to be addressed more immediately and directively; other problems are best addressed through collaboration and seeking a broad range of perspectives.[4]

One of the most highly rated tools for developing your capacity to make decisions in a VUCA environment is the LDMA (Lectical® Decision-Making Assessment) by Lectica. The organisation specialises in developing leaders' capacities for bringing together all the relevant considerations into coherent solutions. The kinds of skills conscious leaders can develop using this tool are:

» Their collaborative capacity and skills: the ability to effectively bring together diverse people and their perspectives when there is a need to deal with complex problems and innovations;

» Their contextual thinking: the ability to consider problems in terms of the broader systems and contexts in which they are embedded; and

» Their cognitive complexity: the ability to think well about complex issues.

We know that leaders who are more vertically developed cope better with complexity and can think in broader terms. This is of great advantage in the VUCA environment of business today. If leaders are also developing as a conscious leader in other areas, they are likely to be invested in taking a systems-wide view and balancing the diverse perspectives of multiple stakeholders, as well as acting responsibly in the system while managing themselves in the process at the same time. The tools for exploring how to develop your capacities as a conscious leader can be found in the section on key tools in the back of this book.

Endnotes

1   Laloux, Frederic. 2014. *Reinventing Organizations: A Guide to Creating Organizations Inspired by the Next Stage in Human Consciousness.* Belgium: Nelson Parker, p199.

2   Adapted from Laloux, Frederic. 2014. *Reinventing Organizations.* Belgium: Nelson Parker, p200.

3   Ram, Sudhakar. 2014. *The Connected Age: Being the Best You Can by Reinventing Your World.* India: HarperCollins, p.45.

4   https://dts.lectica.org/_about/showcase. php?instrument_id=LDMA

16

HOLDING
THE SPACE

have previously referred to the phenomenon known as 'holding the space'. Holding the space affects many levels of the conscious leader's style of leading: the way they engage others; the way they make decisions; the way they help innovation happen; the way they shape the future and their own organisation's contribution to it. What does holding the space mean in practical, tangible terms, that enables other leaders to replicate it in their own lives and their own organisations?

WHAT IS 'HOLDING THE SPACE'?

Holding the space is about holding the context for the organisation. It is a natural extension of getting, at a visceral level, that everything is connected. It becomes intrinsic for these leaders to hold the space for their organisation to contribute to the world to which it is connected, in some way. This becomes linked to the organisation's higher purpose and very often to the conscious leader's individual higher purpose. A case in point is Paul Polman, CEO of Unilever, whose heartfelt connection towards ecological responsibility plays out in the initiatives taken by the company to act responsibly in the world and which drives its strategic direction, something about which Polman is very vocal and takes a strong stand.

Holding the space is of a different order from what we normally think of in leadership. Traditional leadership, especially at the CEO level, is about envisioning and energising, and so the behaviours that follow on from this are often about directing and controlling in order to make action happen. What we've seen in conscious leaders is that they view the world, and their role, differently. We've seen that it is not about control – in fact, control is actively given up (not an easy ask for leaders in traditional mindsets and traditional organisations). Instead, leading is about assuring, stewarding, listening and becoming an instrument for the organisation to live and evolve into something that contributes to the world around it.

In doing this, conscious leaders may need to hold at bay the conventional urges of their organisation – and even their own – to put in place structures and processes that control, secure and marshal life into straight lines. The illusion of control needs to be replaced by trust. Even where 'mistakes' are made because the conscious leader is holding the space rather than controlling the organisation, the leader's role is to ensure that the rules of freedom, information flow, connection, transparency and agility are upheld.[1] It's important to maintain an agile, alive system. You want to prevent that one transgression suddenly becoming a set of rules that applies to everyone and limits the creativity and free flow of information and energy in the organisation.

Bob Fishman told me that someone in his organisation once took a company car for her son to use at college. Since this was a sackable offence, Bob came under pressure to put in place policies for everyone regarding theft of company property. He refused to do this, upholding the principle that just because one employee had misused the system, this did not mean that everyone was not to be trusted. He consciously chooses to trust people first, and this is a stand that he takes in holding the space.

Joseph Jaworski, in his fascinating book, *Synchronicity: The Inner Path of Leadership*, describes holding the space in this way: "One of the most important roles we can play individually and collectively is to create an opening, or to 'listen' to the implicate order unfolding... True leadership is about creating a domain in which we continually learn and become more capable of participating in our unfolding future."[2]

In this beautiful quote, we can see the conscious leader's invitation to be still and listen to his or her inner wisdom, not to drive things in a rushed and overly energetic way, coming from the egoic will. This doesn't mean, of course, that conscious leaders won't also get into action and help to shape their organisations alongside others. It just means that they have a balance in this; they do both.

There are, in fact, a range of qualities that conscious leaders can employ to hold the space: qualities like listening deeply and sensing into the system, consulting widely to multiple perspectives, taking a stand for the organisation's purpose, and holding the line on the importance of creating win-win solutions for all stakeholders, even while analysts and Boards are breathing down your neck for short-term results, measurements and controls.

There is also a sense of playfulness or, at least, light-heartedness, in the way conscious leaders tend to hold the space. The traditional need to control, report and force can have a very heavy, worrisome and stressful energy about it. There is a lightness of touch in the way conscious leaders observe and interact with the system and see what happens through its feedback loops, all the while holding an attitude of stewardship and safe growth for people and the organisation.

Just one of the reasons why it makes sense to adopt more of this approach is, to put it simply, that many minds are better than one. Bob Fishman told me: "In terms of the consciousness in a company that we could aim for, there are many paths to success. There isn't one right path, one right answer. If the world is infinitely varied, then corporations' futures are unknowable until we have tested them and found them to be successful."

It makes sense, therefore, simply from the perspective of an organisation's responsiveness, agility and fitness, to spend more time as a leader holding the space and less time controlling it or allowing yourself to be the source of all the answers.

LEADING A LIVING COMPANY

Sudhakar Ram has travelled the road from traditional to conscious leadership, and in the process has ushered his organisation towards new levels of self-management. Sudhakar has a fascinating way of describing how he holds the space and interacts with his company as a living system, which gives us practical insight about what this approach looks like in action. Like many of his conscious leader counterparts, he has been influenced by the idea of the 'living company', as proposed by business executive and theorist Arie de Geus. "When I look at Mastek and being at the helm of the affairs of the company today, my job is only to *steward* Mastek to its true potential. I have to keep listening to what is right. I keep watching it and sometimes I pick up something and I throw it out there, assuming that maybe that's what Mastek is saying, but actually it's not; it doesn't stick. Then I have to withdraw and I say, okay, let me try another thing and see if it sticks. I find if something is natural, it sticks easily and there is no resistance. So, we've been able to do a huge amount of organisational change with hardly any resistance and I know that this is right for Mastek. If there is any resistance, then I pull back on that because I know that I'm imposing my own mental models upon it."

His perspective on leading a company is that any form of organisation, any business, is an opportunity for people to come together to achieve something big. Individuals can only do so much on their own, can only perform certain activities alone, but if you want to create something larger and more meaningful, you need to get people together. Organisations, he believes, are the best way of making this happen.

> *Leading any form of organisation,*
> *any business, is an opportunity*
> *for people to come together*
> *to achieve something big*

He doesn't see much difference between, for instance, the organisational forms of a business or an NGO or a government. All are quite similar entities in what they are potentially capable of delivering to the world – in fact, to make anything large and meaningful happen. "Businesses have become derailed because of this quaint notion that it's all about shareholder value," Sudhakar said, "which is a very warped and one-dimensional view, because it shouldn't be all about that for any organisation."

Traditional leaders, of the kind who are paid to chase goals and march towards strategies in straight lines, will think this approach very strange. But to the conscious leader, watching and listening and sensing the response needed is as important as acting and guiding.

> *"Hints of the future are all around us, if only we can*
> *learn to listen for them."*
> Bob Johansen

Here are five ways in which conscious leaders can approach this practice of holding the space.

1 Taking a stand

Is it only about being fluid and watching and offering interventions to see what happens? Not really. Solid actions in the leader's role come from taking certain stands that relate to the organisation's higher purpose, and also upholding some of the 'rules' (that are more like guiding principles) that are in place to help make this happen.

So, for example, in Sudhakar Ram's case: "My job is to hold the space. We stand for certain things which are wholesome, which are about people. We want to do good business; we don't want to let any customer down; we don't want to let any stakeholder down. So it is a win for all. That is the space. All I need to hold is this. I don't even need to do anything about it. It's beautiful to see how the organisation makes choices and how to assist it. Choices will come from completely unexpected quarters. If something is not right, you will sense it if you are paying attention. And this may not be from the next level of management because they normally fall in line with what you say. The signals and choices will often come from some other quarter of the organisation, for example a customer may say something."

Hold the space. Hold the context in mind, the purpose of your organisation, the 'big rules' that bring it to life. Then pay attention to the signs of where guidance is needed.

As we've seen, this notion of holding the space rather than being at the top of a pyramid is so countercultural to traditional organisations as to seem quite nonsensical. Operating in this way requires a huge amount of trust and the willingness to let go of control – indeed, to let go of the fixed mindset that leadership is all about control. As Laloux points out, "Fighting the inner urge to control is probably the hardest challenge of founders and CEOs in self-managing organizations. Over and over again, they must remember to trust."[3]

The role of CEO then becomes, in these kinds of conscious leaders, a role in label only. All of the social constructs that have traditionally been associated with this kind of leadership role fall away and are replaced by a light touch: watching, making suggestions and looking at the ways the organisation wants to shape up and the contributions it can make. Immediately we can see that traditional leaders, especially those at earlier stages of development in terms of their mindset, will tend to be identified with the role of CEO and its labels. They will have a fixed idea of what this means, and they will enjoy the power and control that comes with it. In fact, it is likely that this is why they went for the role in the first place. In conscious leaders, this needs to be replaced by recasting what we mean by CEO and leadership, and what comes through is a desire to be of service and a fascination with seeing how this can play out, differently from day to day.

Sudhakar describes it thus: "This role that is called CEO is a legal structure because we need someone as a CEO role – but really the role is somebody to hold the space and you don't need a whole lot of people to do that. I can keep the Board informed in the right way. I can keep the leadership team informed in the right way. Most of the time their interpretation of what is happening on the field is most important. If they interpret this in a particular way, it could trigger a whole lot of reactions, so my role becomes about how to hold what is happening in the field and put it in the right context. Most of the time the organisation is like a body: if you are observant about it, if on a daily basis you pay attention to the various things it needs to contend with, then most of the time it can heal itself. You don't need to intervene."

There is a deep wisdom in Sudhakar's approach that sees him being the upholder and guardian of the organisation's principles, and ensuring that these are lived in the way the organisation goes about its business.

2 Upholding a higher purpose

Sometimes the vision and higher purpose that a conscious leader holds for his or her organisation can be too vast to be easily translated into terms that others can immediately grasp. For a conscious leader like Laura Roberts, her bigger vision – the sense of responsibility she feels towards the world and the wider contribution she wants to make – is to transform the chemical industry to be more responsible in the way it produces chemicals, and to think about the end-to-end chain from how these chemicals are designed and where they end up at the end of their life. She says: "Even though not everyone in the company may be able to see the possibility of a transformation this big, I can still hold the space for it and make decisions from that space. I can work to develop the team so that they can hold a bigger space for themselves. In this way, decisions can come from these long-term considerations instead of being short-term decisions based on current circumstances. I'm really working on getting people not to let current circumstances dictate what a possible future could look like."

> *"I'm really working on getting people*
> *not to let current circumstances dictate*
> *what a possible future could look like."*
> Laura Roberts

Keeping the higher purpose of the organisation as our 'north star' enables us to stay humble, by reminding us that we are working for something greater than ourselves and our immediate challenges and ambitions. "Service of a higher purpose," says Laloux, enables us to be, "both fully ourselves (rather than full of ourselves) *and* to be working toward achieving an organization's deeper purpose."[4] We get to be more whole when doing this by bringing our whole selves to the leadership role we fulfil and, in ideal circumstances, we get to link our personal purpose to our organisation's purpose and create maximum alignment and flow.

Good questions conscious leaders can ask themselves (and their organisation) in regard to upholding a higher purpose, and which they can role model, are:[5]

» What decision here will best serve the organisation's purpose?

» How will this change/initiative/movement/action serve the organisation's purpose?

» How does working with this client/supplier/stakeholder further the organisation's purpose?

» What needs to happen next to further develop this organisation's purpose in the world?

» What is the best next step to make real the higher purpose?

3 Courage in being an outlier

Holding the space as a conscious leader in your way of being and operating is not necessarily easy. In most organisations, this is a countercultural thing to do, and there are plenty of examples within the mainstream where reacting to fear has driven many a leader to snatch back the company into some kind of centrally managed control state.

Conscious leaders need a deeply held sense of purpose in the world and the ability to navigate some pretty intricate human dynamics in order to succeed. They will often be dealing with other leaders, stakeholders or analysts who don't see the world in quite such nuanced terms and who are far more black and white in their thinking.

As we have seen, Laura Roberts provides a perfect example of how to play the game in this respect: to both honour where other people are coming from and to uphold her own purpose and vision for the company and the chemical industry, finding ways to merge these two wherever possible.

Many conscious leaders nevertheless still find themselves grappling with this dilemma. Lorna Davis heads up Danone's transition to become a socially responsible corporation by 2020 in line with its manifesto. Part of her role requires her to find examples of socially responsible innovation and amplify these, which does not lend itself well to mainstream measurements, especially in the eyes of more traditional stakeholders. She told me: "This is the area where I am most challenged. There's this strong, visceral awareness that I need to hold, to wait, to stay open, to be a space. And then there's this desire at the same time to demonstrate progress. I got asked, 'What's your plan for this? What are your KPIs over the next five years?' And I said, 'I don't have any!' This was really uncomfortable because I thought I should have. But actually, I don't think I should have because I'm waiting to see what emerges. It's hard when people ask you that question because you want to look smart, and my ego says to me, I'm supposed to have a plan! This new relationship between being and doing is the big thing. And I think it's a dance. There is no recipe here. There is, however, something about the momentum we are gaining from the bottom of the organisation. When I hang out with people in more junior levels of the company, it all seems to make a whole lot more sense. This is where I'm much more able to be in the dance of 'being versus doing'."

Lorna's example shows how conscious leaders will need to be answerable to traditional metrics and find a way through this, at least until such a time as the new narrative for business develops and becomes more mainstream. At the moment, these conscious leaders are outliers who are trying to navigate the frontier between traditional and more conscious forms of business. Part of the reason for this book, of course, is to highlight the ways in which they do this, so that others may find ideas for themselves from their stories and so that more momentum develops behind these ideas.

4 Being an instrument

Another thing that conscious leaders can do when holding the space is to 'be the instrument'. The other image that works for this is to think of being a tuning fork as a leader, one towards which others around you can begin resonating.

Conscious leaders describe how they do this through being a role model in their organisation. This might involve role modelling what the organisation stands for, as in the case of Sudhakar Ram. It's also about role modelling what it means to act more consciously. Conscious leaders are keenly aware that their presence, their words and their actions carry a particular weight. Not unlike any leader in any position, where everyone is watching what you do and is taking their cue from this, they are also watching for the gap between what you espouse and your actions. Therefore, how conscious leaders remain conscious becomes important, and this ranges between everything from how they manage themselves to how they conduct their relationships; how they act in a way that takes the whole system into account and all the stakeholders within it; how they uphold the organisation's higher purpose and welcome a diversity of voices; and how they role model trust and don't over-control the situation.

Sometimes it's about the way they role model moral authority. Dominic Sewela spoke to me about the importance of integrity, which to him means doing what he says he will do by when he says he will do it, and coming clean with others when he hasn't. It takes a lot of humility, but it lights the way to respecting oneself and others. Integrity demonstrates self-management and self-responsibility. "When I'm out of integrity, I actually ask for others' forgiveness. For example, in my organisation, coming late is not tolerated, and this starts with me. When I'm late for a meeting, for example if this meeting with you overruns, it means I'm going to be late for my next meeting and there are people waiting for me at that next meeting. It's not like they don't have anything else to do. I keep my word because I have given them an appointment at a particular time. I cannot have one set of rules for myself and another set for others."

Because Dominic role models self-responsibility at the most senior level of the organisation, there is no excuse for others to become lax in their own management of themselves and their arrangements with others. So often in organisations we see people blaming the traffic or other meetings overrunning as a reason (excuse) for not being in integrity to their commitments to each other, even around something as simple as timekeeping. Conscious leaders like Dominic demonstrate how it's possible to bring about a different kind of conscious culture by being the instrument for this in their everyday actions.

Making mistakes role models our humanness, and in our humanness, our vulnerability and our strength need not be in opposition

Frederic Desbrosses agrees: "It's easy to be in the business of role modelling if you want to talk about the principles and make a nice speech about it. People like the speech because it's inspiring. The demonstration of it comes from what you do in your day-to-day life. I'm an extrovert and I've been working a lot on listening so, to me, this is about being connected, sharing how I see things with people and listening to them. I am trying to role model having the right attitude."

This, of course, is not about being perfect. Conscious leaders would be the first to say that leading in this way is a journey, not a destination. In fact, leaders who want to be more conscious and who espouse these values may find themselves under even more scrutiny than usual by people comparing their words with their actions. In becoming more conscious, there is always a new level of clarity to reach, another layer of identity to dissolve. Making mistakes role models our humanness, and in our humanness, our vulnerability and our strength need not be in opposition.

5 Transformation is an individual choice

A final note about holding the space relates to the issue of freedom. Conscious leaders may take a particular stand in the world, both for themselves and their organisations, and this stand may include wanting the highest development for the individuals in their organisation, but these leaders recognise and acknowledge that everyone is on his or her own journey and there is no forcing the pace on this. In fact, some say that the only thing we can really take care of is our own evolution and, in doing this, we might become a beacon for others.

Sudhakar Ram told me how he used to hold a view about his responsibility towards developing others, but he now realises that actually this is a freedom of choice you have to give to individuals. Everyone develops and learns at their own pace and in their own time. He told me: "An organisation cannot have any expectations about an individual transforming. It can only have expectations about people's performance and their ability to grow professionally. Whether personal growth happens or doesn't happen is completely up to the individual. Having said that, we can provide the space and the opportunity to stimulate growth in various ways, for

example through some of the programmes that we have implemented at the company."

Laura Roberts has reached a similar conclusion. In Chapter 12
we learned how Laura had originally been impatient with people's
development, wondering why they didn't get as quickly what was
so clear to her. "I had an 'A-ha!' moment in 2012," she relates,
"where I realised that as a conscious leader it is important to be
okay with wherever someone is on his or her developmental journey.
It doesn't actually matter where they are on this. Really what it's
about is getting them to commit to their development in whatever
way that means something to them. We have reading material and
we have coaches, but it's more of an art than a science. In a sense
you throw spaghetti at the wall because different things resonate
with different people. Frankly I can't even put my finger on what it
is that suddenly makes people get it. I think it's partly the way you
coach in real time and also the way you role model it."

*An organisation can be a conduit
and a container for individual
development and even
enlightenment*

In my experience, when coaching leaders, I find that the more
present I am in the moment, the more space there is for some
kind of magic to enter and do its transformational work. It almost
feels like it's not even me doing it; it is as if elements of transformation enter the conversation by grace. Suddenly, we're talking about
how they're seeing the world and their perspectives rapidly expand
in a quantum leap. There's a rush of energy as we both see the

possibilities for ourselves. I think what counts in transformation is more about our being than our doing.

Ultimately, the conscious leaders' acts of holding the space are about freedom. "The idea of freedom that Gandhi had is different from the Western notion of freedom, which is about entitlement," says Sudhakar. In fact, freedom comes with a sense of duty and responsibility; it's about the freedom to achieve something, not just the freedom to enjoy everything.

"Freedom needs to be accompanied by compassion and the wellbeing of the world at its centre. These are ideals. We're never going to have every individual feeling completely sovereign and free, nor are we going to have a world in which everything is working perfectly. You need enabling mechanisms and this is where the power and potential of the organisation comes in – and where the constructs of the organisation matter."

What Sudhakar is articulating very ably here is how the organisation can be the conduit and a container for individuals' development and even individuals' enlightenment, a view that is shared by a number of conscious leaders.

The construct of holding the space is one that these conscious leaders continue to play with. Perhaps the most playful of all is Jean-François Zobrist, who is joyfully irreverent in the freedom he grants everyone within FAVI – which, incidentally, performs very well as a company. He told me: "I've never taken any decision. I've always consciously made sure that things happen by themselves. To do without doing, which isn't to do nothing; that is the way of leading; letting it be in order to ensure that things happen by themselves. The problem is that all bosses are not free. Usually they have very big egos and think that everything needs to come from them. As far as I'm concerned, all I'm doing is witnessing, basically showing where it's working and sharing my experience. This is what I have done for the last 30 years. After that, it's up to each one to find his or her own way."

To do without doing,
which isn't to do nothing;
that is the way of leading

Holding the Space

»   To be a witness to what is happening and emerging in
    the organisation;

»   To encourage where it is working;

»   To try some things out and see if they stick;

»   Sensing if something is not right by paying attention;

»   Holding the context for people to refer to;

»   Joining up some dots and assisting the organisation in
    the way it lives;

»   Trusting that it will balance and grow as it needs to –
    and not to intervene too much.

Endnotes

1   Laloux, Frederic. 2014. *Reinventing Organizations: A Guide to Creating Organizations Inspired by the Next Stage in Human Consciousness.* Belgium: Nelson Parker.

2   Jaworski, Joseph. 2011. *Synchronicity: The Inner Path of Leadership.* San Francisco USA: Berrett-Koehler Publishers, Inc.

3   Laloux, op. cit.

4   Ibid.

5   Adapted from Laloux, op. cit.

ZONE 3: SYSTEMS INSIGHT

17

THINKING IN WHOLE SYSTEMS

As much as conscious leaders are characterised by their focus on their own self-mastery, their inner listening, and the way they relate to others consciously, they are also focussed on the external world of which they and others are part. They tangibly sense these connections between themselves, others, their organisation and the world around them and this influences every aspect of their decision-making. It would no sooner occur to conscious leaders to act in a way that explicitly damages another part of the system for their own gain than it would occur to them to cut off their own foot. They cannot ignore the effects of their actions; they cannot trade irresponsibly in externalities.

Of course, conscious leaders have a greater or a lesser developed sense of this connection to the system and so they may act, on occasion, like anyone, in ways that are unconscious and reactive or that overlook the effects of their actions. However, a distinguishing feature of these individuals as leaders is that they are on a continuum of alignment and attunement to the system at large and their direction of travel is to become more sensitive to this. They are expanding their awareness of the unity of life itself.

In this section on Systems Insight, we will look at how these leaders think in whole systems, how they are attuned to the serendipity and synchronicity that occurs within interconnected systems, and their unique perspectives on growth that ensures a sustainable system.

There are scores of books on systems thinking, and the intention here is not to go over this ground,[1] but rather to highlight in a few ways how conscious leaders think about and employ their perspective on systems in the way they run their organisations, for this to have a positive impact in the world.

Conscious leaders are natural systems thinkers

Systems intelligence has been identified by Mackey as one of the four cornerstone intelligences of the conscious leader. Systems intelligence accompanies intellectual intelligence (IQ), emotional intelligence (EQ) and spiritual intelligence (SQ) as an interwoven fabric of intelligences through which the conscious leader sees the world and takes action.[2]

Mackey regards conscious leaders as natural systems thinkers. They see the bigger picture and understand how the different components of a system connect and behave together. They are mindful of the short- and long-term consequences of their actions. As such, conscious leaders can be thought of as systems thinkers, but also as systems feelers, he says, who connect with the system in their way of being, who feel into and intuit their next actions, and who are conscious about the effects of these actions on the world around them.

Cindy Wigglesworth, a world-recognised expert in the field of spiritual intelligence (SQ) and the creator of the SQ21 instrument measuring spiritual intelligence, sees our ability to look at life as an interconnected system as one of the key requirements for spiritual intelligence. At the very highest level, says Cindy, spiritual intelligence asks whether you believe the universe is not only an interconnected system, but an intelligent system. You may give that intelligence any name you like, but acknowledging this interconnectivity and higher intelligence is the most advanced expression of our own spiritual intelligence. [3]

Cindy also reminds us that Albert Einstein promoted a similar line of thought. He wrote that human beings are part of a whole, which is called by us 'Universe', and that we are a part of this, limited in time and space. We may experience ourselves, our thoughts and feelings, as separate from others, but this is an illusion (or, in Einstein's words, 'delusion') of our consciousness. Striving to free ourselves from this illusion of separation is the purpose of religion, but for those who do not subscribe to a particular religious tradition, developing our spiritual intelligence through recognition of our inherent interconnectedness is part of a conscious quest for our own evolution.

This quest for our evolution emerges in various contemporary writings, too, for example in the current work around so-called 'Teal' organisations, described by Laloux in *Reinventing Organizations*. Laloux found that the leaders in the highly evolved self-managing organisations he studied use metaphors about living organisms or living systems to describe their organisations. [4] Leadership merges with nature. We are becoming more aware of ourselves as part of the living system of the universe as we become more attuned to the ecology of the whole, which includes nature and the planet.

A useful way of perceiving the whole system is as a series of interconnected circles within circles. This is described eloquently by Bob Johansen in his book, *Leaders Make the Future*. Bob interweaves phenomena as seemingly diverse as diasporas of people, the availability of food networks, the blue economy of water, developments within neuroscience, and technological innovations in the way we manage our bodies and our health as a series of interconnected circles that illustrate how truly connected we all are in our respective overlapping systems, and how inescapable these interconnections are in shaping our future.

Leadership merges with nature

This interconnected system, or systems of systems, is the environment in which leaders of today work. Their awareness of these systems, and the way they collide, mingle and amplify each other, is what conscious leaders will need to develop if they are to reach a perspective that gives them a high leverage point when working with these systems. Beyond simply understanding and thinking about the interactive effects of these systems, about big data and megatrends, conscious leaders will also need to be thinking about how they and their organisations take responsible action within this Petri dish of systemic collisions.

Some conscious leaders, such as Tom Chi, are thinking on such a vast scale that they see the interconnectedness of our systems not as some conceptual idea but as a fact of life. Previously we heard how Tom regards everything as being so deeply interconnected that every iron atom in our blood cells – in every human being's blood cells – went through the same five supernovas in the creation of the universe as we know it. Tom says, "You can't be more connected than being the sons and daughters of the same five stars."

Behaviourally, this awareness of whole systems is felt as a deep sense of 'mutuality' – of how we are all connected, and therefore how our behaviour has a ripple effect on other things in the system. Conscious leaders like Frederic Desbrosses is clear that the one principle that is very meaningful to him, and which makes a big difference to the business of his company, is mutuality. "Efficiency is quite a clear principle that you will see on the agenda of the Board of every single business in the world," says Frederic, "but I think mutuality is also a very interesting principle. Mutuality is about asking ourselves the kinds of questions about, for example, whether our price increase is realistic for our customers. It's about asking whether increasing our price by 6 or 7% actually extends back to our customers, about whether we are giving back the benefit we have received in the business."

> *"For me, mutuality is very meaningful,*
> *and I think it's where conscious business*
> *and conscious leaders should meet up."*
> Frederic Desbrosses

We often see a similar theme emerging when considering externalities. Conscious leaders have great difficulty assigning the label 'externalities' to actions that cause harmful consequences because they can see that they are part of, not separate from, a system that is being impacted as they act upon it.

A good example of the way this whole systems approach can take effect in a business is through the executive pay at Whole Foods Market. It is a well-known fact that executives' pay is capped at a maximum of nineteen times the salary of the average employee. Compare this, for example, with many big corporation CEOs, whose pay might be as much as 350 times the average employee's salary. What the Whole Foods Market's rule so neatly puts in place is that the only way to earn more money as an executive is to ensure that everybody earns more money, that is to say, that the size of the pie grows. In reality, setting up a pay ratio such as 19:1 is more likely to be an expression of the company's, and these executives', needs for balance and sustainability, rather than for rampant profit-driven growth at any cost.

An additional advantage of systems intelligence is that it enables conscious leaders to plug into the source of human creativity within and outside their organisations. This is about how they can encourage the whole system to work towards achieving a sustainable balance and towards solving complex, previously unencountered problems.

Lorna Davis told me how she had recently left a meeting of a group of nutritionists, paediatricians, agronomists and scientists who had spent their entire lives dedicated to improving the nutrition of the world and setting dietary guidelines. The group recognised that there was no simple way to change behaviour because it's not possible to legislate to fix obesity. They recognised that business was an essential piece of the puzzle and that the pattern of increasing obesity meant co-opting businesses in the discussions. Previously, businesses had been seen as separate from the problem of health, as non-players. However, in talking with Danone it became evident to them that business is part of the system and can play a role in helping to change it. Conscious leaders therefore have a role to include the various stakeholders in the system that draws on this wider intelligence and invites these sorts of discussions which solve complex problems.

Sometimes, thinking in systems is simply a personal approach and choice. Paul Monekosso Cleal conducts his business on the basis of the reciprocity in the system. When Paul speaks about 'business karma', he is referring to the principle that if you are positive and helpful in business, other people will help you. He says: "I see it all the time, both at an individual level and a collective business level. People who go out of their way to be helpful find it easier to get help from others. Narrow self-interest arrives at a different set of results. Even though there's no guarantee, it can be amazing how your helpfulness to others in the system can come back in the way it helps you, either directly or indirectly, through third parties."

How we develop more systems intelligence and insight lies partly in the questions we ask ourselves and the experiences in which we immerse ourselves. The act of thinking as broadly as possible about your stakeholder universe as a leader, and about the needs of all the players within it, can broaden a leader's mindset.

In the words of Mackey, conscious leaders know that every strategic business decision must be made after considering how it will affect and create value for each of a company's stakeholders. These include the employees, suppliers, other business partners, customers, community, society and environment. [5] Similarly, immersing yourself in nature and natural studies can help to develop your systems intelligence by virtue of the connections and relationships in living systems.

THINKING WITH A SYSTEMS MINDSET

Sally Ann Ranney, whom we met in Chapter 3, is a conscious leader who champions conservation causes and combines this with influences in business and politics. She wonders what effect it could have if every politician serving in office or every leader in a company was required to undergo whole systems training before taking on their position. What might happen if these leaders were sent into nature with some amazing minds, she asks, to expose them to what the whole system means and to experience the fabric of life – and in the process to realise how our decisions as the predominant species can make or break that fabric? "We need to realise, deeply," says Sally, "that all other species are subservient to our ignorance or our wisdom."

All other species are subservient to our ignorance or our wisdom

She lives and breathes systems thinking and is a great example of how this quality can come to the fore in conscious leaders. We saw in Chapter 3 how she realised at the age of seven that life was intricately connected with nature, leading to her deep immersion in nature and natural causes.

Speaking to her, I was struck by how she sees, virtually exclusively, in the broadest possible systems. Importantly, she doesn't do this with merely an intellectual, analytical, head-based understanding. She *feels* systems from the deepest and most compassionate part of her heart. Indeed, her heart is huge, the extent of her compassion a palpable force in any conversation with her. She has what can be described as bio-empathy: the ability to see things from nature's point of view and to understand, respect and learn from its patterns. [6]

Sally effortlessly references natural systems and human behaviour in her ways of perceiving and leading. She reminds us that understanding whole systems is endemic to our very humanness and that it occurs in the original knowledge of all indigenous people. At the deepest levels of our origins as humans and living beings, we are all one.

It can be useful for conscious leaders to consider nature's conditions for sustaining life and how this might inform their decisions in their own organisations. It can prompt us to ask ourselves questions about the impact of our decisions and actions on the system we're part of.

Sally talked me through nature's conditions for sustaining life:

1   One species' waste is another species' food.
    Expressions of life are joined up in an endlessly
    interconnected chain that forms a whole system,
    each link feeding into the other.

2   You cannot mine populations (for example, forests or
    fisheries) beyond their capacity to regenerate
    themselves to the levels they were when you
    first intervened.

3   You cannot add more subsurface material (for example,
    acid mine drainage on the Earth's surface) than can be
    reabsorbed over time.

Everything exists in an exquisite balance. Thinking about this
balance asks us to consider what we are doing, what we are taking
out compared with what we are putting back in.

There is a fourth condition, says Sally, which asks us to examine
our own consciousness:

4   How much is sufficient? What is enough? In other
    words, is growth on growth on growth a
    sustainable outcome?

We'll explore further how conscious leaders view growth in
Chapter 19.

Applying these ecological principles to business, Sally encourages
us to question whether what we are doing is depleting the whole or,
instead, how what we're doing can be done in a way that keeps the
whole intact. A conscious leader, advises Sally, needs to be thinking
about the entire supply chain. Simply considering how you get your
raw materials from the middle-man is not enough. We need to be
asking ourselves, where does he get his raw materials from? And
where does that person source theirs? "As conscious business leaders,
we have a responsibility in the production of materials and the waste.
We have to figure out that problem," believes Sally. This is reminiscent
of the seventh generation principle, which asks us to consider the
impact of our actions and decisions on seven generations hence.

Many of us are great fans of Amazon, and their ability to deliver
products to our doorstep within 24 hours is undeniably convenient.
How many of us, however, wonder about the sustainability of
Amazon's packaging? Having recently received six stacking baskets
separately packaged with an abundance of bubblewrap in a carton
the size of half a truck, I stood and observed the huge pile of waste

in front of me and began thinking about the excess of cardboard, plastic, truck space, fuel, traffic and emissions that had gone into delivering this one item to my door. If we extrapolate this to the sheer volume of delivery business that Amazon does every minute of every day, this naturally begs the question: what responsibility is Amazon taking for insisting that the packaging from its abundance of suppliers is carried out more sustainably? One would imagine that a company with the buying power of Amazon should be able to make some pretty large demands about sustainable packaging.

Sally and I discuss packaging. She emphasises that over-packaging goes against the whole ethos of systems thinking. "What we can do," she advises, "as consumers, as leaders, is to identify what is pro- and anti-whole systems, and then choose to do what is whole systems healthy." Additionally, we have the capacity to make intelligent choices and exercise intelligent action in the interests of whole system balance. "If everyone were to send all their packaging back to the producer, don't you think they'd start rethinking it when all this waste landed on their doorstep?" she asks.

> *"We are taught that giving and receiving are*
> *two actions. They aren't – they are one."*
> Sally Ann Ranney

Our conscious use of our systems intelligence can also be applied to our purchasing power. "We are inclined to think," suggests Sally, "that when I give you $1.50 and you hand me a product across the counter, that's a two-person transaction. It's not. There is a whole linked supply chain that hardly anyone thinks about beyond whether it is cost effective or not. What is my money really doing? Where did the raw materials go? What was the impact of getting the raw materials? What is the employment like for the people who got me those raw materials? What is the carbon footprint of this product coming all the way to me? How will it be disposed of?"

These kinds of whole systems questions apply not only to the products that we buy as individuals and companies, but all the way up to where policies are made. A leader like Sally believes that politicians, being the powerbrokers, are out of sync with a whole systems approach to politics. "We are dealing with long-term problems and solutions, yet we have two-year and four-year, sometimes double-term appointments to office," she says. Short-termism in politics runs counter to thinking long-term about rebalancing systems. What would whole systems politics look like? If all decisions were mandated as whole systems decisions, what becomes possible for humankind?

What would whole systems politics look like?

There is an invitation for us to collaborate as human beings across all systems for the benefit of the quality of our life today and in the future. Doing so will require many of the qualities described in this book: overcoming our ego-driven natures that cause us to act in our own self-interest and joining up with others beyond the ways in which we have done so before to leverage our collective intelligence. We need to realise that what stops us is simply the construct of our own minds. Now is the time to realise more acutely than ever before that we are one and that we need to think and act as one.

I wanted to end this chapter by sharing an example that I find particularly inspiring and that also widened the limits of my mind to what is possible in business, regarding taking wider systems into account. This is an example drawn from Tony Hsieh, the CEO of Zappos, and what he has done with his business in the environment of Las Vegas, where the company is based.

Case Study: Tony Hsieh, CEO of Zappos— Pushing the edges of system thinking

Following the thinking of integral philosopher Ken Wilber, a company can be seen as a point in the unified web of the marketplace, the environment, and societal and planetary webs. The implication is that where the boundary of our company lies is a construct in our own minds as leaders. It doesn't have to end at the doors of our office building or the edges of our company's brand. These are all just social conventions gleaned from the dominant narrative of business which we unconsciously employ when thinking about our own organisation. The boundary of our company can end, in fact, anywhere we'd like it to. One such leader experimenting with how we think about business boundaries is Tony Hsieh.

Where the boundary of our company lies is a construct in our own minds as leaders

---

Hsieh is serving as the breaker of the proverbial four-minute mile for the business world. He is someone not just talking about conscious leadership, but actively doing it. Similarly to Tom Chi, he sees vastly outside the box, thinks about the interconnectedness and furthest reaches of the system in which he operates, considers how benefitting many people might also benefit Zappos, and is humble and engaging in his style. All this is done with a clear business focus but, in doing so, Hsieh combines systems intelligence, innovation and good business sense.

Whereas he became known for his initial focus in Zappos of building on the four company beacons of clothing, customer service, company culture and community, Hsieh is now majoring on the beacon of 'community'. He does so by amplifying the variables that play on community: variables such as co-learning, connectedness, density and diversity of the population and, what he calls, 'collisions'. Collisions are the interconnection points between people where ideas are swapped and which become the ground for innovations to be born.

What does Hsieh's approach mean in practice?

Through the Downtown Las Vegas project, Hsieh invested $350 million of his own and a handful of other investors' money to reinvigorate, rejuvenate and refresh downtown Las Vegas when he moved his company headquarters there from San Francisco in 2013. Distinct from other business leaders, Hsieh regards the impact, responsibility and opportunities for his company not as ending at the walls of the Zappos office building, but rather as extending outwards into the entire downtown Las Vegas community. He has, through the project, played an active part in stimulating positive effects in the entire city and, in the process, aimed to rejuvenate what was a flagging community.

Part of Hsieh's $350 million investment was $50 million allocated to small businesses. His criteria for investment was that these were owner-operated businesses that displayed passion and helped promote a sense of community spirit. These businesses also needed to be sustainable, execute themselves well, and be unique or first or best at something so that they were story worthy. These 'big rules' created the container in which emergent business rejuvenation could take place.

Hsieh sees 'collisions' as opportunities for innovation to occur in the community, for the good of the community. Collisions are the conversations and interactions which create innovations, that in turn sustain and enliven the community. Rather than maximising short-term ROI (return on investment), Hsieh zones-in on maximising long-term ROC (return on community and return on collisions).

In addition, he has looked at institutionalising 'ROL' ('return on luck'). By this he means supporting and accelerating serendipity, chance, coincidental encounters that produce opportunities to maximise collisions and create positive impact. ROL is based on findings that when cities double in size, productivity and innovations per resident increases by 15%. Therefore, the train of reasoning is that encouraging collisions increases 'return on luck' by amplifying serendipity, which accelerates learning and, through this, productivity and innovation. This means that Hsieh's business efforts and success have been inextricably woven into the prosperity of the entire community of downtown Las Vegas, and he has a stake in the game.

Hsieh's ingredients for accelerating serendipity, or ROL, are based on a residential density of 100 residents/acre, plus a great deal of street level activity which provide opportunities for residents to 'collide'. By increasing density and diversity, he helps cause the effect of accelerating learning and innovation. The oil in the wheels is a culture of openness, collaboration, creativity and optimism. In so doing, Hsieh embodies many of the qualities of the conscious leaders featured in this book and encourages the development of these qualities in the community. His passion for learning and innovation finds a channel through community activities – whether this be the Zappos community itself, tech start-ups, small businesses, fashion, art and music or communities of local residents.

In fact, the Downtown Las Vegas Project has not been an unmitigated success and Hseih stepped down from the leadership of the project in 2014, saying, "It's just what it is to be an entrepreneur. Not every venture is going to work."[7] Regardless, there are not many business leaders, especially of the stature and success of Hsieh, who would see the opportunity to create a tech entrepreneur village and look to create a win-win result for his business as well as for the community. His responsibility has run deep. Part of his efforts have involved taking care of some of the 'hygiene factors' in the Downtown Las Vegas community. These include establishing a school where children are taught entrepreneurship and innovation using the latest neuroscience techniques – effectively bringing together three emerging trends to educate children for the future – and a re-worked and revamped medical centre which addresses some of the crippling factors in the US healthcare system.

In summary, Hsieh's 'big bet' has been based on three guiding principles: accelerating Collisions, encouraging Co-learning and amplifying Connectedness. With this, he has experimented with everything else falling into place: productivity, innovation, growth and happiness.

I find his example utterly inspiring, irrespective of its results and because of its vision. Imagine what would become possible in the world through business if more leaders collectively thought and acted like this?

Endnotes

1   See: Meadows, Donella. 2008. *Thinking in Systems: A Primer.*
     USA: Chelsea Green Publisher.

2   Mackey, John and Sisodia, Raj. 2014. *Conscious Capitalism:
     Liberating the Heroic Spirit of Business.* USA: Harvard Business
     School Publishing Corporation.

3   Wigglesworth, Cindy. 2014. *SQ21: The Twenty-One Skills of
     Spiritual Intelligence.* New York: SelectBooks, p70.

4   Laloux, Frederic. 2014. *Reinventing Organizations: A Guide to
     Creating Organizations Inspired by the Next Stage in Human
     Consciousness.* Belgium: Nelson Parker.

5   Mackey, op. cit.

6   Johansen, Bob. 2012. *Leaders Make The Future: Ten New
     Leadership Skills for an Uncertain World.* San Francisco. Berrett-
     Koehler Publishers, Inc., *a BK Business Book,* pp95-98.

7   http://www.recode.net/2016/5/18/11698318/
     tony-hsieh–zappos-amazon-code-commerce

18

SERENDIPITY AND SYNCHRONICITY

W hether it's innumerable examples of strange but helpful coincidences where life seems to come to our rescue, or Tony Hsieh's somewhat more scientific approach of 'Return on Luck', synchronicity provides one of the most intriguing windows into the minds of conscious leaders. Their stories are fascinating, but perhaps no more fascinating than what happens in everyone's lives. The difference seems to be that many conscious leaders are very aware of the play and interplay of the forces of synchronicity in their lives and they actively seek to nurture and develop these.

The future metric of success will be synchronicity

Synchronicity is described as 'the ability to find meaning in coincidence'.[1] As we are required to find ways to lead in ever more complex circumstances, with multitudinous factors and the need to bring in the collective human dimension more than ever before, knowing how to find meaning in coincidence becomes our ally in leadership. It has even been suggested that the future metric of success will be synchronicity.

"Leaders need to see patterns before others see them," advises Bob Johansen in his study of what makes future leaders successful. "The ability to see links between personal experience and future possibilities will be essential. Great leaders have always had this ability, except that in the future the underlying patterns are likely to be more difficult to discern. Meaningful coincidence is important for leaders: they must listen and sense the patterns, sense the links."[2]

> *"The ability to see links between personal experience*
> *and future possibilities will be essential.*
> *Great leaders have always had this ability."*
> Bob Johansen

At one level, we're talking here about intuition. Intuition helps us to make leaps of connection without needing to have the dots in between filled in. It is our inner knowing of how things are connected, even though we may not have the evidence to prove it – to ourselves or to anyone. It is simply a sense of knowing.

At an even deeper level, this skill is about the ability to stand still in the forest and listen into something bigger than ourselves, to life itself, through our own deep and quiet inner voice. Inner knowing speaks loudest when we are still within, because the inner voice is often quiet and easily drowned out by the noise and bustle of the day-to-day, with its hoots and beeps from a thousand events, people and devices.

While there are things that leaders can do to develop the way in which they tune into the patterns of synchronicity, there is no guarantee that these coincidences will arrive on schedule.

Mariana Bozesan, who we met earlier and who conducted a study of the inner worlds of conscious leaders, found that one of these qualities is the capacity to flow with life's events, rather than trying to force or control life. In place of this, conscious leaders practise a deep underlying willingness to trust life. They adopt an attitude of abundance, rather than scarcity, and a belief that life will, in the end, provide perfectly what we need, even though this may not be what we think we want.

This doesn't mean that we are not 'being in action', creating our lives the way we would want them to be. However, much of this quality of living that seems to coincide with the magic of synchronicity has to do with surrendering our little will (our ego) to the larger will of life itself and our place within it. It is about listening inwardly to what we are being called to do and serve. Essentially, it is about being clear in our intentions and then getting out of the way, being unattached to the outcomes. In these circumstances, life can surprise us by providing just the kinds of support that we least expect, from the places we least expect it. Our lives become somewhat of an adventure where we co-create outcomes and become an agent for life, rather than acting from our egos as if we are separate from it.

While this might sound like quite a mystical approach, some conscious leaders adopt a very pragmatic and even scientific view of the way synchronicity works. Tom Chi explains his view in this way: "People treat synchronicity as if it's a belief. It's not. It's a priming function of the reticular activating system in our brains which allows us to notice things more. The noticing of things – whether we call them coincidences or not – against a primed intention tends to be a useful thing. If we notice the things that would be helpful to us and put ourselves in the position of being around a lot of stimuli, our chances of accumulating a lot of useful inputs is very high. If we don't do this, the probability becomes very low. I think that what people call 'synchronicity' or the 'law of attraction' is really a mathematical function of the reticular activation system and the number of exposures that people put themselves into."

While some of us might appreciate Tom Chi's very pragmatic approach, others allude to the existence of something that seems to sit quietly, more deeply and universally connected, just behind the fabric of life that we see. Many conscious leaders also have what can be described as a faith in life, as well as a faith in themselves. Their approach emerges as a combination of trusting in life and taking action in life.

Lorna Davis told me: "I've got two angles on this subject. I'm a huge fan of synchronicity. For example, many years ago I was travelling the world and arrived in Australia thinking, I'll call up this company and if they give me a job I'll stay, and if they don't I'll move on. As it happens, when I made the call the guy on the end of the line told me they'd been looking for a manager for the exact product brand I had been representing for the past six months. I borrowed a dress, went in the next day for an interview and got the job. This was a wonderful coincidence. However, I made the call and I got a good reference from my previous company because I acted. That's served me well. Synchronicity is about putting ourselves in places that suit us better than other places. It's not only about dealing with the reality that comes to us; we can also be more active in choosing to be in the places that nourish us."

Lorna's views are shared by Paul Monekosso Cleal: "This is very much about intuition and serendipity. Recently I went to see a new client, a senior government politician who was unhappy with how he was perceiving us and who was refusing to spend time with me. As a result, I ended up waiting to go into his office, standing in the corridor outside it. Someone who was another potential client happened to come past and we ended up chatting. It turned out this person was going in to see this senior politician about a big project where he might employ us. By coincidence, even though I hadn't got the meeting with the senior politician, this other person went in and essentially sold the project for me without me even having to be there. Weird things like that happen to me all the time. Almost weekly I have coincidences where I think, if I hadn't been standing in that place at that time, or called that person, this thing wouldn't have happened."

Paul actively uses his network to encourage synchronicity: "There is an element of making your own luck, of encouraging serendipity. If you keep in touch with people, if you create a good network, if you are regularly helpful to people and you give them your time when they ask for it, then it's interesting how they think of you when they need help or they respond when you need help. By using your network positively, you can create greater chances that these so-called 'random' events will occur."

How to Develop Synchronicity

The picture that is emerging of the way conscious leaders enjoy and develop synchronicity in their lives and roles as leaders is to combine a clear intention of what you need at any point in time with an act of faith in life itself, sometimes trusting that what you need will come to you and sometimes just marvelling at the coincidences that arise to support you. It is helped by staying in action of what you want, whether this is keeping an open mind and noticing the patterns around you or putting yourself in the right places, or by actively nurturing your relationships and connections. Noticing the play and interplay of coincidences in your life can give you a huge boost in confidence about life's support of you.

Taking a more scientific approach can equally help to build this confidence, whether this takes the form of noticing occurrences that link to your specific intention (pattern recognition) or taking a measured approach, like Tony Hsieh, to tap into the collective intelligence of stakeholders by increasing the number of 'collisions' or interactions between people in an atmosphere of openness and collaboration so that greater creativity and innovation can occur.

If we do choose to take a more magical, mysterious view of synchronicity, then the words of Joseph Jaworski can guide us: "A true leader ... sets the stage on which predictable miracles, synchronistic in nature, can – and do – occur." Participating in this process, says Jaworski, has more to do with our leadership being than our leadership doing. "Leadership is about creating, day by day, a domain in which we and those around us continually deepen our understanding of reality and are able to participate in shaping the future." [3]

> *"A true leader sets the stage on which predictable miracles, synchronistic in nature, can – and do – occur."*
> Joseph Jaworski

This collective and collaborative intelligence is the way we will lead into the future. Creating this kind of domain requires all of the skills of conscious leadership described in this book to be brought into the foreground. These skills include:

» The ability to think in whole terms, not separately;

» The ability to manage our egos as they cause us to react and want to separate from and win over others at our own and everyone's expense;

» The way we hold ourselves in relationship to others that encourages collaboration and collective thinking;

» The ability to get out of the way as the positional 'leader' and let the intelligence of the many shine through;

» The way we are able to join the dots and see the patterns in what others bring to the fore through their intelligence, thinking and innovation;

» The way we can hold the space and context for a bigger
   purpose to shine through for everyone's efforts; and

» How we recast competition to make it about benefit to
   the many and not the one.

In their way of being, this is how conscious leaders serve life
itself, by allowing life to come through them in the service of something greater that supports the common good, not by acting as if
they are separate from it.

Similarly, Jaworski advised three shifts of mind to encourage the
'predictable miracles' of synchronicity to occur:

» Shifting our mental model of the world from a clock or
   a machine to an interconnected, open, dynamic and
   living whole;

» Recognising that everything lives in relationship to
   everything else, and it is only through these
   relationships that things exist; and

» Accepting that it is not so much about our will (our ego
   minds) but about our willingness (our surrender).
   Listening to our inner voice helps to guide us and we
   trust that we are part of the unfolding universe, which
   is to say that we are co-creators in the emerging future.

We commit to our part by taking a stand, by asking ourselves:
what is our part in this whole? As we take a stand, Jaworski describes
how people gather around us because of our authentic presence.
We find ourselves in a coherent field where the flow of people taking
collective action supports the larger unfolding of the future. It is
also at this point that conscious leaders need to take responsibility
for the effect they are creating, by asking themselves: how am I being
that is helping people to take collective action? "At this point," says

Jaworski, "your life becomes a series of predictable miracles."

I find Jaworski's words beguilingly mysterious and deeply appealing – and equally recognise that their poetic nature may not appeal to all leaders, especially those looking for more 'crunchy' approaches to their leadership challenges. It might be that in the descriptions of the leaders above, and the pointers to the behaviours that help to support synchronicity, that these more pragmatic ideas and suggestions will be helpful to a wide range of conscious leaders.

A NOTE ON ABUNDANCE

It seems that alongside the qualities of trust, surrender, deep listening and noticing patterns, there is another quality that accounts for synchronicity, and that is an open, generous and abundant heart. Where conscious leaders are perhaps very different from more traditional leaders is that they operate from a mindset of abundance rather than scarcity. Giving things away is not a problem for these leaders. They don't feel that if they give things away – control, money, power – they will lose out and have less.

A key question that leaders can ask themselves is whether, at any moment, they are operating from an abundance mindset or a scarcity mindset. A purely commercial mindset is grounded in the scarcity model (win-lose), while an abundance model is grounded in creative principles. Creativity is not a zero-sum game. Rather, more creativity emerges from creativity.

> "The most important decision we make is whether we
> believe we live in a friendly or a hostile universe."
> Albert Einstein

Conscious leaders like Ramesh Kacholia, Founder of Caring Friends, the successful India-based organisation that acts as a bridge between outstanding NGOs and donors, speaks with an open and grateful heart about his own sense of abundance and the creative outcomes that flow from this. He says: "I realised that when we are helping others, our resources never get reduced. On the contrary, I always found that I was better off, even financially, when I was helping others. I feel that I have been given more than my fair share of resources, and the only way is to share these resources with those who are really in urgent need of help and support from us. By sharing these resources, they are never reduced; they are truly always increased."

Neal Gandhi: an abundant entrepreneur

Neal Gandhi has made the transition from successful, yet stressed and over-achieving entrepreneur, to even more successful, relaxed entrepreneur and angel investor in socially conscious companies, integrating the principles of conscious leadership and, in the case of his story below, of abundance and synchronicity in particular.

One thing I noticed about Neal is that he never seems rushed. He always has time to become involved in things that seem, intuitively, to make sense for him. He is actively observing patterns, noticing synchronicities, and opening up to these opportunities. He told me the story about a company he has just invested in: "Somebody had moved jobs and a huge business opportunity came out of my name being mentioned three times in a week, with the result that this person noticed and picked up her phone to say, 'Your name's come up three times this week and we need to meet.'"

I asked Neal how he achieves such an abundance of time: "Because I trust," he said simply. "If you don't trust, you can't have an abundance of time, because you're trying to do everything yourself." He related the story of his Bulgarian business and how he gave 40% of it to others and 30% of this to the new CEO: "As a consequence, I don't have to spend any time on this. I don't even have to look at any decision he makes because he's absolutely doing it for the best of the business. If you set up the right conditions, you can trust. That trust gives you the space to create. This deal will double the size of the company and there are people who are much better equipped to handle contracts than I am. I don't need to control it and it frees me up to do bigger stuff and better stuff."

I asked him whether he had a sense of where he was heading or whether he lived in the moment. Although Neal has a strong inclination to not want to control anything, he says: "In business I do have a crystal clear idea of where I'm taking each of the companies. I'm on top of what we're out to do, how we're going to get there, and I continue to drive the vision across all of them."

With such clarity, yet with the willingness to let go of the need to control outcomes, Neal makes things really simple. Most leaders need to work really hard to stay on top of the complexity, and then all of the human dynamics come into play as well. From what Neal describes, he stays open and spacious and drives the vision in his companies towards success, but he doesn't control the detail. He trusts life, and a great team, to do the rest and he doesn't obsess about it.

> *"I know and trust that something will happen,*
> *and it does."*
> Neal Gandhi

I wondered about the wider market forces that can make any attempts to live as a conscious leader more difficult or miserable. Neal agrees, and recognises that as a CEO of a listed company with the market's expectations on you, this can be a much more difficult challenge and the stress can really take its toll. "I used to think that conscious businesses and public markets couldn't actually go together, because analysts control all of the markets and are often just on the same old treadmill as everyone else. However, in my new venture I am going to go public and how I'm approaching this is to create a network of conscious CEOs across the business. We will develop these CEOs as conscious leaders and they will support and reinforce each other and set the tone of their organisations, so that we have consciousness and strength across the business. This way, the business is actually creating a positive impact on the market through the collective weight of these conscious CEOs."

It is in his description of the changes in his life, however, where the thread of abundance can be seen most clearly: "I have a real feeling of abundance," he says. "I want for nothing. This is a huge shift from where I've been. It doesn't mean I don't go out and do cool things or buy cool stuff, but I don't chase the money in order to do it. Since I've started doing this, the money just comes in and, even though I've got major financial commitments, I know and trust that something will happen, and it does. As long as I keep putting positive energy in, connecting to a set of values, and express ongoing positivity to everyone that I meet, life and the energies of the universe seem to be supporting me."

In summary, although conscious leaders interpret in an individualised way how they use the principles of serendipity and synchronicity, there are common threads between all of them that are worth mulling over if we want to consider how we might tap into life working in our favour.

Endnotes

1   Johansen, Bob. 2012. *Leaders Make The Future: Ten New Leadership Skills for an Uncertain World.* San Francisco. Berrett-Koehler Publishers, Inc., *a BK Business Book,* p23.

2   Ibid.

3   Jaworski, Joseph. 2011. *Synchronicity: The Inner Path of Leadership.* San Francisco USA: Berrett-Koehler Publishers, Inc, Chapter 24.

19

THE CONSCIOUS LEADER'S VIEW ON GROWTH

The attitude of conscious leaders towards business growth is fascinating. Central to their whole approach to this topic is the difference between whether they are focused on volume growth or growth by the value they are creating. Volume growth can perhaps be thought of as the less conscious approach to growth. What is driving this?

As far as the traditional narrative of business is concerned, we are highly conditioned by our current economic model, which tells us that growth is required. Our mental models dictate that successful business is about growth. This drives us in the pursuit of ever greater growth, acquisition, numbers, percentages. For many in mainstream business, it is unthinkable and downright irreverent not to be aiming to be the biggest, or the best, or the most innovative, famous, 'out there' (apply any label). When our egos get engaged, we fall naturally into comparing ourselves and our companies with others and don't want to be found to be lacking or inferior. We chase the competition in the hope of catching them up or keeping them behind us. We are all about acquiring a larger percentage of market share. This obsession with growth in volume and size narrows our perspective down to a single thing that can be measured with a ruler. We don't even question the assumptions within whose influence we are caught up; it seldom occurs to us that there can be a different way of looking at growth. In doing so, we lose sight of the wider system in which we are operating.

> *"Why do we have to be number one?*
> *What's wrong with being number four?"*
> Erika Uffindell, The Global Centre for
> Conscious Leadership

Laura Roberts has this to say about growth by volume: "I think growth for growth's sake has created some negative behaviours in capitalism. For example, private equity groups are driven to increase evaluation of their investments to make a profit in 3 to 5 years. I believe growth that is organic and driven by the needs of the market-place is a much healthier situation. Growth that is driven primarily by acquisition is not proving to be sustainable and is, unfortunately, driving many adverse outcomes in business."

Compared to this, growing by the value that is created is a much more conscious way of regarding how we grow as a business. Value growth occurs as a result of wellbeing in the system, not because growth is the target in and of itself. The key to value growth lies in our attitude: how wide is the view that we are taking? Taking a broader, macro perspective on growth is a direct antidote to the micro, unconscious assumption that 'we must grow'. While being driven to achieve dominant market share might seem a healthy attitude in a business context, it doesn't necessarily address the system that our business operates within, which includes the factors of the environment, human relationships and our responsibility towards the effects of our actions on the greater system. A more conscious approach to growth is therefore a philosophy we can adopt when operating a business.

A mindset of growing the value we are broadly creating seems to be enabled by three things:

» An attitude of abundance rather than scarcity;

» The consideration of balance and the tendency to think of all of life as being part of an interconnected whole; and

» Taking a longer-term, sustainable mindset.

Some examples taken from the conscious leaders interviewed for this book, and their attitude towards growth, help to illustrate these mindset shifts.

Jean-François Zobrist, whom we met in previous chapters, is a fervent supporter of freedom and trusting employees to organise themselves in the best way to get a job done well. He told me: "Growth cannot be an objective. Growth is a result of wellbeing. We have gone from 70 to 600 employees in 25 years, then we stabilised ourselves, then we went down to 450 employees due to people who have retired and also by following the decrease in market share, despite all our efforts at diversification. So there it is. Just a statement of fact. The market will continue to migrate towards Asia and it is essential for us to invent a new organisation. I'm convinced that only those who come back to the principle of trust will survive."

We can see in Jean-François' attitude his ability to consider, consciously, the facts of the balance within the system he and FAVI operate within. There are interconnections, there are knock-on effects, and these are part of the realities of life. Rather than narrowing his perspective down to a sliver, driven by the unconscious narrative that 'FAVI must grow', Jean-François shows the ability to keep his perspective wide and to consider the interplay and ebb-and-flow of life in front of him. He deals directly with these facts rather than moulding them around the assumption that volume growth is an inevitable destination.

Similarly to Zobrist, Sudhakar Ram has this to say about business growth: "Growth comes from a sense of abundance that there are enough opportunities and that there is enough choice. At Mastek, we have an inner knowing that we will always create something and that there will be enough work for us. Therefore, we don't worry about getting to a particular level, or winning against specific competition – those are in some ways secondary notions. Primary considerations for us are: are we doing things which are valuable to the customer; are we doing things which help us to learn and grow; and are we doing things which create long-term value for the company? Growth is a natural outcome of this. If growth happens, it happens; if it doesn't happen, it doesn't happen, so there's no point in worrying about that. This is the kind of environment we aim to create."

While businesses clearly need to be viable in order to sustain themselves, what Sudhakar is pointing to here are the benefits of taking a broad and balanced perspective on growth, that means growth occurs as a result of the wellbeing of the system, rather than in spite of it. As these conscious leaders exemplify, it is not sustainable to put growth ahead of the survival of the system that supports it. We cannot destroy our host, the planet, in the interests of doing successful business.

It is not sustainable to put growth ahead of the survival of the system that supports it

This is also not to suggest that growth is not important to conscious companies. The business environment is far too dynamic and businesses are in far too much of a state of constant flux and creative tension for them to rest on their laurels and be complacent. The point is rather that value growth comes in many forms which need not be solely focussed on revenue and size. These might be quality, learning, customer happiness or any other forms of growth that avoid stagnation.

> *"These days, I'm focussed on the concept of good growth. I constantly ask myself and my employees, 'how do we grow in ways that are sustainable, and ways we can be proud of?'"*
>
> Eileen Fisher

The irony of approaching value growth in this way is that it can also be good for volume growth. There are numerous examples in which we can see that companies that aim for the wellbeing of the system and the fulfilment of their purpose in the world show huge growth rates, sometimes far in excess of those companies that aim for profit alone.

Some of the work illustrating this trend has been done by Raj Sisodia, Professor of Global Business at Babson College who, in his book, *Firms of Endearment*, shows how conscious and purpose-led companies outperformed their more profit-only orientated peers on returns by 10 to 14 times. In many ways, this makes perfect sense. Although it seems a paradox that not focussing on profit can, in fact, lead to more of it, as thinkers like Laloux[1] and others point out, this kind of attitude unleashes tremendous energies which, when a noble purpose meets a deep hunger in the world, leads to fantastic stories of growth.

> *"As long as we're doing the work we're doing and doing it well, we will grow organically. We're not only doing the work for growth's sake. If we're making an impact, and it's a sustainable business where people are thriving, that is the most important thing to us."*
>
> Laura Roberts

Choosing to grow in this way takes some not insignificant courage from conscious leaders. There are still shareholders to satisfy who need a return on their investment at some point, and who often demand this sooner rather than later. What seems to help with these decisions around growth is to consider how it can happen in line with the company's purpose and principles.

In the case of Frederic Desbrosses, it is all about qualitative growth in line with the company's founding principles. He asks: "Are we aligned with our principles when we say we want to grow by 10% or should we be happy to grow by 4% because we are doing better work, because we are investing in our people and our capabilities, in food quality and food safety? The question is: what do you want as a profit? The Mars family's dream is not to win in five years; their dream is to be there in 50 years, so their growth reflects that and they want to be proud of what the next generation will do."

What an enormously different attitude from the one that dictates we should focus on measuring quarterly results. The ability to look long-term characterises these conscious companies and their leaders. They are in the game not to win over others as quickly as possible, but for everyone to win, even where this takes longer. In fact, the way the game is played over the long term is often the joy of what it is all about, alongside a desire to create greater benefit for all as a result of doing business in the first place.

It therefore seems important to be in touch with the purpose of the organisation and its founding principles to have a reference point against which to make decisions about growth. Sometimes these are not just the principles settled upon by the founders of the company, but reflect the very system in which the business sits.

Dominic Sewela picks up this theme: "Because we operate in a space – in Southern Africa – where there are a lot of endemic chal-lenges such as corruption, when you feed growth you've got to establish certain principles or it will be detrimental not just to the organisation but beyond it as well. In a company like ours, which has a high code of ethics, there has got to be a balance between growth and what we stand for as an organisation. We are willing to walk away from the idea of growth if that doesn't align with our principles. And we are willing to wait things out, even if this means we stay flat for two years, because we see that there is a greater good that can come from that. While growth is very important, a conscious attitude towards growth is what is sustainable."

It is clear to see that conscious leaders hold this line in relation to their organisations' growth.

ATTITUDES TO PERSONAL GROWTH

Apart from their attitudes towards organisational growth, what conscious leaders also agree on is the need to avoid personal stagnation by focussing on their personal growth and continued evolution.

Conscious leaders are committed to their personal growth and development, and they recognise they need to be an active participant in their own evolutionary process. Because we are fortunate enough to be able to reflect consciously on our own awareness, we are able to take part consciously in our own evolution. No other species, as far as we know, has this amazing ability.

Conscious leaders recognise they need to be an active participant in their own evolutionary process

---

Much of this book covers edges for personal growth, whether this is to continue developing our levels of self-awareness, examine our purposes, look more deeply into the ways we relate to others, critically appraise how much we need to be in control versus how much we're willing to let go, how we bring people together to leverage collective intelligence for innovation and the health of the system, and evaluate how skilfully we can read these systems, amongst many other facets of conscious leadership.

"Conscious leaders are not static, because human beings are not static," says Mackey.[2] He reminds us that we are dynamic and evolving towards higher levels of consciousness and complexity. In Mackey's view, we have an ethical imperative to grow and evolve.

That said, personal evolution takes courage. Staying in our comfort zones is easier because it simply takes less effort to repeat the well-worn grooves of our own habits, patterns and processes. In the short term, we might get some modicum of comfort that we know what we're doing and the security that goes along with this. In the long term, we begin to wonder why the same circumstances happen to us again and again, almost as if life is forcing us to sit up and take notice of some aspect of ourselves.

Ultimately, there are two possibilities for a human life: to strive to move beyond where you currently are or to continue doing what you've always done. We are all gifted with this choice. As Richard Barrett points out, "The only choice we have is between conscious evolution and unconscious evolution. Unconscious evolution is the default choice. It is going to happen whether you sign up for personal evolution or not ... Signing up for conscious personal evolution makes the process so much easier and successful ... if enough people sign up for their own personal evolution, we have the possibility of accelerating the evolution of consciousness of humanity."[3]

The choice we have as leaders is how conscious we want to become, and we get to choose the stretch that will break us out of our existing moulds. We have the choice to develop aspects of ourselves, our teams and our businesses. Conscious leaders step into unknown domains and expand into new spaces; they discover new possibilities and they integrate aspects of themselves and the system that have previously been regarded as separate. It's a more conscious, intelligent way of living and leading.

Conscious leaders equally inspire others to do the same. They might consciously encourage others to step outside their comfort zones or simply be an example that others look up to to follow.

> *"Leaders who make personal and professional growth*
> *a priority not only build remarkable businesses,*
> *but lead remarkable lives."*
>
> Tony Hsieh

All this is in the service of conscious evolution, in which there is no standing still, no stagnation. In a healthy system, there is always renewal and the free flow and right circulation of energy. The decision for leaders interested in the journey of the conscious leader is which renewal edges they will choose.

Endnotes

1   Laloux, Frederic. 2014. *Reinventing Organizations: A Guide to Creating Organizations Inspired by the Next Stage in Human Consciousness.* Belgium: Nelson Parker.

2   Mackey, Johnn and Sisodia, Raj. 2014. *Conscious Capitalism: Liberating the Heroic Spirit of Business. USA: Harvard School Publishing Corporation,* Chapter 14.

3   Barrett, Richard. 2011. *The New Leadership Paradigm.* p318 (Available via Amazon Books, Marston Gate.)

ZONE 4:
COLLECTIVE RESPONSIBILITY

20

RESPONSIBILITY
TO THE WHOLE

The fourth cornerstone of conscious leadership is the sense of responsibility these leaders feel towards the greater whole of which we are all part. It takes our ability to think in systems one step further. Once we have become conscious of ourselves as something other than a bundle of thoughts, feelings and conditioned habits, and developed our degree of choice over this; once we are engaged in relating to others in more conscious ways; and once we have developed our capacity to think in systems, the fourth quality that distinguishes conscious leaders from other leaders is an inner urge to act with an unwavering sense of responsibility towards the world, and life, at large. In this respect, conscious leaders are stewards of the whole.

John Renesch points out in his book, *The Great Growing Up*, that this recognition requires a new level of maturity, of being accountable for our choices, individually and collectively. In John's words, "It is time to grow up".[1]

WHOLENESS

The principle of wholeness is equally one of three characteristics identified by Laloux in his study of organisations that are at the leading edge of how we think about business and work. Indeed, these organisations are at the leading edge of our own evolution. This desire for wholeness seems to be a direct effect of disidentifying from our ego, says Laloux, and "one more step of liberation on the human journey."[2]

"With this stage", he continues, "comes a deep yearning for wholeness – bringing together the ego and the deeper parts of the self; integrating mind, body, and soul," an incorporation of both the masculine and feminine, and an awareness of our deeper connection to life and nature. Often this shift comes with, "a profound sense that at some level, we are all connected and part of one big whole." While we may have had many successive steps in becoming "independent and true to ourselves, it dawns on us that, paradoxically, we are profoundly part of everything." [3]

This yearning for wholeness has emerged in various ways for all the conscious leaders interviewed for this book. They have transcended the traditional business mindset which has been telling us that it is possible to separate business from its connection to society and life. They have moved past the idea that we can somehow break organisations up into rational boxes which we control through logical org charts, flow diagrams and processes. Conscious leaders are much more likely to see the integral multiple connections between their organisation and life itself. For these leaders, there is no 'in here' and 'out there'. They see in wholes, in patterns, in systems, and they think more in terms of natural balance and stewardship than machinery and control.

There is no 'in here' and 'out there'

"How do we do business in a way that people are whole?" asks Sally Ann Ranney. "How do we conduct business so that wherever the resources come from are left whole? We can create a different narrative around business. What is profit? How do we create a triple bottom line that incorporates equality? Growth, growth and more growth is unsustainable. How do we move quickly into a different economic structure that is sustainable?"

> *"There are no such things on this planet as side effects."*
>
> Raj Sisodia

CHANGING PURPOSE

Conscious leaders no longer buy-in to the social construct that business is about profit alone and that this is all that matters. As we've seen, they are creating a different narrative around business and its role in society and in life.

We've seen that the shift in the way business is perceived as having a role in society and for the planet, can have a profound effect on the purpose of a company. Lorna Davis, whose role is to bring Danone's sustainable business manifesto to fruition by 2020, has this to say about Danone's changing purpose: "Right now we have this manifesto: a statement of what we believe in and what our convictions are. We are moving from a company that sells bottles and jars of food and beverages to a company that influences the way people eat and drink. And we believe that food is not just about nutrition; it's a complete system and it is a socio-cultural experience. It needs to be seen in context. We are defining and refining what we mean by that."

Lorna's description of Danone's aspirations shows just how far these companies have travelled from the traditional production-and-profit model as they begin to take into account their collective responsibility towards the greater whole in which we all operate.

Danone is the first big corporate to apply for 'B-Corp' status in support of business being a force for good – a move that reflects how it sees its role in society and its wider planetary impact. B-Corp (or benefit corporation) provides a legal framework and certification for companies wishing to benefit society as well as their shareholders.

"What I imagine in ten years' time is that the metrics of big corporates won't just be P&L," continues Lorna. "I think that having B-Corp status is ultimately the way things will end up, a double set of KPIs: P&L and another set of metrics that are not destructible by takeover."

"My catalyst is the inability to ignore something that I can affect."
Ibrahim AlHusseini, FullCycle Energy Fund

With these kinds of structural changes afoot, we are fast seeing how an organisation's responsibility towards the planet and everything on it is being built into its internal architecture, a far cry from having a single department taking care of corporate social responsibility.

In many cases, a conscious leader's personal purpose is reflected in the organisation's purpose. This is not the easiest thing to do within a company already in existence; it is much easier to do when starting a new enterprise, as we saw in the case of Neal Gandhi.

Another example of a conscious leader forging links between personal purpose and company purpose is Ibrahim AlHusseini, a venture capitalist, entrepreneur, philanthropist and Founder and Managing Partner of the FullCycle Energy Fund, which funds companies with the goal of turning municipal waste into clean energy. AlHusseini sees his responsibility as an impact investor as, "creating the future we want to live into". He invests in ways that solve the problems of an undesirable future. "My catalyst is the inability to ignore something that I can affect," he says. This sums up perfectly the deeply felt sense of responsibility that causes conscious leaders to act.

Reassigning a company's purpose to be more responsible to the world at large is a complex challenge, but one which a leader like Paul Polman, CEO of Unilever, is renowned for taking on. Polman has an unshakeable conviction in the importance of businesses today taking a sustainable approach. "Business can be the biggest contributor to ending poverty or it can be one of the biggest causes of the challenges we are facing," says Polman. "There is no business case for enduring poverty. We need a new way: open, inclusive and sustainable. That's the business model of the future." [4]

BIO-EMPATHY AND SYSTEMS

For leaders such as Polman, there is no dividing line between a company and the life that surrounds it, and systems come naturally into their field of vision and influence all their decisions in business. This is defined by some, for example Bob Johansen, as 'bio-empathy': the ability to see things from nature's point of view. [5] Respect for nature is a basic requirement of bio-empathy, along with an essential long-term view of what is needed for life to go on for generations beyond the present. It prompts leaders to consider timelines of generations hence (seven generations in the case of John Replogle or a thousand years in the example of Tom Chi), which means that these leaders act in ways that take responsibility for the effects they create and make decisions that will have a positive impact on the long-term wellbeing of humanity in the future. A thousand years to influence a business decision of today is a remarkable example of just how far ahead a conscious leader can look in his or her decision-making process and how much responsibility he or she can take.

I asked Sally Ann Ranney, who as we've seen thinks naturally in terms of whole systems, how she came to have such a highly developed degree of bio-empathy. "I got into this whole business through being a cattle rancher," said Sally. "What gave me the whole systems picture was living on a ranch and seeing how everything is connected to everything. My former father-in-law was a remarkable man who had three timeless rules about the interconnectedness of life:

» Always leave half of your grass; you don't know what the next year is going to bring.

» Always be willing to share your water with your neighbour; you never know when you may need to ask them to share their water with you.

» Do not shoot predators unless it is absolutely the last resort. They were here first; put them into your bottom line."

These lessons on the interconnectedness of life emerged later in her work on conservation and biodiversity, where she began to feel a deep sense of responsibility towards upholding and protecting the genetic archives that are encoded in biodiversity. She realised, for example, that in nature if you protect indicator species – grizzly bears, wolverines and wolves – then you protect everything else.

What might be the 'indicator species' for business that ensures the health of the business system and thereby the planet? Is it responsibly-made profit? Is it us considering the broader impact of our actions? How can we ensure that if we look after certain core indicators of business, we can assure ourselves that business will contribute a sum positive effect on life for all of us?

"If this is the way nature works, and we are part of nature, you have to ask how do we fit in within business?" says Sally. "We are not separate from nature; we are part of it. If we're going to keep the fabric of life intact, then whole systems responsibility applies to business and to our personal choices, too. One of the things that conscious leaders look at is what happens to the whole system given what I choose, given what my company does. This is an invitation to be mindful, to be very present, to be eternally curious, to ask deep, deep questions not just about how we are going to make money, but to look at the whole cycle of cause and effect. Every business needs to consider its role in this."

CONSCIOUS RESPONSIBILITY IN THE REAL WORLD

The way that Sally Ann Ranney and other conscious leaders exercise their choice to act responsibly in the world is best illustrated through the examples of their lives and their businesses, which demonstrate their thinking in action. We have seen glimpses of this throughout this book, but four examples are brought together here to demonstrate just how far conscious leaders can go to demonstrate their sense of responsibility towards the whole through the way they do business.

Tom Chi – The Democratisation of Genius

Tom Chi is a genius who equally doesn't take this aspect of himself seriously at all. He's far more concerned with how the practical actions he and his teams take can have a long-term beneficial impact on the world. At age 15, he was an astrophysical researcher, and in his career has been Head of Product Experience for Google X, part of the creation team for Microsoft Office, and the initiator and project visionary for a multitude of products and tools for advancement in the world.

Tom thinks big: "I started out wanting to understand the whole universe," he says.[6] Then a near-death experience, which left him one minute away from death, caused him to re-evaluate everything. "When I woke up in the morning, I realised two things: that I was only alive due to the generosity of eight people that I will never be able to meet nor thank, and that, due to the extent of my blood transfusions, I was more other people than I was myself."

This caused him to rethink a lot of his life: what it means to be a leader, what it means to create things, what it means to serve at all. "If you can afford a self-driving car (one of his projects at Google X)," he concluded, "you can afford a car, and if you can afford a car you're doing all right in the grand scheme of things. Who, however, is going to do anything for the two billion people living on less than two dollars a day? I don't see anyone jumping out of their seats for that job."

He is referring to the shifting distribution of global wealth as a disturbing trend: the way that the richest 66 people in the world now have as much wealth as the poorest 3.5 billion people, half the world's population. "If it's not enough that there is this disparity, the acceleration of the disparity is the thing that is the most problematic. This is a very unstable trajectory," Tom says.

His experiences got Tom into teaching and, in particular, into the business of how to solve real-world problems incredibly quickly and pragmatically, and innovate at speed so that humanity and the planet can be served. "We have to bring the best tools in the world to the people who are solving the most important problems in the world," he says. "If we keep thinking in the same way, we'll end up creating the same problems."

Tom realised that the problem is not 'out there', but rather 'in here'. He saw that the many gaps and problems in the outside world are a result of the gaps on the inside, in our minds. As an engineer, he felt a responsibility to figure out how to solve this. Through working with very practical, 'what works in reality' approaches, he has pulled together what he calls the 'psychological antecedents to global prosperity'. These have to do with setting up the right mental conditions so that we might think together, innovate collectively and prototype quickly to come up with solutions to global problems that accelerates prosperity for everyone in the world. In effect, Tom is concerned with 'democratising genius'. He has identified simple, user-friendly ways to dissolve what limits our mindsets and our actions. We've seen some of these described in this book, for example, 'knowing is the enemy of learning' or 'metabolizability is more important than truth'. Tom calls these 'mental debugs', because thinking differently, beyond our mental habits and conditioning, enables us to collectively take leaps forward for the benefit of all of us into the future.

Like many conscious leaders, Tom employs context to influence and shape the work he and his teams do. One context we've seen, for example, is how he uses the construct of time. "In my life, I have two timeframes: right now – plus or minus two weeks – and a thousand years. In this way, I do the things that are practical right now, but I do them in the context that if everybody were to do this for a thousand years, the world would end up a much better place."

The extent of Tom's mental reach shows the breadth of perspective that a conscious leader can take. Staying conscious of how our actions in the current day are linked to the effects many years down the line makes us ultimately responsible for what we are creating in the present moment. "When you think on a scale of a thousand years, then you are thinking about major shifts in civilisation," says Tom.

"Right now companies are the primary interface between humanity and nature. I want to reconstruct business in such a way that humanity becomes a net positive to nature."

Tom Chi

What Tom is aiming to do, at the point of highest leverage, is to create shifts in our levels of consciousness, because this is what is needed to make life sustainable for all of us. In terms of one area of application – business – he is experimenting with rapidly forming and reforming companies with different formats to see which formats lead to better, more constructive behaviour in the company and in the relationship between the company and society. (See Chapter 8 for a more detailed description).

"The work I'm doing is about trying to change the fundamental nature of companies," he says, "because right now companies are the primary interface between humanity and nature. I want to reconstruct business in such a way that humanity becomes a net positive to nature. Only in that world would the addition of hundreds of thousands of years make the Earth richer."

As I've alluded to at various points in this book, talking to someone like Tom Chi makes one realise just how vast a perspective we can take. For Tom to see the connections between business, people, global prosperity and nature, and to be experimenting with different forms of business to find the right combinations that are a game-changer for humanity's future, shows how responsibility to the greater whole can play out in these kinds of conscious leaders through innovation.

Laura Roberts – a Conscious Chemical Company

When we think of some of the more unsavoury corporations that have negative effects on the world, then chemical production probably is there alongside the destruction of rainforests and rampant industrialisation. One CEO who is determined to change this is Laura Roberts. "Our bigger purpose isn't one we necessarily say to the world, but it is one we speak to internally. We really want to fundamentally transform the chemical industry. Right now, we are living in one huge Petri dish of chemicals and we have no idea how they're all interacting, but they're all ending up back in our bodies and certainly all throughout the ecosystem. It's just not sustainable and we can do better."

Laura has used her energy over the years to move away from being angry with the way things are to being focussed on what Pantheon can make happen in the world. In doing so, she thinks very much in systems that involve all the sets of interconnected stakeholders. Some of the stakeholders are the initial investors, who in the early days would ask the standard questions about what Pantheon was doing about its competitors. At the time, says Laura, she would list her competition. Today, however, she sees the irony that the people who she listed as competitors over a decade ago are now Pantheon's partners. Her leadership of the company is very much more geared towards being collaborative within the wider system and taking a long-term view with all stakeholders, including Pantheon's competitors.

For Laura, her responsibility towards the greater whole is about transformation of the entire chemical industry and even of the education system – how we educate our business leaders and our scientists of the future. She believes that sustainability needs to be a discipline throughout all education sectors, so that the next generation of people going into the world of commerce have the lens that whatever we make to put out into the world, we need to be thinking about where it ends up and what it does in the long term.

> *"In essence, we are wanting to see chemistry using*
> *nature as a design template and then designing*
> *with end of life in mind so that chemicals,*
> *when they've done their job, break apart."*
> Laura Roberts

In raising Pantheon's profile within the chemical industry, Laura is playing not only a long game but also a highly inclusive one. "Our strategy is to first get our name out there in the world through some big transformational accomplishments that we've done and be the 'thought leaders' who raise public awareness so that people start to demand better chemistry. We endeavour to partner up with chemical companies to be part of the solution with them, perhaps by being an innovation wing for them or to have them take our products to market because they have the distribution infrastructure and the brand. We are aiming towards the industry at large being forced, at some point, by critical mass demand to change the way chemicals are designed, how they are made and where they end up. In essence, we want to see chemistry using nature as a design template and then designing with end of life in mind so that chemicals, when they've done their job, break apart."

Laura's sense of collective responsibility to the whole comes from something she cares about deeply. In her leadership of Pantheon, she is able to combine personal passion and vision to make a difference with the company's purpose in the world. In so doing, through her business she is taking responsibility for the impact of her industry on the whole of humanity and the planet.

Lorna Davis – Transforming the Purpose of the Business

"Having a social responsibility has been a long-term distinguishing characteristic of Danone," says Lorna Davis. The company was founded in the late 1960s, and in 1972, in the aftermath of the French riots of 1968, the company founder made a famous speech in which he talked about it not being good enough for business just to make profit. It also needed to fulfil a greater good. 'Our responsibility doesn't end at the factory gate,' was the strapline, with a recognition that it needed to be a 'double project' that kept business and social impact in mind.

"In those days," says Lorna, "it was seen as a social mission: trade unions and workers. But that backbone has been in the company since the beginning. People used to talk about it all the time and they still do."

In 1997 the founder's son took over with a vision to shift the purpose of the company much more towards wide-scale health. The purpose of Danone became: 'To bring health through food to as many people as possible.' "He began," says Lorna, "by systematically cleaning up the portfolio. We used to sell beer and champagne and mayonnaise and we had a biscuit division. We sold all of those businesses and made a big acquisition – Numico, a baby division – and acquired a medical nutrition division." The purpose-driven element of the company has therefore been around a long time and has now become fine-tuned towards health.

The new CEO, Emmanuel Faber, who took on his role in 2014, is determined to take this development to the next level. With a long history in the company of seeking to differentiate itself on the basis of a purpose that got more and more refined over time, the new CEO is currently saying, "I think the issues of the world right now are so big that we can't avoid it. I think Danone is a place where, morally, this is what we as business should be doing." This growth of the company's purpose in the world has developed to the point where, in December 2015, Danone signed a partnership agreement with the B Corp movement by joining their advisory council, thereby pledging to help more people use business as a force for good.[7] This demonstrates how seriously the current CEO takes his particular stand on socially responsible business and the impact of Danone on the world at large.

As Danone has ventured further into the world of social and planetary responsibility, it has prompted them to launch a series of experiments to see how this plays out in reality. Their social business initially grew out of a conversation with Muhammed Yunis, the Bangladeshi social entrepreneur, banker and economist, who was awarded the Nobel Peace Prize for founding Grameen Bank and pioneering microfinance and microcredit.

The conversation with Yunis led to considering how Danone might make a difference in Bangladesh. They now have a business called Grameen Danone which microfinances the purchase of cows for Bangladeshis. Danone collects the milk and then, in a purpose-built factory, turns the milk into yoghurt, which is fortified for the local population and sold back to them, using as employees women who have no other means of financial self-support. Many Bangladeshi women are left alone without income when their husbands go to work in Dubai and don't return. Including these women in the business cycle contributes to the raising up of communities, health and prosperity in Bangladesh.

Danone's other social business investments, which take the form of investing in ten companies with social purposes, include a waste-picking project in Brazil, where the company supports waste-pickers to organise themselves and ensures they get a fair wage for what they do. Danone takes the bottles that the waste-pickers find and recycles them into the company's water business. In Senegal, the company's ecosystem fund supports a vet who is working to make a difference to the lives of herders, whose cows supply milk that is processed in the city. "We have a whole lot of initiatives that have been going on around our business," says Lorna, "but now we think it's time to put these two things together: purpose and profit."

Danone's shareholders have voted that their only conditions surrounding the ecosystem fund is that it is driven by local businesses, that the initiatives the fund support need to partner with an NGO and that they needed to be sustainable in five years.

In reality, what has happened with these initiatives is that they have driven a larger number of significant benefits for the company as their social contribution has taken hold:

1   The initiatives have allowed people in Danone who are interested in social enterprise to participate in them, and have attracted to the business talented people whom they might otherwise not have attracted.

2   Danone has learned a lot from a business model point of view as to what is sustainable and what is not. For example, their herder project in Senegal is actually going to make a profit for the first time in seven years. The Bangladeshi project has yet to make a profit after 10 years. Lorna believes these different results are partly because the company is trying to do too many of these things at the same time. Equally, these experiences have created a lot of learning for Danone about how to make a sustainable business.

3   Critically, it's taught them a new skill set around
    collaboration, which is the go-to requirement of the new
    world. Lorna gave an example of a partnership forged
    between a local company General Manager and a
    pro-breastfeeding activist in Romania, who had given
    up her house to support breastfeeding within the
    Romanian culture. There was an unlikely match in
    temperaments between the two, but they now have a
    new-found respect for each other, having learned to
    collaborate and understand the world from each other's
    perspectives. "It was amazing to me to see how much
    they had learned from one another," says Lorna. "When
    I spoke to the GM, he had never realised there were
    people like this in the world. Her view was that three
    years ago she would have taken the money rather than
    the partnership, but is now really happy to partner with
    the GM and with Danone."

Lorna is quick to acknowledge that transforming into a socially
responsible company is easier in smaller enterprises; a lot harder
in big companies. "It's a tougher call, because you have to get so
many more people turned around." Her strategy is bottom-up: the
company's manifesto was launched globally via a webcast in July
2015 and was followed by a social media platform for people to
comment and get involved.

"We got support from the bottom, from 2,500 people who are
inspired and demonstrating that they are up for it because this is
consistent with their values. What I'm doing with the more senior
people is to identify and amplify where things are going well. I find
examples of where we are doing things that are completely consistent with this approach to demonstrate what is working. I have found
a number of great early examples of new shoots in the right direction. Where we are getting good results, we tell everyone what a

great job these people are doing, which helps the company continue to do those initiatives. It also helps to grow similar initiatives elsewhere. Basically, my job is to go around the company blowing on the coals and tending to the fires."

What Lorna's example shows is how an entire company can become more conscious and intentional about its part in the greater whole. It can shape its business around this and, with the right people to help lead it, can refine its purpose and make this part of the mainstream business.

Dominic Sewela – Upholding the Role of Business in Society

Barloworld is, through its rich history and involvement in the politics of South Africa, woven into the fabric of that society. This is something of which Dominic Sewela is acutely aware. He leads his business with this connection to the surrounding society firmly in mind and stays conscious of the ripple effects his decisions and the company's actions make in the world around it.

In many countries, businesses can stand alone, making social conscience a luxury or a 'nice-to-have'. Conscious leaders in India tend to have a heartfelt sense of connectedness to the whole of which they're part, perhaps as a reflection of their spiritual traditions. In the case of Barloworld, its context is South Africa and the wider African continent, and the social fabric is difficult to ignore. Companies operating in Africa could easily go in and plunder resources, but Barloworld is standing for something different in a continent that is dealing with problems such a HIV and AIDS. These challenges help to form its objectives and are integrated into what the company is looking to do in business.

Dominic picks up the story. A company established some 112 years ago by an English immigrant entrepreneur, Barloworld eventually became a Fortune 500 company which at its peak employed

250,000 people in South Africa and touched every corner of South African society. Barloworld played a significant role interfacing with the historic National Party government, the architects of apartheid. The company took up positions that could actually have endangered its own survival, by promoting affirmative action – the appointment of employees to reflect the cultural ratios in the population – a move that was very unwelcome at the time. In so doing, the company embarked on various programmes to change the fabric of South Africa during the apartheid era.

"Some of the executives were men of significance who participated heavily in the Peace Accord, even while they were running the organisation," recalls Dominic. "With this kind of history and pedigree, we have a higher expectation from Barloworld about the way in which we impact society and the role that we play within it. I have an institutional memory that tells me about my predecessors, and I see the role of this company being to properly impact all its key stakeholders in a meaningful, sustainable way. I've got a legacy of 112 years to live up to and I want to make sure that I create a foundation which, when I pass on the baton to the next generation of new leaders, they are able to continue with this work."

For Dominic, conducting his business is clearly about more than just profit. This doesn't mean that they don't have rigorous monitoring of operations, but it does mean that when decisions are made – for example to make people's roles redundant – then the wider implications are naturally considered. As a leader, Dominic mirrors other conscious leaders who recognise that there are cycles of business and the company doesn't usually make redundancies, but rather offers them the opportunity to move temporarily elsewhere in the company where there may be a higher demand at that time. "Had we made people redundant at the time of our financial and operational pressures," says Dominic, "then we're simply creating a different kind of crisis, because these people have got kids, and the kids are going to school. They have families and there are all sorts of issues around health challenges."

Considerations for a leader like Dominic extend not only to the impact of his decisions on society, but also to the unique characteristics of that society itself. Barloworld operates in Angola, the Democratic Republic of Congo and Mozambique. "I know the challenges that war has created there," says Dominic, "so when our company enters those societies, we also take a more active than usual role by asking: *How do we impact the community there so that we make a complete social investment?*"

This question leads the company to take stands on, for example, health, which is a fundamental consideration in these countries. Dominic explains: "Health may not be fundamental to other people, but where we operate, we have got to address these challenges. Alongside this, we take a ten-year view rather than a short-term view, because we understand that in the long term, if you don't do certain things, you'll not be sustainable."

These four examples show some of the ways in which conscious leaders, through their companies, can take collective responsibility for the greater whole of which they and their organisations are part. Taking responsibility in this way lives through the company, and these leaders help to usher in this new way of relating business to society and the planet. As we've seen above, they do this through innovation, through taking responsibility for the effects of their industry on the planet and stakeholders, by growing socially responsible initiatives as part of their company purpose, and by taking responsibility for a positive effect on society at large. These are just four of the many ways that conscious leaders live out this quality in their lives and in their leadership. There are as many ways to do this as there are leaders. The differentiator is that these leaders feel that part of who they are is the pull towards acting for the benefit of the greater whole.

IMPACTING THE WORLD
AS INDIVIDUALS

We'll conclude this section with how conscious leaders can impact the world in their individual capacities. While they can make a contribution through their organisations, reflected externally in the way their business is conducted in broader society and on the planet, these leaders can also contribute and take responsibility through the ways they encourage their employees to grow and evolve.

The difference between being a leader invested in the learning and development of your people, and being a conscious leader, is that as a conscious leader you see it as part of your role to catalyse the growth and development of consciousness of those within your organisation. This doesn't mean you get to control it. As we saw in chapters 12 and 16, a number of the leaders interviewed for this book have realised that they can create the right conditions, but they cannot demand or even expect anyone to evolve. This is an individual freedom we all have.

Other conscious leaders, such as Mackey, believe that the leader's role in this capacity is to make a positive difference, to enable people to derive meaning from their work, help them to grow and evolve as individuals and leaders in their own right, and enable them to make tough moral choices with clarity and consistency. Mackey is consistent with all conscious leaders in the way he embodies transpersonal values, those that connect us to each other, which can lead to people being inspired to develop higher levels of awareness in themselves. Talking to some employees of Whole Foods Market, one of the distinctive qualities they mentioned to me was the way the organisation provided encouragement to them to grow and evolve.

Since conscious leaders are not attached to making this kind of growth and evolution happen in their organisation, they tend to provide the space and opportunities for growth to occur but stop short of forcing the issue. GD, who advises businesses, says that a conscious leader's sense of responsibility is first and foremost to himself, so that he is being the best he can be. He continues: "We must always remember that we are doing this for our own evolution. No matter how big we become, we always maintain the position of an open-hearted student. If you get too entangled in trying to change the world, there is a danger of forgetting yourself. So make sure you stay in touch with your own evolution, allowing your organisation also to be a training ground for that. As you evolve, everything around you evolves too."

Sometimes conscious leaders play a very active role in the growth and evolution of those in their companies by providing tangible opportunities for this to occur. Leaders like Dominic Sewela believe that amongst the various stakeholders of the business, employees are crucially important because he is only able to achieve what he does through these employees. He raises the awareness of his employees by getting them to think through and clarify their significance in the world. He employs coaches throughout his organisation and instructs them to coach for performance as well as for significance. "You want people to achieve so they feel they have succeeded, and then once they have succeeded, they can move on and get on to the journey of becoming significant," he says.

Dominic recognises that the roles that people play in the organisation are only part of the roles they play throughout society. Impacting employees at work creates effects, good or bad, out into wider society through their family and communities. "The people we employ are a microcosm of society. It's important that they realise the roles they have to play and consciously think beyond just their immediate work. That's how you get to impact society – it begins at a micro level in the community that you live in."

By helping people to grow not only in their performance and awareness, but also in their significance in their lives and the impact they make, leaders such as Dominic Sewela create a kind of ripple effect out into the system, from employees out into the world, through all the different dimensions of their lives. This quality of conscious leaders is about not just seeing in systems, but thinking about what you can do to create impactful positive effects in the system all around you, using your organisation as a vehicle to do so.

The only thing we can try to do is help other people by having a positive impact on them

We end this chapter with a comment by Prabhmeet Singh, a wisely conscious Millennial who is featured in the next chapter. Prabhmeet was a financial analyst who is now a management consultant engaged in projects that have a greater impact on society as a whole. He has this to say on the subject of creating positive ripple effects: "This universe we're living in doesn't care whether we're alive or dead, because we're part of it. From a divine perspective, from a spiritual perspective, all is connected and there is no difference between you and I. The universe doesn't really care about little things that we think are significant to us. There is no 'my house' versus 'how much money you have in your bank account'. Nobody cares. At the end of the day, it's more about realising how we might have an impact on our one being. The reason why we want growth, the reason why we want promotion, why we want more money, usually all comes down to ego, to looking better than others. The only thing we can try to do is help other people by having a positive impact on them. Nothing else is actually worth it, everything else we're going to leave behind."

This chapter concludes the tour we've taken of the qualities of conscious leaders in the four zones of our conscious leadership model: Self-mastery; Conscious Relating; Systems Insight; and Collective Responsibility.

Through exploring the examples of these leaders' lives, their behaviours and their approaches to leading their organisations, you'll have hopefully gathered some inspiring ideas for how you might further develop the qualities of conscious leadership in yourself.

We'll conclude this book with two final chapters: a look into what it takes to lead conscious Millennials as the new generation of employees coming through our organisations and, finally, we'll hear some advice from the conscious leaders featured in this book on developing as a conscious leader.

Endnotes

1   Renesch, John. 2011. *The Great Growing Up: Being Responsible for Humanity's Future*. Arizona: Hohm Press, p15.

2   Laloux, Frederic. 2014. *Reinventing Organizations: A Guide to Creating Organizations Inspired by the Next Stage in Human Consciousness*. Belgium: Nelson Parker.

3   Ibid., p48.

4   https://brightfuture.unilever.co.uk/stories/473110/GLOBAL-CITIZEN-FESTIVAL-THE-STAR-STUDDED-CONCERT-THAT-INSPIRED-MILLIONS-TO-TAKE-ACTION-.aspx

5   Johansen, Bob. 2012. *Leaders Make The Future: Ten New Leadership Skills for an Uncertain World*. San Francisco. Berrett-Koehler Publishers, Inc., *a BK Business Book*, p95-98.

6   https://www.youtube.com/watch?v=25fUDjMtkuI

7   http://bcorporation.eu/blog/partnership-agreement-with-danone-opens-doors-multinationals-to-measure-what-matters

21

LEADING
CONSCIOUS
MILLENNIALS

W e all know the rumours about trying to lead Millennials. The digitally plugged generation born between 1980 and 2000 evoke cries of frustration, accusations of 'laziness' and runaway entitlement. They want responsibility and to advance too quickly without paying their dues, we hear. They dislike feedback. On some of the leadership programmes I run, managers of Millennials scratch their heads in consternation and ask each other, "How do I motivate these people?"

If you find yourself faced with these sorts of problems, the issue is not that you're stuck with the wrong kinds of people, it's probably that you're not asking the right kinds of questions.

THE CONTRIBUTIONS OF MILLENNIALS

In reality, conscious Millennials are a rich seam of gold for companies, an unending source of energy and contribution – if you know the right questions to ask and the right way to lead them. Managed in the right way, Millennials – and especially conscious Millennials, of whom there are many – are willing to give a great deal for the right cause. Companies and leaders who get this right get the pick of the talent in the market-place and an enormous source of innovation and development.

Laura Roberts is a firm believer in the power of Millennials coming through industry to revolutionise the way we do business. Like many conscious leaders, she sees her role as shepherding these future leaders who are more sustainably and responsibly minded. "The baby-boomers have been at the helm for so long in most segments: public, private and non-profit," says Laura, "and the Gen Xs are now moving into these leadership positions. If the Gen Xs do their job well, they will mentor Millennials in their careers and support them in rapidly changing the business conversation. Previous generations need to take care not to discredit Millennials with stereotypes, such as being entitled and demanding. Instead, they can tap into their rigorous search for meaning and their desire to use business as a force for good. Millennials to a large extent have had the opportunity to grow up in the higher layers of Maslow's hierarchy of needs, which allows them to ponder meaning much earlier in their lives. If we develop them with all this in mind, then they will be uniquely poised to create positive transformation on a large scale when they take the helm."

Conscious Millennials are a rich seam of gold for companies

We know that Millennials are a significant source of innovation and creativity. Lorna Davis told me how she often feels at home speaking to the Millennial generation in her company. "What I'm seeing is that the young people in Danone are completely inspired by the opportunity to innovate to make a difference, and are saying that this is the kind of company they want to work for. They are rapidly generating ideas and creating practical, financially sustainable solutions for more responsible business. At its simplest level, once you help people to wake up, they move in a direction that they weren't moving in before for the good of the business, because that's who they are; they're achievement orientated."

> *"Millenials in Spain were involved in a project where,*
> *in order to encourage kids to drink more water*
> *and less sugary drinks, we've got a programme*
> *to put the water in these fun little bottles*
> *shaped like the characters from Frozen.*
> *Kids say that's more fun than fizzy drinks.*
> *Small things, but they make the difference."*
>
> Lorna Davis

WHO ARE CONSCIOUS MILLENNIALS?

It's not the case that all Millennials are conscious Millennials. Conscious Millennials are natural systems thinkers who deeply grasp the connection between actions and consequences, not just locally to them but right across the globe. Millennials who see the power of business to transform the world are even more useful to companies. Conscious companies who can identify this kind of talent are able to exponentially leverage the contribution these young people can make. In contrast, Millennials who attract negative comments and uncharitable labels often suffer from a profound sense of being lost in a digitally powered world of overwhelming choice.

Jennifer Wilson, a Millennial who works with The Global Centre for Conscious Leadership (alongside a diverse portfolio career – one of the hallmarks of Millennials) explains it this way: "Millennials find it hard to focus because they are surrounded by so much choice. Many of these choices bring immediate gratification, yet no amount of gratification works if its disconnected from a sense of purpose. The feeling that accompanies this is underlying anxiety and a lack of fulfilment. It comes from being inherently disconnected from others, despite being ultra-connected through technology. Connection is so important to our generation, yet we can lose our way through an abundance of choice."

This can lead to the behaviour popular thinking often associates with Millennials: a seemingly unquenchable thirst for being validated by others through belonging and social media and of needing to be constantly reinforced (through, for example, the number of 'likes' on Facebook). "At an extreme," says Jen, "there are some in my generation who will expressly go to a place to have their photo taken, not for the purposes of going to that place and experiencing it, but to have a cool, coordinated photo taken of being there that will get them validated by their social group. It's a desperate way of living. We can be more concerned with eating the menu rather than the meal." Later in this chapter we'll explore what leaders can do to capture the attention of even these more distracted and restless Millennials.

Conscious Millennials are born with the human upgrade already in place

For the more consciously-minded Millennials, how does this new generation differ from its predecessors? First, it's worth saying that conscious Millennials don't see themselves as particularly different from their predecessors. Andrew Brady, a 20-something entrepreneur, development consultant, coach and leader in the Conscious Capitalism® Rochester Chapter, says: "I'm not entirely convinced that the Millennials are any different to the idealistic 20-somethings of generations past. They want to make a contribution in the world, they want to work in a different way. The difference is that through technology there are now more avenues open for us to make this happen. We don't have to get caught up to the same extent in the system that's quarterly-earnings driven. We can – and want – to take a more holistic perspective."

Jennifer Wilson agrees: "None of this is significant to my generation," she says. "We're not born with a special chromosome of consciousness or anything. It's just purely the context we're born into, the newest context there is. We're born into the forefront of what evolution has to offer. In 2016, this is about having more choice than ever before."

> "We're born into the forefront of what
> evolution has to offer. In 2016, this is about
> having more choice than ever before."
> Jennifer Wilson

I agree with Jennifer and Andrew, but only partly. I was astonished by the interviews with conscious Millennials I carried out for this book. In many ways, at an incredibly early age (in their early to mid-twenties), they instinctively know all sorts of things about life that people of my generation, in our forties, had to learn through repeatedly knocking our heads against the walls of life until we had no option but to wake up and become more aware.

Conscious Millennials are born with the human upgrade already in place. Conscious Millennials might not have a great deal of life experience yet, but they have a great deal of innate wisdom and, in conscious terms, they are awake. They understand that the world is an interconnected system where their actions have knock-on effects. They realise that they can create themselves in the way they want and that they can design their lifestyles to a much greater degree than previous generations realised. They somehow already know about the difference between operating from your ego and operating from your higher self; between being conscious and unconscious.

What, then, becomes possible when we add wisdom and life experience to the mix of this potential? In talking to these Millennials, I saw the possibilities of taking humanity to the next level of our evolution. And, as conscious leaders of today's companies realise, existing leaders have a responsibility to help nurture and develop this incredible potential that, more than any generation before it, is acutely conscious of how it is evolving, while it is evolving.

How do these innate 'human upgrades' play out? Two stories of conscious Millennials interviewed for this book illustrate to some extent the shift that happens at a very early age.

Bethany Hilton is fascinated by good business. A musician until the age of 16, she took the opportunity to work in an office, where she experienced first-hand how business is conducted when it isn't completely honest. Now 22, she has read over 100 business books, attends economics meetings and forums to understand how business works, and has benefited from a range of excellent mentors.

"I fell in love with the concept that business creates value," she says. "Business is service; showing up every day and trying to create something of value is my way of serving to the people around me and my community. I'm passionate about the engine of business itself, rather than any specific product: how good business is put together, how I bring value to the table and how you exchange your own creation of value with me for that, and together we partner to make that happen. I appreciate CEOs and founders and entrepreneurs who've had the courage to say, 'I'm going to start something' and, as a result of that, a lot of people have benefited."

The oldest of ten brothers and sisters, Bethany has always been aware of her role as an inspiration and as an example to others. "I think about the choices that I make in my life and how I create and design my life, and the effect that will have on others. You have to know yourself, to be aware, be conscious. You have to start by leading yourself. How I live my life is what my siblings are going to believe is possible for themselves."

This sense of responsibility extends to business as well. "To me, personal growth precedes business success. Through my personal growth, I want to role model good business and conscious business in what I do. If business can better understand the value it's capable of bringing to the world, this can positively impact those involved and inspire them to push themselves through barriers to reach higher levels."

What is striking about Bethany is that, even at such a young age, she is very conscious and intentional about her choices. She has been an active member of the Conscious Capitalism® Rochester Chapter and recently pursued and secured a role with a growing enterprise in Dallas, Improving, purely based on her first-hand experience of their leadership. She now sits on the board for the Dallas chapter of Conscious Capitalism as well. With such a deeply held sense of purpose, it is astonishing to think what she will be capable of when she is in her thirties, and the positive impact she will have had on the world around her.

A similar wake-up call happened early on in life for Millennial Prabhmeet Singh, a qualified accountant with a highly analytical background in financial modelling. While working for an insurance business, Prabhmeet helped them to achieve their goal of growing the organisation from a start-up to a billion-pound business in five years, and as a result he enjoyed all the material success this brings. However, his dissatisfaction with the lack of purpose of the company prompted him to leave without having another job to go to. "It literally got to the point where I was thinking, what am I actually doing? How am I influencing society in the role that I have? So I resigned and walked out, thinking, what have I just done? I don't have a job but I have a mortgage!"

As a result of his actions, he became clear about what he wanted to do, which was to make a change to society. Currently, Prabhmeet is employed as a principal consultant for a global consulting firm: "I work on really fascinating projects that impact society, using all of my professional background and skills, but in a way that can have an impact. For example, I am working on developing business cases for improving the lives of children at school by changing their environment, which impacts the education system. It feels like I've got a purpose here that is also using my skill set."

A Sikh by religious background, Prabhmeet is also deeply conscious. "We grow up believing you should be humble, serve selflessly. This doesn't really match up with the corporate world and begs the question: how can I marry my corporate life with serving?" While religion does play a big part in his life, he believes he is more 'spiritual' in nature. A large proportion of Millennials ascribe themselves to the category 'spiritual but not religious'. "This is a way of life which is about how we can impact other people, help others and our role in this. It's about the feeling that you get when you help somebody without wanting anything in return, a feeling that you can understand but you can't put a price on it."

NATURAL SYSTEMS THINKERS

Even in cases where conscious Millennials are not necessarily spiritually minded, they are consummate and natural systems thinkers. As a result, they are much more inclined than previous generations to see themselves as part of a greater whole and to consider the knock-on effects of their own and others' actions, making them particularly conscious about what they do, where they work and what they are involved in.

Millennial Andrew Brady says: "We're growing up in a world where we don't know any differently to having a social conscience. We know that we're living in this interconnected web and that something that happens across the world is going to impact our economy and impact us in some way. When you're living in that interdependent system, you start to see the ripples that some random person across the world makes and you think, perhaps I have the potential to make that sort of impact. Part of waking up is that the more your consciousness evolves, the more you see those ripples. It's not that they weren't there before, it's just that now, whether it's through technology or through the expansion of consciousness in general, we're seeing more of the interdependencies and we're taking them into account."

> *"We're growing up in a world where we don't know*
> *any differently to having a social conscience."*
> Andrew Brady

These Millennials realise that we're getting ever more interconnected the more we have the technology and tools to do it. Jen Wilson agrees: "Every single action is connected to something else and has an effect and an impact. Being awake is realising that every thought that's converted into an action has got an impact beyond your little world. It puts a lot of responsibility on you, and this can come with some anxiety. Being a conscious Millennial in today's world is about stopping to look right now at the environment, at what's happening, and being willing to say, let's pause – where do we go from here?"

For many Millennials, seeing the interconnections in the wider system can be a deeply rewarding experience. It connects them with a sense of awe and wonder, with being part of nature and increases their positive emotions and wellbeing as they care for systems outside themselves. "Your moral circle expands," explains Andrew Brady, "the circle of concern that expands to it being about something beyond just me."

As a result, conscious Millennials think deeply about the implications of being a piece in a larger puzzle and what this means for being human. "The two threads I see for the evolution of consciousness," says Andrew, "are the expanding moral circles – seeing the interdependencies – and seeing further out into the future. These are seventh generation principles. Every decision I make I want to make knowing what the impact is going to be on seven generations hence. When I'm thinking about not only whether my decisions are going to have ripples in the present but also in the future, I start to ask myself: am I making positive effects? Are these decisions I can be proud of?"

HOW DO YOU SUCCESSFULLY LEAD CONSCIOUS MILLENNIALS?

The urge to be responsible in the world and for the world is one of the keys to successfully unlocking and leading a generation that is waking up. Leaders who are slow to grasp this miss out on one of the biggest powers to motivate their upcoming and ever more conscious talent. The trend of the Millennials is towards perceiving interconnections, and their heart is pulled towards wanting to make a contribution to this system of connections, to take care of it, and to have an impact that matters. So, it is important to know how to channel their desire for connection and their abundance of choice. We'll consider this under the three categories of:

» Using purpose as a tool for creating belonging and increasing relevance

» Highlighting the impact of their contribution

» Amplifying connection and creating immediate feedback loops

USING PURPOSE AS A TOOL FOR CREATING BELONGING AND RELEVANCE

Taking all that raw talent and need for connection and harnessing it in some way is one of the main tools leaders have to access the potential of the Millennial generation. The wise leader taps into this generation's need to belong and to be relevant, and holds a compelling context with which the Millennials can identify. We've already seen earlier in this book how conscious leaders are masters at creating and holding context.

This context can easily take the form of the purpose of a company or a project that has an impact on the world and which Millennials find meaningful. These companies or projects send pipelines to their values, which leads them to naturally want to contribute. As we've seen throughout this book, a company's higher purpose should ideally be plugged into a social impact and Millennials are watching for this as they choose where they'd like to become involved and how they'd like to invest their energy.

Jennifer Wilson describes what this experience is like: "When you're connected to a bigger purpose, you can relax and feel that you're part of something. Without that connection, I'm just in reaction to the day. If I'm connected to a purpose, to the meaning of what I'm doing that day, it drives my actions and then I can meet the day knowing what I'm here to do."

The challenge of helping conscious Millennials to make choices is another useful tool which leaders can use. In a hyper-connected world, this generation is often trying to be attentive to too many things at once. Leaders can help by holding the strong context that orientates Millennials, that aligns their values with purpose, responsibility and impact. "There's so much choice for us," says Jennifer. "We're a lucky generation because we're spoilt for choice, though it can create high anxiety levels from having so much choice about what you can have and how you can behave. If you're not working amongst people who are aligned with your values, it's bewildering."

"If people are showing up disengaged and on Facebook
all day, it's quite possible there's a leadership problem.
We want to work, but my generation won't give our best
if we don't feel connected to a purpose and a cause."
Bethany Hilton

In a world of choice, these factors – higher purpose, contribution, impact and connection – create a sense of belonging and encourages the best from socially conscious Millennials. Companies like Airbnb have captured the essence of this perfectly in their simple advertising campaign, #mankind. The message is that I can belong anywhere and we are all a global, connected community. More importantly, I can choose where I belong and I can personalise it. Airbnb is a highly individualised experience that lets you choose what you want to do and where you want to belong. This is the same approach used by Spotify® – you can belong through having highly tailored music piped into your ears at any time, and share this with the community of your choice. It's all about connection.

Leaders can tap into this desire to belong and amplify it in the community of their organisation. It helps to build communities and tribes. "Because we experience so much disconnection," says Jen Wilson, "creating a sense of belonging at work ties into our needs to feel connected and relevant. If you're working at a company that doesn't match your values, and you're being led by leaders just for the sake of getting a pay cheque at the end of the month, it doesn't fulfil the deeper question of why am I actually doing this? Where do I belong?"

Some questions that conscious leaders can ask themselves about purpose, belonging and relevance are:

» What is the purpose that is drawing the attention of your Millennial-generation employees?

» How explicit and aligned are the values of the work compared with the values of the people?

» To what does this generation feel it belongs in your organisation?

» How does this reinforce their social identity and how is it relevant to them?

» What difference does their involvement make?

HIGHLIGHTING THE IMPACT OF THEIR CONTRIBUTION

Rather than the 'me' generation, Millennials can more appropriately be labelled as the 'meaning generation'. Conscious Millennials need to know that their work is making a difference in some way to something bigger than themselves – preferably in a way that aligns with their values – and that what they do is an extension of their authentic selves. Conscious Millennials are more likely to see that business doesn't have to be at odds with making a social contribution in the world. They are less likely to shun profit-making business for a non-profit alternative – as long as the conditions are right. However, for this to work in a business's favour, the links between the purpose of the company and the impact out in the world needs to be clear. What Millennials aren't prepared to do is work in a sweatshop until they secure the corner office. They've got to see the impact that their efforts are making.

Andrew Brady admits that Millennials get a bad rap: "They want all the responsibility; they want to advance really quickly, without perhaps doing all the groundwork. What this comes back to really is just wanting to see the impact of what we're doing. When you connect people with their end users, it increases our motivation. Impact is easily measurable and available these days because of transparency, and we want to feel like we're having some kind of contribution from Day 1."

This theme of contribution is huge with conscious Millennials. Bethany Hilton adds: "We are likely to ask: what's the point of all this? Why are you exhausting yourself for this business – to drive a flashier car? I'm not going to be inspired by that, I'm not going to last there. It's not enough to work because we have to. Our generation doesn't really care about making the boss rich and we can no longer be guaranteed the safety that if we stay with a company, they will take care of us for the remainder of our careers. So, we're going to put our heart into our work if we really believe we are making a difference. What's the point if we're not doing that? We are looking for leaders who don't put profit before people so we can get behind them and make their vision happen. We're less concerned about how you are going to get there; we just want to be part of it. No matter whether I'm a secretary or the engineer on the project, the question is: how is the work that I'm doing contributing?"

> *"We're going to work if we really believe we are*
> *making a difference and are helping people,*
> *because what's the point if we're not doing that?"*
> Bethany Hilton

"Leaving the world in a better place than when I arrived is a big motivator for me; it's the bigger picture," agrees Prabhmeet Singh. "True leadership for me is getting people to understand they have options. In the corporate world, you don't even know why you're doing it sometimes, you're just doing things because everyone else is. When I work with teams, it's not just about what we've produced, it's about how I've developed others to understand there's a bigger picture here. For example, in a consultancy project I might ask, why are we doing this, how are we going to impact other people? For me it's about developing and touching each person I come across in a way that they have a bit of an awakening to what it is that we're doing here."

Conscious businesses provide an important opportunity to

attract and keep Millennials because in these businesses profit and impact are so solidly welded together. This can help to prevent the attrition of Millennial talent being lured away to social enterprises by corporates that are too slow to change and too divided to honour the whole person.

Crucially, conscious Millennials believe in the power of business. They are pro-profit and they recognise business for the potential contribution it can make to the world – if it's led properly. "Business can change the world. It has access to resources, it has leverage in politics, the platform to champion change. It is an incredibly power-ful tool that can be used for good or bad," says Bethany Hilton. "I want to use this tool as an opportunity to create something of value in the world by doing business better and raising the game for everyone."

Some questions that conscious leaders can ask themselves about impact and contribution are:

» How clear is the impact of your company's efforts on the world?

» What are the knock-on effects – for good – in the wider stakeholder system in which your company exists?

» How is your business doing its part to change the world in some small or large way?

» How clearly can you articulate this vision to your younger generation of employees?

AMPLIFYING CONNECTION AND CREATING IMMEDIATE FEEDBACK LOOPS

As well as highlighting purpose, contribution and impact, leaders can inspire conscious Millennials into action by amplifying the connections that create a sense that they belong to a network or a community. When this network or community is linked to personal values and higher purpose, this creates a tempting context to belong to.

Once leaders set up this frame, perhaps the biggest difference with the Millennial generation is their need for immediate feedback. Yearly performance appraisals, ad hoc feedback or missing feedback sessions all create an experience for Millennials that they are working in a vacuum – one that is easily filled by distractions such as social media.

This is a generation which is able to get instant answers off the internet, a generation that is constantly online, which in itself provides constant, instant feedback. This trend will only increase as we head into the era of the Digital Natives, the first generation in history to become adults in the emerging world of social media, having known nothing different. Bob Johansen, in *Leaders Make the Future*, defines digital natives as those who were 16 years old or younger in 2012. [1] By 2021, everyone on the planet 25 years and younger will be a digital native. We don't yet know how the digital natives will be different from us, nor how they will change the world, and we don't know the impact on the formation of their brains, but what is certain is it will be significantly different from the way we grew up and now function as human beings.

Even amongst the Millennial generation, there is a recognition that the constant connection to technology can either be a distraction or a blessing. "Most people are just using connectivity as a bit of morphine," says Andrew Brady. "It's a desperate need for connection but without consciousness, without being awake and aware or having a purpose you don't see what it's for – you're just longing for connection."

How can a leader use this longing for connection and desire for immediate feedback to an advantage when leading Millennials? If Millennials need it, show them the impact they're having every day. "We're bored and disconnected!" says Bethany Hilton. "So shorten the feedback loop between what we're doing and the impact we're having. Find ways to articulate and reinforce the 'why' with us, regularly. When we can see the results of our work, we will be able to come up with more creative and innovation solutions to the problems we're solving."

Some questions that conscious leaders can ask themselves about connection and immediacy are:

» How short are your feedback cycles to point out the impact of Millennials' efforts?

» How frequently are you, as a leader, providing opportunities for connection to the central purpose of your company or project?

WHAT DO CONSCIOUS MILLENNIALS WANT FROM THEIR LEADERS?

A few years ago, I attended a Conscious Capitalism conference and decided to interview some of the 20-somethings there. I was fascinated by how they'd come to be at a conference full of middle-aged consultants and coaches, all of whom were answering an inner calling to do business in a better way.

One Millennial had travelled for 54 hours on a Greyhound bus to get to the conference. He simply said, "I just needed to be here." Another was there with his father, a leadership consultant. Both father and son were interested in doing business differently and supported each other in their respective ways. These young people spoke about being more conscious and working more responsibly in a way that I had seldom heard in adults. The general theme of the conversations was: we (the Millennials) need you (the existing leaders) to open the doors for us, to break the mould. You know how the power dynamics and structures work. Our role is to come in after you upset the status quo and embed this new way of leading and doing business.

These were wise words. The best thing a conscious leader can do for the Millennials in their organisation, particularly the conscious Millennials, is to bend or break structures where necessary, champion conscious efforts in the company, and allow this generation the opportunity to express their ideas and potential.

As Laura Roberts described it earlier, existing Gen X leaders have the responsibility to pave the way and mentor Millennials into different and more conscious ways of doing business.

WHAT DOES BAD LEADERSHIP LOOK LIKE FOR MILLENNIALS?

"The worst thing is if somebody were to tell us to do something that has no purpose, something that was just keeping someone else's ego happy or to tick a box," says Jen Wilson. The question Millennials are asking is, is what we're doing really necessary? Is it relevant?

Is what we're doing really necessary? Is it relevant?

Forgetting the purpose of a business and following a process for the sake of itself is the kiss of death to the ever more conscious Millennials who are thinking about the impact of the work they're doing. As we've seen, being free to do something with a higher purpose in mind and being able to do it quickly with immediate feedback is the way to activate their energy. Reaching targets and dangling the carrot of bonuses is unlikely to motivate many Millennials, especially the conscious ones. Seeing no end in sight or failing to make a contribution that seems relevant is likely to get them draining the company of whatever learning they can acquire and then leaving to set up a smaller company of their own. This is neither a virtuous nor a sustainable cycle for any leader to pursue.

SUCCESSFULLY LEADING CONSCIOUS MILLENNIALS

Here are five markers leaders can keep in mind to successfully lead conscious Millennials:

1 Connect them to a Purpose

Having a higher purpose can't be overstressed. Conscious Millennials need meaning in their lives far more than they need security. In fact, they don't believe that security in large organisations exists any more. They've replaced this with experimentation, innovation and social contribution. Show them the link to the bigger picture, right upfront. Get Millennials engaged and fulfilled by connecting them to a purpose and making them feel part of something. Let this purpose be linked to a more effective solution for the world.

"Good leadership would be any person in any position able to inspire something in me that I would be willing to sign up for that's good for moving the world forward and that aligns to what moves me most," says Jen Wilson. Help them to make choices in a world of overwhelming possibilities by connecting them to a purpose through their values that creates a sense that they belong. Enable them to see themselves in the project and show them the value that they could bring, based on who they are.

2 Dial-up your Authenticity

The global trend towards 'wholeness' at work has become more than a moral case; it's a business case, according to Will Reynolds, coach and 21st-century career strategist.[2] He points out that for Gen Y, the Millennials, the opportunity to design their lifestyle is the number one paradigm shift that characterises this tech-enabled 21st-century career sector.

They're not interested in the 'deferred life plan', where they work now for reward later, but are looking to bring more of themselves into the work that they do every day, and to be more fully themselves in every moment. If leaders are to capture the attention of conscious Millennials, they need to include the whole person in both the purpose and in what's being produced. The proactive and ambitious Millennials who will build and power the organisations of the future demand this from their careers and, as Will Reynolds points out, in time, the only organisations left standing will be those that have the values of wholeness and balance built into their DNA.[3]

The only organisations left standing
will be those that have the values
of wholeness and balance
built into their DNA

Not only should work be more authentic, leaders need to be authentic, too. To lead this generation, leaders need to bring their authentic selves into the room. "They need to have the guts just to be who they are," says Prabhmeet Singh. This means being willing to share what it means to them to work on whatever project they're doing. "This inspires me to get on board," says Jen Wilson. "If I resonate with it, I would sign up completely. If a leader can bring through the art and purpose of what they're trying to make happen in the world, and it's aligned with what I see in the world, then it's a joint vision."

3 Give them Bespoke Growth and Development

Millennials are not so much an homogenous group as they are a collection of individualistic explorers looking to express themselves in unique ways. While they look to belong, this belonging should be to something that they choose themselves and that is connected to the authentic self-expression of their values and interests.

Their individuality feeds through into their growth and development inside an organisation. Not only do Millennials crave this growth and development, they want it to take place with their unique qualities in mind.

"A conscious leader has an understanding of the individual, why they're doing the things they're doing. It's not just about tactics; it's about understanding who these people really are, the fabric of them as individuals, and as a generation. The best leaders don't see everyone as just a lump sum – the sales team, the x team, here's the rule book," says Bethany Hilton. "They see individuals and they understand how to maximise and leverage those different strengths." It's the direct opposite of depersonalised systems and routine procedures.

"We want to be led in a way that the person leading us cares about our growth and development," continues Andrew Brady. "We don't so much mind doing some of the dirty work if we can see what the plan is, what it's for, what some of the experiences are along the way. We need to see the impact that the company is making on the world, and we need to see the vision and how we're part of it, as well as how we're growing from it. It goes far beyond bringing a ping-pong table into the breakroom. It's about what lights people up."

"A true leader will understand what individualistic expression means and bring this out," says Prabhmeet Singh. "We often have to put on this mask when we come to work. We can't express who we are but we have to express the culture of the tribe that we've joined. This kills self-expression. When you kill self-expression, you can't identify talent because you don't know what that person can actually achieve."

The message is clear: take an interest in your Millennial generation on an individual basis, and provide them with development that uses their strengths and allows them to be the best versions of themselves.

To successfully lead a generation of conscious Millennials, it's also important for leaders to be on the road to becoming more conscious themselves. This extends beyond managing yourself and your reactions and emotions to something much more: with personal growth being so high on the agenda of Millennials, the best conscious leaders are dedicated to their own growth and development, as well as the growth and development of others.

"The conscious leader is the one in front of the troops helping to awaken them," says Andrew Brady. "Part of the responsibility of the conscious leader is to grow the consciousness of the folks that are working for him or her. If people are interested in working only for themselves, then the question to ask yourself, as a leader, is how you can broaden that to get them to care about their work teams and their families, to see how they're impacting the company as a whole. Then, how do you get them to see how they're impacting the world or the planet?"

> *"The conscious leader becomes an architect*
> *of the experiences that can expand*
> *the consciousness for their people."*
> Andrew Brady

4 Distribute and Share your Leadership

Who knows better what appeals to Millennials than Millennials themselves? Millennials in your organisation are a source of talent and fresh thinking waiting to be tapped. The most successful leaders of conscious Millennials recognise this and invite them into the strategic processes and decisions.

Paul Monekosso Cleal describes how important he believes it is to invite the contributions of the younger generations: "I'm very non-hierarchical. Typically, people use the hierarchy to reinforce their power. They can't get the best out of the more junior people because they're not allowing them to speak their minds, but in doing so they're missing the point that younger people know more about what's coming through, especially technologically, and there's a shift in knowledge and power as a result. As leaders, we need to involve everyone and give everyone a chance to speak."

Being able to see the situation without the blinkers of habitual perspective, Millennials bring fresh eyes to a project or to a business. Good leaders know how to allow this fresh perspective out, let it play a part and to learn from it.

Similarly, Millennials tend to see work as a partnership more than as a situation of 'us' and 'them'. True to the spirit of partnership, this involves transparency in sharing the desired outcomes, generously ascribing responsibility and including their views. Autonomy and trust are important parts of the mix. "We need to hear that you hired us because you believe we're capable," says Bethany Hilton, "that you believe we're going to become better than we currently are because we're going to develop. Be clear with us about what 'good' looks like and give us the freedom to engage and the tools to manage ourselves and get there."

Conscious leaders create sparks in their younger generation employees, first by attracting those who share the vision and possibilities they see themselves, and then giving these people the freedom to go and explore their own directions and ignite others with their ideas. It is the exact opposite of controlling outcomes and it's all about stewarding the right kinds of environments for these Millennials to come alive.

5 Create Adventure Through Experimentation and Spontaneity

While the idea of providing degrees of freedom might leave some leaders cold because of the apparent risks involved, there really is little alternative to successfully leading Millennials, especially conscious Millennials who cannot think other than about wanting to make a contribution and seeing an impact. Because they are motivated by spontaneous and unique experiences that reinforce who they are, a cardboard-cutout role with predefined borders will have them feeling bored and seeking stimulation elsewhere, probably on social media, or outside your company.

How, then, to provide these opportunities? Think safe container with plenty of opportunity for safe risk. "There's got to be an opportunity to experiment, to reinvent, to risk," says Jen Wilson. "A portion of the project should be a risk, and this risk is that something greater than me could come out of it."

"Create opportunities for us to be challenged and trust us enough to let us occasionally fail," agrees Bethany Hilton. "To keep us from being bored and to get the best out of us, we need big responsibility and a safe environment to test and experiment, to fail and push our limits. We also need the leader to keep in front of us, reminding us of the vision that we're trying to accomplish, that we connect to. It's the kind of environment where you are almost running your own small business within the larger company."

The outcomes may not be the ones you thought of at the outset

For conscious leaders trying to source Millennial talent for their projects, a good rule of thumb to keep in mind is to sell the cause authentically and let it resonate with those to whom it naturally appeals, then provide a clear vision and an experimental container in which the magic of new ideas through fresh eyes can happen. Keeping the vision and desired impact in the world in front of them, while providing quick-cycle feedback on the results and the actual impact achieved, will keep Millennials engaged and energised towards outcomes. Bear in mind that, with fresh perspectives and new ideas, these outcomes may not be the ones you thought of at the outset! However, with the right Millennial combination in place, you can be guaranteed that they will be relevant and innovative outputs, with quite possibly a business-changing genius idea or two in the mix.

Without these five markers in place, leaders will be likely to experience some of the worst kinds of disengagement from their talent pool. Ideas that could spring from these kinds of containers and change the face of the business will wither in the face of leadership that isn't willing to flex. Lack of experimentation will crush a young person's soul if they have a creative spark that isn't even tried out. This is likely to create a sullen and resigned response of 'why should I try to create anything then?' or a desire to draw from the company what is worthwhile and then leave to try out their creative ideas elsewhere.

On the other hand, considering these five markers and how they can come alive in your own organisation is likely to spark the interest of your Millennial generation and get the best contributions from them.

THE APPEAL OF
CONSCIOUS LEADERSHIP

Ultimately, many of the ideas in this chapter aren't necessarily new to Millennial thinking and they are as applicable to conscious Millennials as to everyone else in Gen Y. However, there are distinct differences for leaders wishing to get the most out of conscious Millennials and to develop themselves as effective leaders of this expanding section of the talent pool.

The conscious Millennials interviewed for this book do see differences in the way they view the world, compared with their contemporaries. In many ways, they are much more requiring of their leaders.

For Andrew Brady, there is a requirement to be more responsible as a business: "With social media and technology out there creating so much transparency, companies can't control their marketing messages in the same way any more. You can't have companies putting out great commercials but behind the scenes producing products in sweatshops. Leaders these days need to be much more transparent and have much more integrity to look at all aspects of their business. Millennials are noticing and that's why the conscious companies are getting their pick of the talent. It's creating a shift and it's exciting."

From Prabhmeet Singh's perspective, there are those who think like him and there are many who have yet to wake up. This group sees the world in the traditional way and works for their pay cheque. Prabhmeet regards this group as very different from those who want to change society. He believes that championing this new guard of Millennials is very important for the role of conscious leader. "With the existence of social media and all the transparency it brings, we get to hear about leaders who are great role models. We have more knowledge and awareness about how they're actually operating and we can implement that for ourselves. Previously, we were left with academic ideas of leadership or what we observed or what our parents told us. When this generation comes into leadership positions, our mentality will be different. We'll bring in an awareness that the world doesn't have to be this way."

What Prabhmeet is pointing to here is that Millennials are watching their leaders keenly and are looking for their wisdom and authenticity but not for their close control. It also suggests that they have some very distinct views about what constitutes good leadership and which leaders they will respect.

There is a real drive in conscious Millennials to make a difference, to use business for good and to have an impact on the furthest reaches of the system. They are ready and hungry to be utilised, and they ignite responsibility in others in the process.

"The financial crisis of 2009," says Prabhmeet, "showed us that this change is not even a nice-to-have, it's a necessity that we need to change the way that we run businesses. The VW emissions scandal has shown us that this need goes far beyond just the banking sector; it's manifest in every sector. When we get to the stage where we think of all of us as humanity, as one big family, then business will be set up to serve rather than to make profits. This will herald a complete shift in mentality at that point."

When Millennials come into leadership positions, we'll bring in an awareness that the world doesn't have to be this way

---

In many ways, the conscious Millennials are forcing the leaders of today to wake up. They won't work for a meaningless goal. They won't contribute their all unless they can see an impact for the greater good. Old-fashioned leaders, the type that usher workers in straight lines towards predetermined, profit-only goals, will quickly lose the talent of their organisations to more exciting entrepreneurial ventures. Leaders who are unconscious to the impact of their organisations on the world around them, and who fail to take into account the responsibilities of their businesses to the wider world, are further likely to alienate this upcoming generation of talent. These conscious Millennials see the world differently and they are demanding to be led in a way that makes sense to someone who knows that we are all part of an interconnected whole. Leaders who fail to wake up to these factors will lag behind in engaging the raw talents of the new generations.

As Prabhmeet Singh says, "It's just not cool to be that type of leader any more."

Endnotes

1   Johansen, Bob. 2012. *Leaders Make The Future: Ten New Leadership Skills for an Uncertain World*. San Francisco. Berrett-Koehler Publishers, Inc., a *BK Business Book*, p10-12.

2   Reynolds, Will. November 2015. 'Why Generation Y are designing their lives before planning careers'. www.virgin.com

3   Ibid.

22

ADVICE FOR CONSCIOUS LEADERS

As part of the research I conducted for this book, I asked the conscious leaders I interviewed what advice they had for those considering the journey towards conscious leadership for themselves. While the list of suggestions here is by no means exhaustive, it does come from those who are on the path themselves and, as such, is grounded in their real-life experiences of how to lead differently.

WHAT IS YOUR CATALYST?

The first area to consider is what you might be going through at the moment that is prompting you to think about why you and your life might need to be different. In Chapter 3 we explored how these experiences might be accompanied by the loss of your previously felt certainty, how it might overturn what you once took for granted. Whereas before, pursuing the achievement of goals was a reason for living in itself, as we deepen our levels of consciousness, the things that used to be so meaningful to us are not as meaningful any more and we begin to seek some other answers for our purpose in life.

Occasionally, it is simply that our life experiences shape us in their own way. At other times, it might simply be an inner knowing that has been with us our entire lives. But, for most of us, the path to expanding our own levels of awareness requires the shell of our previous selves to crack open, allowing the new version of ourselves to come through. This is not always a pleasant experience. It asks us to let go of the layers of ourselves, of the fundamentals of our identity that we have been clinging to that give us a sense of our own significance. We are required to allow ourselves to be vulnerable, to not know, to trust and to watch while the new version of ourselves emerges.

In consciousness terms, there is the saying that goes, 'what we resist, persists'. This can sound somewhat trite; however, in the experience of those undergoing this journey of self, it is in the act of letting go and surrendering that our expansion lies.

What are the circumstances of your life, therefore, that at the moment are calling you to become a more enlightened version of yourself? The catalyst that may even be a crisis right now for you, could be an opportunity for further awakening.

It is in the act of letting go and surrendering that our expansion lies

---

We have met throughout this book the successful entrepreneur Neal Gandhi, who described so well the process he went through of realising that everything he had unconsciously held dear had become meaningless. He describes this process as 'a massive awakening'.

Neal says of how people can get on with the journey of becoming a conscious leader: "I'd like to hope that it wasn't some sort of personal crisis, but I can't help but feel that there has to be a jolt that moves people from the old place to the new place. Something has to shift them and, more often than not, it is a crisis. Or, maybe, it's that point where you are in your forties and you work out that there's got to be more to life than this. You look ahead, and you think, do you really want me to do this for another 20 or 30 years?"

So that is the first piece of advice for getting on with the journey of becoming a conscious leader: look for the catalysts and, if you are currently in a crisis, ask yourself what change or act of letting go might be being asked of you. Though it's certainly not an easy thing, the right support through, for example, coaching, mentoring, therapy, spiritual practice or other forms of meaning-making – or, indeed, meaning-losing – can aid you in your process.

CHOOSING HOPE

If we are not being pursued by the events of our lives, then the other approach to developing as a conscious leader is to anticipate what this might mean for us as leaders in our organisation, and simply as human beings. The inspirational aspects of being a conscious leader are what I had hoped would be conveyed by the stories in this book. Those that have gone before us give us the power to look at our own lives in perspective; to realise that where there are breakdowns, these are likely to be part of breakthroughs and, when taking a wider perspective, we might acknowledge the inevitable process of ebb and flow that is our own life.

"The first thing to say to those drawn to conscious leadership is that it's possible," says Peter Matthies. "There is a different way that we can operate. If we delve into our authenticity, and work from there, then work is not work any more. When we click into this genuine part of ourselves, life becomes so much easier: our relationships are easier and our work is easier. It's a longer-term transition, it's not going to happen in six months, but there are support systems which can take you through this transition."

This pattern of proactively choosing the path of the conscious leader is echoed by Laura Roberts. Her advice? "It's about realising that the most important work you can do is to create the elevation in your own universe. World peace starts at home."

> *"It's about realising that the most important work you can do is to create the elevation in your own universe. World peace starts at home."*
>
> Laura Roberts

IT'S ABOUT THE JOURNEY, NOT THE DESTINATION

Conscious leaders agree that getting on the path is not about getting to an ultimate destination. There is no destination. It's all about the practice of who you are being on the path. "First and foremost, conscious leaders need to be clear about why they want to be this way," says Sudhakar Ram. "Consciousness is not a means to an end; it is an end in itself. You don't become conscious in order to do something."

These are very wise words from a wise, conscious leader. Developing ever further as a conscious leader is the entire point. This can be difficult or uncomfortable to comprehend, especially for those leaders whose reason for being, doing, living and working is very much linked to pursuing goals and knocking down challenges. This is probably why crossing over into conscious leadership tends to be accompanied by leaders becoming dissatisfied with what previously drove them, causing them to question the meaning and the purpose of their lives.

There is no destination

"If you are clear that becoming more conscious is part of your life's purpose and journey," says Sudhakar, "then you can be willing to treat this as a game in which you will learn various things. But there is nothing to achieve at the end of it; it just makes every day more enjoyable in some form."

Steve Hall agrees: "My advice would be to make sure your journey is about being true to yourself. It's about knowing that this journey of yours is lifelong; it's not about there being a destination and becoming attached to the destination. Instead, it's about getting attached to the process of exploration of yourself. In the past, I got attached to the destination and when I reached the destination it was a real let-down. Going forward, I don't want to get attached to a destination at all, I just want to continue with this process of living true to myself, to my values, every day, no matter what I do, whether its business or time with friends and family. This is what I want to show up as and enjoy, regardless of the results."

ASK THE DEEP QUESTIONS

Being a conscious leader has a lot to do with asking yourself the big questions. It doesn't have to be this way; some conscious leaders are content with the simple act of being in the moment and enjoying life as a flow. Others are more concerned with the contribution that they are being called to make, and this has direct links with under-standing their life's purpose.

Leaders like Dominic Sewela believe that a key element is humil-ity: "I could only advise people to the extent of how things have evolved for me. First, it is necessary to have a level of humility that enables you to really look at yourself, because it takes a lot to criti-cally look at yourself as a leader and when you really try and be humble, you get to ask yourself: what other things do I really need to transform about myself? What is my purpose?"

It is when you ask yourself those fundamental questions that you embark on the journey to change yourself, and to becoming aware and more conscious. "I think this is a journey that a lot of leaders are sometimes too busy to embark upon, or they are so caught up in what they think success is that they never pause to ask those deep questions," says Dominic. "For me, it's really important that leaders have this self-reflection, because they are likely to do more, they are likely to be more impactful and they are likely to achieve significance in the world."

> *"Everybody has the chance in their forties to ask*
> *themselves whether there's more to life than this,*
> *because everybody questions their purpose,*
> *and some just bury it again or they choose to listen*
> *and do something about it."*
> Neal Gandhi

DECIDE ON THE IMPACT YOU WANT TO MAKE

The whole question of impact is deftly handled by Millennial conscious leader Andrew Brady, whom we met in Chapter 21.

Andrew believes it really starts with the inner compass of figuring out what's most important to you: "Because, if you want to have an impact, well you can have an impact in an infinite number of ways, so how do you want to dedicate your life, your 10,000 hours to becoming an expert? We have to be careful. Having all this technology available to us leads to the fear of missing out and it defeats the whole purpose of wellbeing and being present. The person who can focus and get really clear on the impact he or she wants to make amidst the infinite number of ways to potentially impact the world is the one who can make all the difference."

Like most Millennials, it is easy to see how Andrew folds technology, purpose and leadership into his vision of what successful leadership will look like in the future. In upcoming generations, now and increasingly so as we move into an ever more technologically connected, globally driven future, a ludicrous amount of choice becomes available. The value of having a clear sense of one's life purpose, gained through asking the big questions, is a distinct advantage – some might say even a necessity – for our wellbeing and personal navigation.

Also clear to see in Andrew's perspective is how our clarity of focus about the impact we want to make as leaders can call together around us a tribe of like-minded people that enables this vision or purpose to become a reality. As we know from the Conscious Millennials, leaders play an incredibly important role in sifting out purpose from pulp and creating the opportunities for Millennials to identify with something they feel passionate about and towards which they want to contribute.

> *"The person who can focus and get really clear on the impact he or she wants to make amidst the infinite number of ways to potentially impact the world is the one who can make all the difference."*
> Andrew Brady

"When a leader gets really clear on the impact he or she wants to make, together with self-awareness, it starts to unlock the capacity to find some other people who have complementary skills and who may want to work in a similar direction," says Andrew. "It really starts with the self. And you may change the focus of your impact over the course of your lifetime, but it is key to focus on a couple of areas so that you're not trying to make an impact in a hundred different ways and not doing a good job at any of them."

JUMP IN

So what we have as advice in the ways of becoming a conscious leader is to notice what the catalysts are in our life right now that are calling us to shed our old skins and emerge with the new; we have the reassurance that there is another way and the inner pull or yearning towards a higher version of ourselves and the work we can do both for ourselves and for other people. We know that the conscious leadership journey is the destination and that this is a continual opportunity to hone our own levels of consciousness simply as part of living and leading every day. And we have the invitation to ask ourselves the big questions about our purpose, linked to who we authentically are and the impact we want to make in the world.

Don't dally, just jump in

The final piece of advice from conscious leaders is simply: jump in. "I see people who we might think are 'in the process of waking up' gathering lots of information, reading lots of books, going to lots of seminars, getting ready to say, 'right, I'm part of this group,'" says John Renesch. "The advice I would give is: don't dally, just jump in. The worst that could happen is that you jump back out again because the water's a little too cold or too hot. If you don't like this pool, swim into a different pool. But get wet."

Peter Matthies agrees: "Don't dip your toe in. Seriously consider that there is a different way, go in and try it out. Talk to people who are intriguing. Watch things that inspire you, where your soul says, 'this is cool'. Follow the steps on this path and you're on the right track."

Practices seem a great place to start. The mindfulness revolution

– which is so accessible now that it can be entirely technology-driven – helps make us all more conscious, even if we're not thinking about conscious leadership. It's a great doorway into becoming more conscious as a leader.

"It starts with us," says Laura Roberts, "and, therefore, whatever intentional, mindful practices you can enter into, like being self-observant of your emotional state, or working out ways to reboot quickly so that you can be fully present, or really paying attention to how loud your internal conversations are and learning how to turn them down so you can be fully present with the other person – all these practices help us to become more conscious leaders."

> *"I keep watching for what triggers me – there are always*
> *some things that you haven't discovered about yourself*
> *but that you need to get in touch with and transform."*
> Sudhakar Ram

> *"Stay connected and be present. Look around you and*
> *the answers are everywhere. There is nothing you cannot*
> *learn from being connected."*
> Frederic Desbrosses

In my experience, certainly, the process has been about 'losing stuff', rather than 'adding stuff'. Rather than adding layers or information or points of view or certifications in through the top of your head, to get somewhere, which is going to make you something, it's about losing layers, exfoliating your ideas about yourself. What's left is a state of being in which we can live more in joy rather than be imprisoned by ideas of who we should be, or what we should know. As I mentioned elsewhere, my spiritual coach has a saying: "We are mostly just empty space with a few stories attached." This, for me, epitomises the freedom of being human – yet, like everyone interested in this path, it requires a great deal of letting go in order to embody it, and this letting go is an ongoing practice, like any other.

It's about losing layers, exfoliating your ideas about yourself

---

Perhaps the biggest obstacle in the path to becoming an ever more conscious leader is to think that leadership belongs to someone else. If we are inclined to think of leadership as 'out there', attached to the positions of others in our organisations, then we are missing the point.

Conscious leadership is not a position but a way of being. It is a verb rather than a noun: leading consciously rather than being 'a conscious leader'. We do not need to have a position or a title to get on the journey ourselves. Leading consciously is about self-leadership before it is about other-leadership. Our journey of waking up is our own.

This means that any person, in any position, in or outside any organisation, can lead consciously. Self-leadership, which requires us to wake up to the choices we have over our conditioning and our automatic patterns, is the entry ticket for being a conscious leader and, as we have seen from the leaders featured in this book, it never stops. There is always more to discover about the stories we tell ourselves that define us and that limit the space we have available to play in.

Waking up to the choices over our conditioning is the entry ticket.

Those who embrace this journey for themselves, who invest in the practices and stay aware and connected in the present moment, those for whom being shines through, become natural beacons for others. We cannot help but affect those around us through our ways of being. We become leaders of others, either informally, in the way we influence them, or formally, in the way we fulfil our leadership roles and positions. Whichever way, how much responsibility do we take for our way of being in the world? This is the adventure of conscious leadership.

Anyone can be a conscious leader

In the future, as we move away from hierarchical models of organisations and towards ever more self-organising modes, our ability to be conscious leaders of ourselves and to engage with others consciously will become more and more important. Multiple points of connection and opportunities to collaborate and create will strip away hierarchy as we come to rely on the skills needed to create commons with other people, driven by technology and human-to-human contact, in order to rapidly innovate solutions that benefit all of us. In this kind of world, anyone can be a leader and the more conscious will be better able to engage others. While we are not there yet, and while hierarchical, triangle-based organisations are still the norm, becoming a more conscious leader is a wise path for now and for the future, even simply as a means to be happier within ourselves.

SOME BIG QUESTIONS

Self-Mastery:

- » What is your definition of success?

- » What is the game, bigger than yourself, that you want to play?

- » What is the difference you would like to make to the world and others?

- » How can you catch your ego's three strategies (being right; looking good; controlling and defending) at play and convert them to more open, inclusive acts?

- » What are you resisting right now, in this moment, that you could accept?

- » How can you practise and role model curiosity?

- » What are the other 'right answers'?

- » What are your top three values that form your roots?

- » What are the most courageous stands you need to take in your organisation? How does this relate to your personal purpose and/or to your organisation's purpose?

- » What is your story of the future and how is it provoking insight and invoking action in the present?

- » How are you role modelling a more conscious way of being in your organisation, every day?

- » Is the universe hostile or friendly? If hostile, how can you notice more friendly, supportive cues?

» Where are you being supported in your life right now, without even asking?

» What do you feel grateful for, right now?

Conscious Relating:

» What's your relationship to hierarchy?

» Where can you let go of control in your organisation and stand in a space of 'not knowing'?

» What 'big rules' can you put in place instead for others to experiment within?

» How are you leveraging collaboration and collective intelligence? From which undiscovered corners of your organisation can you seek input?

» How can you create psychological safety for others in your organisation?

» How are you amplifying connections, strengths and diversity, and dialing down unhelpful comparisons, judgements and criticisms?

» Are you listening from your head, your heart and your intuition? What does your intuition tell you about your biggest conversation today?

» What is the context (the bigger purpose) you are holding for your team or your organisation?

» What are the qualities of the stories you are telling and encouraging to be told in your organisation?

» Are you speaking primarily from the past? The present? The future?

» What is still possible, even though the circumstances look like this today?

» What are the bigger conversations you need to have?

» How are you helping to bring the 'maker instinct' alive in your teams and your whole organisation? How could you do this to accelerate experimentation and innovation?

» What opportunities for personal transformation are you offering in your organisation right now for those who want to take them?

Systems Insight:

» Who benefits from your purpose? What are the outer reaches of those whom you impact?

» Where would you choose to recast the boundary lines with your competition?

» What opportunities exist to create potential partnerships with your competitors around a common purpose? What does win (you), win (them) and win (society) look like?

» Who do you need to trust?

» What is the value that can be created from innovating with your widest circle of stakeholders?

» Who all benefits when your organisation benefits?

» What level of responsibility are you engaged in for what others do to others in your organisation? And for the impact your organisation is having on your stakeholders, the world and the planet?

» How might you play in the dynamic space between giving shape to your organisation and listening in to the shape it wants to take?

» What is your organisation telling you right now about the direction it wants to head into in the future? How can you test this out?

» What experimental intention can you set right now, to notice the meaningful coincidences and patterns relating to this?

Collective Responsibility:

» How is what you're creating through your organisation adding to the net benefit of humanity? In a decade? In half a century? In a hundred years? A thousand?

» What are your views on growth? How much is sufficient? What is enough?

» How much responsibility are you taking in the effects of the end-to-end processes in your supply chain? What do you need to speak up about?

» What does whole systems healthy look like for your organisation?

» What are the core indicators for your business that will help to ensure it contributes a net positive effect on life for all?

» What question has most energy for you to begin with right now? How will you begin?

SOME KEY TOOLS TO BEGIN

Vertical Development:

» The Leadership Development Framework (LDF) http://harthill.co.uk

» Lectica: The LDMA (Lectical® Decision-Making Assessment) https://dts.lectica.org/_about/showcase. php?instrument_id=LDMA

» The Leadership Circle 360 https://leadershipcircle.com/?lang=eu

» The Global Leadership Profile http://www. williamrtorbert.com/global-leadership-profile/

Personal, Leadership and Organisational Values:

» Barrett Values Centre https://www.valuescentre.com

Spiritual Intelligence:

» The SQ21: https://www.deepchange.com

Meaning-making:

» The Map of Meaning: http://www.holisticdevelopment.org.nz

We-Q:

» We-Q Collaborative Intelligence tool: https://www.we-q.com

Perspective Taking:

» Polarity Management:
http://www.polaritypartnerships.com/#home

Contact Gina at http://consciousleadershipconsultancy.com to discuss individual conscious leadership coaching work, team work and organisational work.

NEXT STEPS

I hope the stories and examples in this book have inspired you in thinking about the conscious leader you are continuing to become, whether you're heading up an entire organisation, leading a team, leading yourself or simply being an integral part of your community and your family. In an ever more complex and technologically connected world that often seems alienating and frightening, what we long for is human connection and the sense that we are all in this, together. I hope this book, and the work and many ideas that might come out of it, will serve this purpose.

None of us does this alone. In this growing field of responsible and conscious leadership, it takes all of us bringing all our insights and collective intelligence. I am grateful for any idea, practice, organisation or leadership example you want to share. I would love to hear from you if you have an idea about how this book can reach others or if you want to share with me what this book has meant to you.

If you're interested in exploring your own conscious leadership capacities further or thinking through how conscious leadership can help you and your organisation, you might consider contacting me about:

One-to-one leadership coaching: focused work on developing yourself as an extraordinary conscious leader.

Working with your team or organisation: consulting solutions to support your organisation's change via myself and my trusted network of skilful and highly experienced consultants in all aspects of conscious business.

The Conscious Leadership Executive Programme: A tailored and transformative leadership development experience enjoyed amongst a group of your leadership peers.

Speaking engagements: for keynotes, conscious leadership workshops and facilitated sessions.

You can reach me directly at:
gina@becomingaconsciousleader.com or call +44(0) 7957 306 706.

Visit:

http://consciousleadershipconsultancy.com
https://becomingaconsciousleader.com

Publicity and Press:

For interviews, podcasts, in print or online media, please contact:
lorna@thewritefactor.co.uk or
gina@becomingaconsciousleader.com

I look forward to connecting with you.
Gina

ABOUT THE AUTHOR

GINA HAYDEN has worked with leaders across the world for the past twenty years developing their capacity to lead themselves and others with more awareness, wisdom and choice.

In addition to coaching executives to lead more consciously, she consults widely in global companies such PwC, AT Kearney, AlixPartners, Novartis and Arup amongst many others, working with their teams, designing and delivering development programmes for their leaders and consulting on strategies to align their people for effective results.

Gina is the co-founder of The Global Centre for Conscious Leadership and a Director of the Conscious Capitalism UK Chapter. She is passionate about bringing more conscious and responsible leadership to business and how business can be a powerful force for good in the world. Some of her most rewarding roles involve working directly with leaders one-to-one, exploring their meaning-making, establishing their self-perceived boundaries and limitations, and expanding their horizons so that they can make their desired impact on the world.

Gina lives in London with her ever-inspiring and wise young daughter.

Find out more and connect with Gina via:
e: gina@becomingaconsciousleader.com
t: @GinaCoach
f: facebook.com/Becoming-a-Conscious-Leader
LinkedIn: https://uk.linkedin.com/in/ginalhayden

The book: https://becomingaconsciousleader.com
The Conscious Leadership Consultancy:
http://consciousleadershipconsultancy.com
The Global Centre for Conscious Leadership: http://gcfcl.com
Sphere Consulting: http://www.sphereconsulting.org

INDEX

A

above the line   129– 130

abundance, abundant   57, 94, 131, 142–143, 214, 219, 220, 232, 236, 256, 266, 268, 276, 367, 372–375, 381, 420, 426

acceptance   230–236

action logics   78–82, 229

Adam Smith   13,14

adult development theory   75–83, 126, 333

advice process   191, 209, 319

altrocentric leadership   42

Amazon   355

Andrew Brady   19, 410, 424–425, 432, 437–438, 442, 452–453

authenticity, authentic leadership   42, 162–170, 281–282, 371, 429, 436

B

B-Corp   395–396

Barloworld   63, 98, 166, 174, 408–410

Barrett Brown   86–87

Barrett Values Centre   119, 120

Barry-Wehmiller   63

Benjamin Zander   142, 175, 187–188, 269–270

Bethany Hilton   218–219, 430, 437, 439, 440

Bill George   42, 166, 169

Bill Torbert   78

bio-empathy   354, 397

Bob Chapman   63

Bob Fishman   21, 36, 103–104, 182, 186, 188, 208–209, 214–216, 218, 243, 246, 293–294, 318–319, 328, 329–330, 366, 432

Bob Johansen   18, 161–162, 163–164, 232, 261–262

business narrative   101

Buurtzorg   189, 255–256

C

capitalism   11 -12, 14, 16, 17, 113, 325, 313

Cindy Wigglesworth   52, 110, 112, 119, 348–349

collaboration   20, 21, 129, 143–144, 184, 218, 323, 402, 407, 457

collaborative economy   21

collaborative intelligence   260–262, 320, 370

collective intelligence   87, 143, 184, 190, 216, 282, 300, 369, 386

collective leadership   87

collective responsibility   59–61

comfort zone   386–387

common creating   261, 282, 457

competition   143–144, 213, 253–256, 259, 379, 402

complexity   20–21, 144, 323

complexity of mind   74, 126

conditioning   72, 115–117, 148, 393, 400

connection, interconnectedness   241–242, 247, 327, 397, 420, 421, 424–426

Conscious Business Institute, The   11, 96

Conscious Capitalism   17, 28, 35, 46, 113, 314, 420, 423, 433

Conscious Capitalism: Liberating the Heroic Spirit of Business   22

conscious competition   24–25

conscious growth   379–385

conscious leader model   51

conscious relating   54–56

conscious social media   20

context   140–144, 323, 327, 421, 427

control   296, 328, 386

courage   335, 384, 386

Cranfield University   17

curiosity   145–147

D

Danone   64, 97, 174, 395–396, 404–408, 418

decision-making   315–313, 426

Diana Chapman   129, 235, 288

diasporas   161–162

Digital Natives   26, 218, 432

distributed leadership   87

Dominic Sewela   63, 98–99, 166–167, 174, 244, 337–338, 384–385, 408–410, 412–413, 451–452

Donella Meadows   18, 128, 146–147

Downtown Las Vegas Project   359

driversselect   94–95, 158, 173, 231, 274–278

E

ego's strategies   130–134

Eileen Fisher   186, 383

embodied leadership   73

emotional intelligence   281–282

externalities   113–114, 320, 351

F

Fast Company   18, 19

FAVI Enterprises   63, 173, 185, 381

fear   267–269, 296

feedback   432, 441

Fernando Flores   216

fight, flight, freeze   120, 138, 232

Firms of Endearment   22, 383

Frederic Desbrosses   89, 173, 183, 230, 243–244, 308, 319, 338, 350–351, 384

Frederic Laloux   31–34, 35, 83, 247, 294, 332, 334, 383, 393–394

fundamentalism   116, 183

G

GD   160, 235, 412

generous speaking   289

Global Centre for Conscious Leadership, The   419

growth   355, 395

growth (volume; value) 379–380

H

Harthill Consulting 78

hierarchy 243, 439, 457

Holacracy 32, 202, 209, 295, 300

holding the space 327, 332, 411

horizontal development 76, 82

human operating system 73–75

I

IBM CEO studies 21, 144

impact 429, 452

innovation 22, 129, 138, 184, 257–260, 323, 386, 400, 417, 418, 433, 441, 457

inside-out approach 30, 34–36

Institute for the Future, The 18

integrity 167–168, 337–338

intention 221, 367, 369

intention and attention 222–223

intuition 86, 281, 285, 287, 318, 319, 366, 368

invisible hand 13

J

Jaworski 123, 211, 329, 370–371

Jean-Francois Zobrist 63, 173, 185, 268–269, 341, 381

Jeff Carreira 128

Jennifer Wilson 419, 421, 425, 440

Jo Confino 128

John Mackey 35, 45–47, 167–168, 216, 227–228, 232, 242, 267, 348

John Renesch 28, 43–44, 45, 73, 84, 91–93, 116, 140, 198, 229, 289, 454

John Replogle 28

join the dots 86

Jon Freeman 15

K

Kegan   160

Ken Wilber   84, 183–184

L

Laura Roberts   24, 105–106, 233, 259, 271, 289, 334, 340, 380, 383, 402–404,
      418, 434, 450, 455

Lectica (LDMA)   323

lifelong learning   234

Lorna Davis   64, 96–98, 145, 174, 182, 200–201, 233–234, 336, 352, 368,
      395–396, 404–408, 418

Luke Nosek   65

Lynda Gratton   129

Lynne Twist   198–199

M

maker instinct   214–216, 218, 248

Mariana Bozesan   47–48, 123, 221, 366

Maslow   138, 418

Mastek   36, 91–92, 140, 296–299, 330, 382

mastery and transcendence   235–236

Me to We   71, 114, 122

meaning   25 -26, 64, 139, 140, 155, 418

meaning making   76, 79, 80, 82,229

meaning making, ways of   78–82

mental debugs   187, 400

metabolizability   271

Michael Bernard Beckwith   29

Michael Porter   17

Mike Griffiths   216–217

Millennials   26, 155, 218, 413

Milton Friedman   13, 14

mindfulness   88–89, 122, 233, 454–455

Muhammed Yunis   405

multiple perspectives   78, 181, 210, 218, 229, 243–244, 248, 321, 329
mutuality   350–351

N

nature   59, 101, 247, 255, 266, 349, 350, 353–354, 394, 398, 401–403, 425
Neal Gandhi   93–94, 174, 219–220, 234, 448–449
Nithya Shanti   45, 201, 222–223, 273

O

Otto Scharmer   113, 283
outside-in approach   30, 31–34

P

Pantheon Enterprises   24, 105, 233, 402–404
Paul Monekosso Cleal   12, 63, 99–100, 143, 182, 189, 210, 220, 234, 245, 282, 320, 352, 368–369, 439
Paul Polman, Unilever   327, 396–397
personal growth, personal evolution   385–387, 411, 437
perspective taking   131, 321
Pete Hamill   73
Peter Matthies   11, 28, 83, 85, 95–96, 248, 450, 454
politics   357
post-conventional thinking   79, 81
post-heroic leadership   87
power   293–314, 439
power, five levels of   309–313
power, ladder of   301–308
Prabhmeet Singh   413, 423, 430, 436, 438, 442–444
presence   88–89, 102, 289–290
Procter and Gamble   23
psychological safety   138
purpose   17, 18, 26, 34, 65, 105, 139, 140, 142, 155, 171–175, 248, 265–266, 329, 334, 335, 384, 395–397, 402, 404–408, 426–427, 435
purposeful partnership   21, 144

R

radical listening, generous listening   287, 288, 329

radical partnerships   257

Raj Sisodia   22, 28, 63, 383

Ramesch Kacholia   168–169, 175, 372–373

rapid prototyping   258–259, 285, 400

reciprocity-based innovation   257–258, 261

Reinventing Organizations   31

relative viewpoints   192–193

responsibility and power   299

responsibility to the whole   393–398

reticular activating system   367

return on luck'   360, 361, 365

RHD (Resources for Human Development)   21, 36, 103

Richard Barrett   119, 386

role modelling   228, 229, 244, 337–338

S

Sally Ann Ranney   100–102, 248, 353–357, 394, 397–398

self-authoring, self-transforming mind   73, 160

self-management   32, 35, 295, 457

self-mastery   51–53

sensing   329, 332, 366

servant leadership   42

seventh generation   28, 356, 397, 425–426

Shareholder value   14

shifting   129, 235

Simon Sinek, Golden Circle   141

social purpose, social responsibility   114, 404, 406, 431

speech act   216

Spiritual Intelligence   110, 348–349

stakeholders   17, 313, 320, 321, 329, 402

stands   198–203, 332, 371

Steve Hall   94–95, 158, 173, 231, 274–278, 451

steward   210, 244, 329, 331, 393, 440, 393

Strategist-stage leaders   80

subconscious programmes   115

success   62–64

Sudhakar Ram   36, 91–92, 140–141, 149, 200, 230, 232, 234, 297–299, 321–322, 330–321, 332, 333, 339, 341, 381–382, 450–451

sustainable business   101, 406

synchronicity, serendipity   123, 211, 221, 329, 365–372

systems intelligence, insight   56–59, 348, 352, 419, 424

T

Teal   31, 33–34, 35, 294

Theory U   283–286

three breakthroughs   32

Tom Chi   112, 114, 116, 149–150, 186–187, 193, 212–213, 247–248, 254–255, 267–268, 271, 350, 367, 399–402

TOMS Shoes   27

Tony Hsieh   22, 300–301, 357–361

transformational change   80–81

transparency   19, 163–164, 248, 328, 429

true north   42, 157, 346

trust   295, 328, 332, 373–374

tuning fork   272–273, 318, 337

V

values   26, 139, 142, 155, 158–159, 428

vertical development   76, 78, 321

Viktor Frankl   309

VUCA   120, 208, 210, 232, 322, 323

vulnerability   169–170

W

We-Q   22, 138, 143, 181

Whole Foods Market   19, 35, 351

whole leader   155–157, 168, 431

whole systems   101, 114, 318, 321, 323, 337, 347–361, 380, 424

wholeness   32, 246, 393–394, 436

worldview   128, 183–184

Z

Zappos   22, 300–301, 357–361

Printed in Great Britain
by Amazon